D0848558

International Monetary
Reconstruction

International Monetary Reconstruction

Problems and Issues

Wilbur F. Monroe

Lexington Books
D.C. Heath and Company
Lexington, Massachusetts
Toronto   London

Library of Congress Cataloging in Publication Data

Monroe, Wilbur F.
  International monetary reconstruction.

International
    1. International finance. 2. Currency question. 3. Monetary policy.
I. Title.
HG3881.M616   332.4'5   73-21612
ISBN 0-669-92551-9

Copyright © 1974 by D.C. Heath and Company.

All rights reserved. No part of this publication may be reproduced or transmitted in any form or by any means, electronic or mechanical, including photocopy, recording, or any information storage or retrieval system, without permission in writing from the publisher.

Published simultaneously in Canada.

Printed in the United States of America.

International Standard Book Number: 0-669-92551-9

Library of Congress Catalog Card Number: 73-21612

332.45
M753

To Walter Krause, John F. Murray
Professor of Economics,
University of Iowa

Contents

Foreword

After a decade of tremendous upheaval, the world is faced in the 1970s with the pressing need for the reconstruction and renewal of international institutions. This is especially true in regard to international economic relations, where the collapse of the Bretton Woods System has precipitated an extended period of monetary instability.

Bretton Woods had appeared to many as the bulwark of international monetary relations. But its fatal flaws were its dependence on governments adopting unpopular domestic economic policies to correct balance of payments disequilibrium and on the dollar to serve as international money. The recent run on the dollar unleashed a wave of currency speculation, which in turn fueled monetary expansion and aggravated inflation in several strong-currency nations. These flows were checked somewhat by internal capital controls, but these have been instituted at the expense of international monetary cooperation.

Controls do not solve the basic problem of international monetary reform, however; for that one needs an effective adjustment mechanism. The international arena is replete with plans for reform, but attaining consensus in a multilateral forum is a more difficult proposition.

Since March, most countries have adopted almost by default the automatic adjustment mechanism implicit in freely floating exchange rates. Adjustment has been tempered, however, by "managing" the floats and limiting convertibility through exchange restrictions. Floating rates have afforded an effective buffer to short-term shocks, of which there have been many, and thus saved the world many financial crises. But floating rates have also hindered progress towards monetary reform and possibly undermined long-run prospects for international cooperation.

On the other hand, a return to a fixed-rate system still presents the problem of developing a new adjustment mechanism that would symmetrically force both deficit *and* surplus nations to alter their parities in response to certain indicators of disequilibrium. Furthermore, the system is plagued with the problem of what to do about the massive pool of liquid funds hanging over world financial markets. It has aggravated the decline in confidence in paper currencies and facilitated the rapid acceleration in the international transmission of inflation.

This points up the problem that in an era of high-powered finance, where massive flows of money can be rapidly generated and transferred all over the world, the ability to control an international system is difficult indeed. The problem is complicated by the fact that the United States can no longer act as the "prime mover" of the world economy. Europe and Japan now play such a large role in trade and monetary affairs that they have an equal voice in determining the international monetary reform, and this compounds the political problem of creating a new order. Attention must be paid to political blocs as well as economic issues if we are to reconstruct a lasting framework for international monetary relations.

These are the difficult problems examined by Dr. Wilbur F. Monroe. He is uniquely qualified for such an investigation, having been trained in international finance and having dealt with the operating issues in both Tokyo and Washington. He has served as the assistant financial attaché at the American Embassy in Tokyo and as a senior member of the international staff of the Treasury in Washington. During the spring of 1973, Dr. Monroe took leave from the Treasury to become a Guest Scholar at the Brookings Institution, and the study was completed at this time.

Lawrence B. Krause

Preface

For a long time it was thought that the international monetary system, known also as the Bretton Woods System, had been operating fairly smoothly. Confidence was shaken, however, by a series of monetary crises which revealed that existing arrangements were inadequate or were somehow inappropriate, in view of how the world economic order had evolved since the end of World War II. Attention of leading experts and international forums was focused on whether the existing system needed to be changed and, if so, how it might be done; numerous ideas and alternative proposals were put forth and debated.

Negotiations to reshape the international monetary system appear approximately at their midpoint at the time of this writing. The main lines of the ensuing debates and the outcome of those negotiations are extremely critical and interesting because so much hinges on the form and substance of final resolution. Indeed, the importance of world monetary reconstruction can scarcely be overemphasized.

This volume is about the momentous problems, issues, and actions confronting monetary architects in the current era. Coverage includes a brief description of the problem, followed by brief attention to how, and in terms of what setting, this problem arose. Then, for central emphasis, attention is placed upon the issues, both in functional terms and in country or power-bloc terms. Finally, implications of alternate courses are explored in terms of overall and sectoral impacts and in terms of possible country or bloc impacts.

It is intended that this book capture the interest of a wide range of readers concerned with international monetary reconstruction: students, laymen, and professionals. The central thrust is on problems and issues in broadest terms; that is to say, major questions as seen by major country participants. Accordingly, readers will gain a perspective and an understanding of what has been involved in restructuring the world's monetary system and will have some basis for making their own judgments as to the implications of an international monetary reform agreement once it is announced.

This book was written while I was on leave from the International Affairs Division of the US Treasury Department. During that time, which ended in autumn of 1973, I was pleased to have been associated with the Brookings Institution as a Guest Scholar.

I am greatly indebted to a host of experts in international finance who generously made themselves accessible to me in order to discuss the topic at hand. Many of them read parts of the manuscript and commented helpfully on it. My special appreciation is due to Walter Krause, John F. Murray Professor of Economics at the University of Iowa, who has been a constant inspiration and source of wise counsel. I should also like to thank Henry J. Bitterman, formerly with the US Treasury Department and now retired; William B. Dale, US

Executive Director of the International Monetary Fund; Walter Gardner, formerly with the Federal Reserve Board and the IMF; Robert Solomon, Vice-Chairman of the Committee of Twenty; Dr. Gottfried Haberler, Resident Scholar of the American Enterprise Institute; Dr. Lawrence B. Krause, Senior Fellow at the Brookings Institution; and Professor Henry C. Wallich of Yale University. I express my appreciation to certain associates in the Treasury Department and Federal Reserve Board who will, I trust, forgive me for not mentioning their names, but who will readily recognize my acknowledgment here of personal indebtedness to them. Finally, I owe my unstinting gratitude to a large number of financial officials of various foreign countries who generously shared with me their personal insights as well as enlightening me on their particular country's interests and positions on key issues.

The views and opinions expressed in this book are mine alone and should in no way be taken as representing the views of the United States Treasury Department, the Brookings Institution, or any of their officials.

Wilbur F. Monroe
September 1973

Part I:
The Problem

1 The Current Juncture

On August 15, 1971, the postwar international monetary system, known as the Bretton Woods system, broke down. Since that date, and even for some months preceding it, it is fair to say that the world economy has been either involved in or threatened by crisis circumstances without letup. Thus far, those crisis conditions have manifested themselves pretty much at the financial level only. The fact that they have not adversely affected real economic activity in domestic economies or international trade may be laid to two separate considerations. One concerns the ingenuity and persistence of international traders and financiers in finding new ways of operating in today's monetary order; the other is connected more closely with luck. That is to say, crisis circumstances that have prevailed since August, 1971 have taken place in an environment of rapidly expanding aggregate demand in almost all leading countries; moreover, there has been a booming demand for raw materials and fuels which provided developing economies a much needed uplift in foreign exchange earnings and their overall level of economic activity. If these particular economic conditions had not prevailed, it is not unreasonable to suspect that the crisis circumstances unfolding on the international monetary scene would have seeped through and would have had a distinct negative impact on world trade and on domestic economic performances of those countries heavily dependent upon world commerce for their very livelihood.

The world cannot and must not hope to depend on continuing reprieves of its sentence of economic disorder and chaos. The nations of the world must move forthrightly and swiftly to reform the international monetary system. What is needed is a system that provides for smooth and orderly adjustment of balance of payments imbalances; a system that injects the right amount of international liquidity so that countries suffering from temporary payments disequilibria may tide themselves over; a system that commands the confidence and respect of all members by issuing the same basic rights and requiring the same basic obligations regardless of size, stage of economic development, or condition of international balance of payments. Such a reformed monetary system will go far in restoring a stable monetary order and in creating the kind of environment conducive to steady expansion of world trade and investment and general economic welfare.

In July 1972 agreement was reached on the format for international monetary reform negotiations. Members of the International Monetary Fund agreed to establish a committee, known as the Committee of Twenty, to conduct such negotiations. The committee is similar to the representational system employed by the Executive Board of the IMF, where membership is broken down into twenty separate constituencies. The first meeting of the C-20 (as it has become known) occurred during the annual meeting of the International Monetary Fund and World Bank in September 1972. Several meetings have taken place since then, and it was hoped that a draft outline of the main elements of a reformed system could be prepared in time for the 1973 annual meeting of the Fund in Nairobi. While that hope did not materialize fully,[1] it is still widely expected that continued progress during the coming months can be followed by agreement on the main issues of reform by July 31, 1974, with a complete reform package to be presented to the Fund-Bank meeting in September 1974 or, what seems more likely, sometime soon thereafter, with ratification by legislatures of member nations to follow. At the earliest, it does not seem possible that a new international monetary system could go into effect before late 1975 or early 1976. The world, therefore, is now at one of those critical crossroads in history which hopefully arise but once or twice in a century.

For the present, however, with a reformed monetary system only a hope and not an accomplished fact, the world must limp along as best it can with exchange rates floating in no particular agreed manner with each other. In its 1973 Annual Report, the International Monetary Fund described the present situation:

A feature of prevailing currency relationships is their lack of firm foundation in their internationally agreed act of rules or code of conduct. In this respect, despite continuing consultation and a substantial degree of cooperation among national monetary authorities, the current situation is not consistent with one of the prime conceptions in the founding of the fund—that exchange rates are intrinsically a matter of international concern.[2]

The present study is concerned with the momentous problems and issues now facing architects of monetary reform. It seeks to capture the spirit of the current juncture and the flavor of the issues. It does not purport to be a tour de force for informed economists of the technical considerations leading to the breakdown of the Bretton Woods system; nor is it a comprehensive review of monetary reform proposals designed to handle difficult problems that arose in the past. Instead, the purposes are to link past resolutions of key international monetary issues and the evolution of the Bretton Woods system to the present crisis conditions; to identify and examine, to put into broad focus and perspective, problems and issues as seen by particular countries or country blocs; to consider alternative resolutions to those problems and issues within the context of monetary reform, and to offer some insights as to how those alternative resolutions might affect the world economic environment and the relative standing of participating countries.

The first task is to explore the background to the current crisis conditions. That background includes the international monetary problems and issues existing prior to the Bretton Woods Conference in 1944 (at which the postwar international monetary system was established), and the problems and issues that followed thereafter. Having acquired some feeling for that background, one gains a better appreciation for and understanding of the origins, the histories, and the relative importance of the problems and issues that have converged at the current juncture.

A final word of caution: there is perhaps no perfect solution to reforming the international monetary system which would enhance everyone's position so that no one country would be dissatisfied or might wish for more relative to some nearby neighbor. Indeed, international monetary matters have always been and will continue to be a complex blend of economic and political considerations. The current movement to reform is no exception, and it may be safely anticipated that any outcome will reflect major compromises by all sides stemming from many months of tough haggling among the negotiators. Readers of this volume will, however, be in a good position to judge for themselves the relative merits or demerits of the final resolutions on monetary reform.

Part II:
Background

2

The Spirit of Bretton Woods

Out of a conference held during July 1944 at Bretton Woods, New Hampshire, was born an international monetary accord that was to serve as the basis for exchange rate and balance of payments adjustment between countries until 1971. The Bretton Woods Agreement, as the accord became known, won the acceptance of the requisite number of countries, and with that the International Monetary Fund and the International Bank for Reconstruction and Development came into being in 1946. In order to understand the Spirit of Bretton Woods and hence the framework of the postwar international monetary system, one must have some appreciation of the times and events that then prevailed, the economic circumstances in which the United States and other countries found themselves, and the important lessons obtaining from international monetary arrangements of the recent past.

The Gold Standard: 1900-1914

An international gold standard in its broadest sense refers to a system in which national monetary units are kept at a constant value in terms of gold. This may be achieved either unilaterally or by common agreement among participating countries.[1] The full-fledged gold system arose in Great Britain and had its roots as far back in time as the seventeenth century. Historians are in disagreement over the actual duration of the gold standard. At most, it endured for approximately forty years up until the outbreak of World War I in 1914. There is greater agreement, however, that it existed in a relatively pure form from 1900 until 1914. Even then, however, there was no international agreement between governments on the matter of convertibility. In Europe, the gold standard was taken to mean that central banks stood by willing to buy or sell gold. In the United States, private banks as well were allowed to transact business in gold. Then, even at its high point, the gold standard resulted from unilateral governmental decree, not a formal international agreement.

Even today, the gold standard tends to evoke images of "the good old days," and not without some justification. For during that period people were more free from governmental interference in international transactions than at any time before or since; they were freer to transact business, to invest or transfer funds, and to travel about the world. Moreover, the era of the gold standard was an era of relative peace in the world, a time during which there were no great wars involving many nations.

According to certain expert opinion, the gold standard, for all its emphasis on gold, was really a pound sterling standard. The pound sterling was far and away the most commonly used currency in settling international payments and was the unit in which trade contracts and international capital transactions were denominated—even transactions not involving British citizens or companies.

What made sterling the international currency was the status of London as the dominant financial center. Britain's position as the world's leading exporter and importer and major source of capital made it convenient for foreigners involved in international commerce or finance to hold working balances in sterling. Moreover, London money markets offered safe and ready investment outlets for funds temporarily in disuse. The twin roles of world commercial and financial leader then enjoyed by Britain stemmed from such historical factors as the country's long-standing policy favoring free trade, its having been the Industrial Revolution's country of origin which gave rise to wealth and savings available for loans and investments abroad, and the establishment of a gold standard as early as 1821.[2] The pivotal role played by the pound sterling was facilitated over time as a result of approximate balance between international payments and receipts. The world was kept well supplied with sterling, therefore, and neither a sterling shortage nor a sterling glut arose.

The Bank of England had the responsibility for administering Britain's gold reserves, which actually were quite small both in a relative and absolute sense, although this did not impinge on the operation of the system; the identification of sterling with gold, the unrestricted transferability of sterling, and its general acceptability promoted confidence. Through manipulation of the bank rate, which affected the price at which discount houses could obtain funds to be deposited with commercial banks, the Old Lady of Threadneedle Street (the familiar reference to the Bank) was able to control changes in the amount of money in circulation and in the international movement of gold and sterling balances.

The outbreak of World War I in July 1914 and the ensuing financial crisis in London signaled the collapse of the gold standard as far as Britain was concerned. Elsewhere, however, the end came gradually as in one financial center after another international gold transfers became subject to governmental control and the convertibility of paper money into gold was either restricted or ruled out altogether. Thus ended an unprecedented era in the conduct of international economic relations.

Vain Attempts to Reestablish the Gold Standard: 1919-1929

World War I had caused deep-seated changes in the political, economic, and financial structure of the world, to say nothing of the physical damage caused and the loss of human life. Government intervention in economies had become widespread and was an accepted fact of life; in order to finance war efforts, most governments had resorted to public borrowing, rather than to taxation, which left them with large sums of public debt and inflated money supplies. For a number of countries, severe price inflation resulted and was followed by a period of business depression. The United States fared far better than most nations, however; it endured only a mild case of postwar inflation and was even able to return to the gold standard by mid-1919 as restrictions on gold flows were lifted. For Germany, France, and other European countries, inflation proved to be especially severe and was to be a problem for some years to come.

Collections of war reparations from Germany exacerbated Germany's other financial difficulties and, along with efforts to settle interallied war debts, were the cause of adverse international monetary relations throughout the 1920s and into the early 1930s. The Dawes Plan attempted to improve German ability to pay reparations by strengthening her economic and financial systems. This worked well for some five years and was then succeeded in 1929 by the Young Plan. Less than two years later, German reparations and other war-debt payments came to an end with no country apparently very satisfied by the outcome of such exercises, but with a general consensus that the ongoing attempts to collect sizable reparations had served to keep Europe in financial turmoil far longer than otherwise.

World War I cost Britain her unchallenged role as commercial and financial leader. Interruption of trade induced industrial development in traditional markets; her pre-eminence as a shipping nation was undermined; and foreign-held British treasure in the form of investments and other holdings had been liquidated in large quantities in order to help finance the country's war effort. Smaller current account surpluses, coupled with increased demand for capital domestically in order to rebuild industries, undercut capital exports and further eroded Britain's position as an international banker. Some import duties imposed during the war to raise revenue and conserve scarce foreign exchange were retained after war's end, and others were added, thus tarnishing her "free trade" image.[3]

The tone of British monetary experience during the 1920s was set in 1918 when the report of the Cunliffe Committee called for a return to the prewar gold parity. Before that could occur, wartime controls had to be dismantled and the exchange rate freed from import and capital export controls. These steps took place in piecemeal fashion over a period of time; meanwhile, in the early 1920s the sterling exchange rate was allowed to fluctuate against the dollar.

In 1925 it was announced that restrictions on gold and silver exports would be dropped and that the Bank of England would redeem its currency in gold for export. This in effect proclaimed the reestablishment of the gold standard. Considerations of international prestige weighed heavily on Britain and, in retrospect, were in large part to blame for a return to parity before British and foreign price levels had come into line. The overvaluation of sterling against the dollar (the figure of 10 percent was the traditional informed guess),[4] along with the emergence of downward rigidities in British wages and prices, led to stagnating industrial production and chronic unemployment. According to Yeager, these features of British economy, which worsened after 1929, "contributed to the growth of anti-capitalist sentiment in Britain, to the increasing strength of the Labor Party and its election victory in 1945, and to the lasting importance of 'full employment' as a political slogan."[5]

The weakening of Britain's international economic and financial position as a result of the war was concurrent with the upsurge in United States economic strength. During World War I the United States had become a creditor nation, first lending abroad during its role as a neutral nation to finance its export surplus, and after that, lending abroad during war involvement to help its allies. The dollar had thus posed a serious challenge to sterling's preeminence while New York offered alternative investment outlets for foreign-held balances during the war. After 1925, London was again able to attract short-term funds in large volume, especially deposits of central banks whose governments had reembraced the gold standard. This short-term capital inflow was a prerequisite for Britain's remaining on the gold standard but was an expensive course to follow (and in fact inappropriate, considering the recessionary economic conditions then prevailing domestically) because of the high interest rates necessary to attract funds from other centers such as New York and, to a lesser extent, Paris.

During the latter half of the 1920s, there was evidence that the gold standard was being reestablished. The United States had returned to that standard in 1919 and thereafter served as the guidepost for other currencies. By 1925 some thirty-five currencies besides the dollar had become stabilized on gold—either at prewar parity, or at some devalued amount in relation to it, or through adoption of new currency units (the old ones having been destroyed by hyperinflation)— or had compiled at least a one-year record of exchange stability.[6] But all of this was achieved through separate acts of national sovereignty rather than, in Nurkse's words, "by simultaneous and coordinated international action." Also, "the piecemeal and haphazard manner of international monetary reconstruction sowed the seeds of subsequent disintegration."[7]

The reestablished gold standard (or more accurately, the gold-exchange standard) was at the same time more complex and less stable than its older brother. The much larger postwar volume of cash and liquid assets could be transferred between financial centers, once there were alternative outlets to London—namely, New York and Paris—thus posing a new problem of "hot money movements." International clearing became more complicated, thus necessitating arrangements to offset claims between centers. A further adjunct to the multifinancial center phenomenon was the competition of dollar deposits and drafts with sterling instruments.

A different consideration in the form of gold shortage, or at least maldistribution of the world's existing gold stock, caused many central banks to hold legal monetary reserves as bank accounts or liquid securities in gold standard countries. This was an important explanation behind the widespread adoption of the gold-exchange standard. Another problem with the reconstituted gold standard was that the traditional balance of payments equilibrating methods were not used; that is, government policies were used to neutralize or offset, not to transmit, international influences on domestic prices, incomes, and money supplies. With nothing to replace the standard equilibrating methods, payments disequilibria accumulated or were papered over. The system, to the extent it was a system, was described by one writer as "a temporary exchange pegging device" consisting of "pegging operations on a vast scale."[8] In the words of another writer, "Too much depended upon ad hoc policies and switches in policy. Mistakes in diagnosis and lags in effectiveness of policies threatened perverse results."[9]

The Great Depression and International Monetary Chaos

If the 1920s proved to be a less than satisfactory era in the conduct of international monetary relations, the 1930s offered something far worse. In fact, the Great Depression, which led directly or indirectly to the raising of import barriers in order to foster domestic employment, other beggar-thy-neighbor policies, and competitive exchange depreciations, had a devastating impact on world trade and payments.

The gold-exchange standard came into being in the 1920s when a number of central banks held portions of their legal reserves in the form of bank deposits or securities in the Federal Reserve Bank of New York, in London commercial banks, or in other financial centers rather than in gold. This in effect was a pyramiding of claims on the narrow gold base and was precarious for the reason that serious pressure on any of the gold standard countries could easily trigger withdrawals of the deposits or liquidation of securities and hence put pressure on the financial center itself. This financial system served to exacerbate the unfolding real economic problems in the early 1930s.

Serious depression did not assert itself until industrial production in the United States turned downward in the middle of 1929 and the stock market crash occurred in October. One of the first international repercussions was a reversal of speculative capital inflow which had been taking place in New York in response to the stock market boom. That development was soon over-shadowed by cessation of American lending abroad, even a repatriation of foreign-held financial assets in several cases, and passage of the Smoot-Hawley Tariff of 1930, with its constricting effects on American imports. By the middle of 1932 the level of world industrial production and the volume of world trade had receded by nearly one-third of their respective 1929 levels. (Such declines in indicators of economic activity reflected price reductions as well as decreases in volume.) Countries that experienced declining exports and/or increasing balance of payments deficits countered by departing from the gold standard and permitting their currencies to depreciate, or by erecting controls on imports and foreign exchange payments. Less developed economies were the first to resort to such measures during 1929-31.

By the early 1930s, an economic and financial relapse of major proportions was taking place throughout most of the world. In September 1931, Britain left the gold standard. The United States departed more deliberately in April 1933 under little or no pressure. It was during this period that the sterling area formally came into being. A number of countries had for some time pegged their currencies to sterling; official reserves of those countries consisted in the main of sterling balances. Members of the sterling area included the British dominions and the colonies, excluding Hong Kong. Canada and the Scandanavian countries, although never members of the sterling area, continued to peg their currencies to sterling. Several other countries as well, such as Japan and Australia, while not regarded as members of the sterling bloc, stabilized their currencies with the pound until World War II.

President Roosevelt signed the Gold Reserve Act on January 30, 1934. In so doing, the United States returned to a variant of the gold standard, called a "limited gold-bullion standard." The dollar's value in terms of gold had been redefined at $35 per fine ounce. The government stood ready to purchase all gold at that price and to sell it in return for dollars held by foreign central banks and privately licensed users. This touched off a very large gold inflow into the United States which ran on until foreign restrictions were imposed during World War II. By the end of 1936, the US gold stock was nearly triple what it had been in January 1934. With the gold price so increased from what it had been before (up by almost 60 percent), American capital that had left the country during the 1933-34 period of dollar depreciation against sterling was encouraged to return; and later on in the 1930s when foreign capital sought refuge from mounting political and economic uncertainty, the high price of gold in the United States again offered an attractive resolution of the problem.

Elsewhere, the main European gold standard countries had assembled in July 1933 to form a "gold bloc." Pledges were signed to the effect that their currencies would remain tied to gold at existing parities. At a conference in Geneva held during September 1934, the gold bloc reaffirmed its determination in this regard. By doing so, members endured economic depression and continued threats of, if not actual experiences with capital flight, balance of payments deficits, and loss of gold reserves, all because of overvalued currencies. However, one by one during the mid-1930s, these countries were forced off the gold standard and turned increasingly to exchange controls and to devaluation. Such developments entailed a far greater degree of official exchange market intervention and management of exchange rates by means of controls than had taken place during the devaluations of the early 1930s. According to the Tenth

Annual Report of the Bank for International Settlements, only four major currencies were free of controls in 1940. They were the dollar, the guilder, and the Swiss and Belgium franc.[10]

Precedents for Future Cooperation

There were some important examples of intergovernmental cooperation involving international monetary matters prior to and during World War II. No doubt those cooperative arrangements were in the minds of the postwar monetary architects and therefore had an impact upon thinking leading up to proposals for monetary reform. A few of the key examples will be briefly sketched here.

Out of the French decision to devalue the franc in September 1936 was born the Tripartite Agreement. According to it, the governments of France, Britain, and the United States publicly concurred on the need for the exchange rate change and together took steps to minimize any resulting disturbances in international transactions. Although no formal institutional mechanism was provided for in the agreement, the basis for consultations was established. The Tripartite Agreement included members of the sterling bloc and French franc areas; other governments joining shortly after inception were Belgium, Switzerland, and the Netherlands.

By way of putting some muscle into the Tripartite Agreement, the Secretary of the US Treasury announced his willingness to sell gold to the exchange equalization funds of those countries willing to reciprocate. (In practice, this was done by switching the earmarks on gold bars held at the Federal Reserve Bank of New York.) This arrangement, which was shortly extended to most major members of the agreement, provided a means by which monetary authorities could obtain gold in settlement for balances of another participant's currency acquired on home markets.

Also in 1936, the Bank for International Settlements, which had been established originally to handle German reparations transfers, began a plan of its own which was designed to facilitate international payments connected with commercial transactions. Participating central banks were offered facilities for granting reciprocal credits to one another in national currencies or in gold. This enabled each central bank to provide its exporters with credit but without simultaneously incurring an exchange risk.[11]

Third, in mid-1937 the United States negotiated the first of a series of bilateral stabilization agreements with Brazil. All in the name of promoting exchange equilibrium, the agreements involved commitments to sell gold, or to provide dollars, to Brazil (with stipulated limits) under conditions deemed to be in the interests of both governments.

Finally, after World War II had commenced, Britain negotiated rather similar bilateral arrangements with France and the Netherlands in order to facilitate mobilization efforts and to conserve gold for purchases of war matériel from the United States. Under the agreements, each party agreed to accumulate balances of other's currency in unlimited amounts. Such balances could be used for purchases in the issuing country or in its currency area.

The Tripartite Agreement and the US and British bilateral agreements had three features in common.[12] They called for an exchange of value for value and did not provide for loans. Second, at least on a temporary basis, they shifted responsibility for settling a deficit from the debtor country to the creditor; this averted the immediate need for exchange rate adjustment or exchange controls. Third, exchange rates of currencies involved in the agreements were stabilized.

Other nascent mechanisms of monetary cooperation, such as currency blocs and exchange stabilization funds, may be traced to the interwar period. As for the first, the birth of the sterling area has already been cited. There were also to be found a dollar area and in the Far East a yen bloc. Emergence of these blocs was prima facie evidence of governments' increasing reluctance to abandon exchange rates to the whims of market forces, and to a growing preference over time for management of those rates in one form or another and in varying degree.

The British, the American, and French stabilization funds served as further evidence of the trend in that direction. The first was intended originally to offset only speculative and seasonal fluctuations, although to do this in practice without affecting the longer-term course of the exchange rate proved difficult. The latter two from their inception were intended to influence exchange rates more actively. According to one writer, the American fund sought to defend the dollar against a competitive depreciation of the pound sterling and other currencies as well.[13] At the same time, the British were unwilling to permit the pound to appreciate very much against the dollar. Collaboration between governments in managing exchange rates, of which the Tripartite Agreement was the most striking example of the period, was therefore a natural outgrowth of the observed trend of individual governments to influence if not to dominate the movement of exchange rates over time.

Changes in World Economic Power Structure

The international power structure shifted radically as a consequence of the two world wars. This had a profound influence on the shape of the postwar international monetary system. The productive capacities of West European nations were impaired severely as a result of physical destruction and population dislocation. The same was true of Great Britain's productive capacity. The international payments positions of European countries and Britain alike had deteriorated sharply. The capacity to pay for much needed imports either by means of exporting or by earnings from invisible trade had been eroded. This resulted in the first instance from physical damage and deterioration of plant and equipment at home, and in the second instance as a result of liquidation of overseas investments, both public and private, during the war in order to help finance war-related imports, as a result of reduced earnings from overseas investments which had been retained, either because of damage or neglect while in enemy hands, and as a result of decreased service income attributable to shipping losses during the war. The same story applied with equal if not greater force to Japan.

Outside of the combat zones, however, productive capacity increased sharply during World War II. Most notably, the United States had recovered from the Great Depression of the 1930s and had gone on to increase its productive plant by some 50 percent and its yearly output of goods and services by more than that amount. At war's end, over one-half of all manufacturing activity in the world and one-third of all goods produced were occuring within the United States. World shipping tonnage rose some 6 or 7 percent during the war; whereas the United States claimed ownership of only 14 percent of total tonnage in 1939, it claimed 50 percent after the war. Even in 1947 the United States was supplying one-third of total world exports while consuming only one-tenth of all imports.[14]

Over the span of just thirty years, the position of pre-eminent commercial and financial world leader had been passed from Britain to the United States. The dollar had replaced sterling as the reserve currency, had become the vehicle currency for some unknown but obviously very substantial proportion of commercial transactions, and was the currency most often used in financial transactions. All of these developments had the effect of placing great and new burdens of responsibility on the United States and at the same time put this country squarely in the driver's seat when it came to negotiating reform of the international monetary system.

The State of International Monetary Order
Prior to World War II

From the experience of international economic relations spanning approximately four decades, architects of the postwar international monetary system distilled key lessons that would color their thinking and planning. First, there was agreement concerning the right of each government, if not the obligation, to pursue policies designed to achieve high levels of employment. This became the fundamental purpose of all participants of reform, since there was great determination to avoid the kind of misery that had beset the world during the Great Depression. Moreover, Keynes's *General Theory* offered new theoretical insights and led to a breakthrough at the governmental policy-making level as to how this could be done.[15]

Second, there was a preference for a system of fixed exchange rates such as had prevailed during the years of the gold standard. Such a system, it was generally felt, created a better environment for growth of world trade. At the same time, there was common agreement that the equilibrating methods prescribed by the gold standard, which had on occasion produced unwanted domestic economic consequences, could not be adhered to fully and that some other mechanism would have to be found.

Third, gold for all its shortcomings still commanded the confidence of public and private officials and therefore would continue to have a useful role to play in any new international monetary system.

Finally, national governments acting individually or in concert could not be depended upon to guarantee orderly operation of the international monetary system. The effectiveness of such arrangements as the Tripartite Agreement was limited and, in the view of the best minds at the time, could not be expected to work satisfactorily in peacetime.[16] Accordingly, it appeared that some international authority, more inclusive in terms of representation, was needed to act as impartial superviser, to judge conduct according to a body of principles already agreed upon, and to act as broker in disputes that might arise among participants.[17]

Prevalent Moods

Coupled with a determination to avoid mistakes of the past, there was an optimistic mood prevailing with respect to what could be achieved in the postwar world. This mood was particularly strong in the United States, where in the very early 1940s we were setting our sights upon a different world—the Brave New World—that could be made to unfold after the war. In the spirit of the times new agencies of an international character were thought of, and it was confidently anticipated they would be able to deal effectively with problems already apparent as well as with those not then foreseen.[18] This mood of optimism, which anticipated cooperation among nations in ways and to degrees never before realized, had its roots in the Atlantic Charter and its high-flown sentiments[19] and in the wartime experience of the Allied countries working together toward common objectives. There was a domestic origin as well that was based upon the "agency approach" to problem solving of the New Deal.

Secondary to the mood of optimism, but working as an important restraint upon it, were isolationist sentiments. Feelings along such lines were to be found in the US Congress; and since that body would have to approve major commitments that the country might make economically or financially to any new international organizations, the isolationist views had to be taken into account constantly by the administration and its postwar architects. Ways were sought to accommodate or otherwise assuage such sentiments.

In Britain and in Europe, where the devastation of war on economies was great, the setting of the postwar world was seen in a different light. There, opinion was more divided than in the United States between those advocating free trade, those who advocated "managed economies," and those who advocated continuation of tariffs and other discriminatory devices (such as Britain's imperial preference tariffs of the 1930s). Optimism and hope were to be found in various British and European quarters. For the realization of these aspirations, however, people looked to the United States.

Major Country Interests

Far and away the two dominant countries involved with shaping the postwar international monetary system were the United States and Great Britain, in that order. Yet in view of the world-encompassing objectives, it was necessary to devise a system attractive not only to those two countries but to as many other countries as possible.

A large amount of indebtedness hung over Britain as a result of the war effort. The lend-lease arrangements were continuing in the early 1940s, and a means of settlement had not been finalized. Moreover, there was clear awareness that substantial amounts of imports from abroad and the financing to pay for them would be needed in order for the country to regain its footing economically after the war. Thus, the British hoped to establish some new mechanism to meet the kind of credit requirements they envisaged. In Britain there was also the Keynesian concern that war's end could be followed by recessionary conditions and unemployment unless appropriate domestic policies were pursued. This meant that there would have to be some sort of adjustment mechanism that did not put inordinate pressure on deficit countries to make adjustments by imposing deflationary policies at home or by repeated currency devaluations. If such a mechanism could not be worked out, then Britain was prepared to continue discriminatory trade and exchange practices, which had been made necessary first during the 1930s in answer to US trade control laws that enforced high tariffs, and even more so later on during World War II.

For its part, the United States wanted to recapture the stability of the gold standard, as represented by fixed exchange rates, but at the same time wanted to avoid the kind of trade restrictions that arose in the 1930s. Accordingly, there was recognition of need for some kind of flexibility along with fixity or stability.

The United States was cognizant indeed of its economic and financial strength compared to all other allied countries. No one imagined the very large US trade surplus would be eroded in the foreseeable future, and it was expected that balance of payments surpluses would continue indefinitely. There was agreement that US capital would have to be made available to help out postwar reconstruction, but the estimates of what was to be involved on this score were naïve, to say the least.

Tempering the enthusiasm of those who anticipated a large assistance role for the United States were the isolationist members in Congress. They had to be reckoned with, since their concurrence would be needed for any such arrangements. Moreover, another kind of restraint was embodied in the view that the sort of world inflationary conditions of the 1920s must not be allowed to repeat themselves. This tended to throw cold water on the arguments that the United States should provide very large amounts of funds in a hurry to its allied friends. Funds should be provided on a business-like basis, it was argued, and financing should not be allowed to become open-ended. It also followed that the burden of balance of payments adjustment should fall primarily on debtor countries; for if it did not, then their impulse to inflate their domestic economies back to prosperity would go unchecked and the virus of inflation would become widespread.

These were the uppermost interests of the two main bargaining countries. Such interests reflected their very different circumstances and hence their anticipated economic and financial needs after the war. There were common objectives, although usually given different emphasis, but the binding forces were the joint determination to construct a more stable, prosperous world and the common agreement that in order for this to occur there must be provision for some arrangement by which there could be international financing of future balance of payments deficits.

Negotiations Prior to Bretton Woods: Keynes and White

British and American proposals for postwar monetary reform evolved independent of each other long before World War II had drawn to a close. John Maynard Keynes, the chief architect of the British plan, had held discussions with US authorities during summer of 1941 concerning arrangements for the lend-lease.[20] The United States had been insisting on a clause specifically calling for avoidance of trade discrimination between the two countries in return for US aid. This proved difficult for Keynes and the British government to swallow in the absence of assurances that equilibrium in international trade would be restored after the war and in view of the fact that British financial reserves were so depleted.

Upon returning to England, Keynes directed his attention to preparing a plan international in scope that would ease pressure on debtor countries and would compel creditor countries to lend resources, thereby facilitating nonrestrictive trade and monetary policies. Keynes's chief interest in his *Proposals for an International Clearing Union*, which circulated within the British Treasury in

September 1941, was to devise a means by which nondiscrimination could be accepted by Britain in spite of her financial plight. This meant there would need to be an international clearing mechanism coupled with specific proposals providing for adjustment of exchange rates to ensure export growth and thereby help maintain a steady expansion of domestic economies.

The US proposal had its origins in the Treasury Department. One week after the attack on Pearl Harbor on December 7, 1941, Secretary Morganthau asked Harry Dexter White and his colleagues in Treasury to prepare a plan for an interallied stabilization fund. The fund would be a means of offering aid to the allies during the war, would serve as the basis for postwar international monetary arrangements, and would provide for a postwar "international currency."[21] By the end of the same month, White had come up with a "Suggested Program for Inter-Allied Monetary and Bank Action," which called for establishment of two separate institutions: an Inter-Allied Bank and an Inter-Allied Stabilization Fund. White's chief interest was to offer a means by which exchange rates could be stabilized and competitive devaluations and payments restrictions that other countries had applied after 1933 against US exports could be avoided. During the summer of 1942 and after numerous refinements, the two proposals were exchanged by the two governments.

The plans of Keynes and White had important characteristics in common. They both envisaged widespread international participation; they contemplated the need for other international organizations to deal with such problems as postwar relief, rehabilitation, reconstruction and development; the need was recognized for some concessions in the realm of national sovereignty in order to make the plans operate effectively; there was at the same time awareness that laissez faire was a thing of the past and that "managed" economies were inevitable and even desirable.

While details of the plans are not necessary for present purposes, it is important to be aware of their major differences.[22] First, the Keynes plan contemplated that the role of international reserves be filled by a new international currency, which he called *bancor*, to be fixed in terms of gold and to be used for clearing balances between central banks. Exchange rates of national currencies were to be fixed in terms of bancor. The White plan in its later versions, which were in response to the published Keynes plan, argued that no such international currency was necessary and that, instead, a pool of national currencies linked to gold, plus gold itself, should fill the role. (The original White plan called for a bookkeeping gold unit, called *unitas*, in which the accounts of the stabilization fund were to be kept. This feature was dropped in later versions of the plan, however.)

Second, and in view of Britain's carry-over of external problems and contemplated internal problems in the postwar era, the Keynes plan called for a means of continued financing, based on the British banking system's overdraft principle, for those countries in deficit. This gave a country under pressure some added breathing room but was not meant to substitute for necessary internal economic readjustments. The White plan, in contrast, insisted on a business-like approach with all members contributing, according to a formula, certain amounts of their national currencies and gold reserves. Under defined conditions, member countries could then "buy" currencies of other members for stipulated periods of time.

Third, the Keynes plan put pressure for correction of balance of payments imbalances on both deficit and surplus countries alike, not just on the country under pressure. (Such correction could come about either by exchange rate adjustment, alteration of domestic economic policies, changes in commercial policy, or international development loans.) Keynes' clearing union was conceived of as a central bank for central banks which would charge a rate of interest on credit and debit balances of bancor. The White plan provided for changes in exchange rates only to correct for a fundamental disequilibrium, and then only when 80 percent of the members' votes were in concurrence. The onus was clearly on deficit countries to adjust their currencies—not surplus countries.

In the months that followed the exchange of the two plans, bilateral negotiations dominated by Keynes and White were held between the United States and Britain. The outcome was a "Joint Statement by Experts on the Establishment of an International Monetary Fund" (April 4, 1944). During those negotiations, and particularly during 1943, the United States government consulted with other Allied governments about the US proposed Stabilization Fund. There was no question, however, that the US-British negotiations were the major determining influence on the emerging shape of the White Plan for a Stabilization Fund and the eventual Joint Statement issued by the two governments. In that same year the Canadian and French governments put forward separate, alternative plans to the Keynes and White plans, but these essentially added nothing to the final outcome.

One alternative plan expounded by Professor John Williams of Harvard University deserves mention, not for its impact on the monetary reform agreement eventually to emerge from the Bretton Woods Conference—for it had none—but for its relevance to criticism of the international monetary system which arose in later years. Professor Williams's proposal, known as the "key currency" proposal, began from the premise that currencies of major economic powers (namely, the United States and Britain) were instrumental to the smooth operation of the international monetary system. By stabilizing the key currencies vis-à-vis each other and by ensuring the health of each, there would be a nucleus around which general stabilization efforts could be carried on for lesser currencies. Williams argued, therefore, that no new agency or mechanism was necessary to the smooth operation of the international economic order, nor would any new agency or mechanism be sufficient to overcome a situation in which either or both of the key currencies became unhealthy or were somehow not in the appropriate relationship to each other. While the Williams proposal had considerable support in financial circles and otherwise generated wide acclaim as well as criticism, it did not gain favor in the US government, where the preference for establishing new international agencies to deal with problems was so very strong.

Prior to the full-scale conference held at Bretton Woods, a preliminary drafting conference was held at Atlantic City during the latter part of June 1944. Representatives of thirteen countries plus the United States were invited. A number of amendments were proposed and were carried over to the Bretton Woods Conference; but in most important respects the United States and Britain were able to reach agreement on the major issues with minimum conditions essential to both governments having been achieved. While it would not be precisely accurate to say that the participating countries at Bretton Woods were presented with a common US-UK plan for a new monetary system that was already a fait accompli, something very close to that did in fact occur.

The Bretton Woods Conference and the Resulting Agreement

On July 1, 1944, the International Monetary and Financial Conference of the United and Associated Nations—forty-four in all—convened at Bretton Woods, New Hampshire. Three commissions were established to draft agreements dealing with the Monetary Fund, the World Bank, and other means of international financial cooperation. The Final Act of the Conference, which embodied the Articles of Agreement of the Fund and of the Bank along with other resolutions of lesser importance, was signed *ad referendum* by representatives of each delegation on July 22. The delegations thereupon returned to their respective countries to seek ratification of the agreements.

The purposes of the Fund, according to the Articles of Agreement, were:

1. To promote consultation and collaboration on international monetary problems through a permanent institution which provides the machinery for such exchanges to take place.
2. To facilitate the expansion and balanced growth of international trade and thereby promote and maintain a high level of employment and income.
3. To promote exchange stability and orderly exchange arrangements and to avoid competitive exchange depreciation.
4. To aid in the reestablishment of a multilateral system of payments concerning current transactions between members and to eliminate foreign exchange restrictions which hamper world trade.
5. To make the Fund's resources available to members, with adequate safeguards, so that they may correct maladjustments in balance of payments without resorting to measures destructive of national or international prosperity.
6. To promote measures which shorten the duration and lessen the severity of balance of payments disequilibria.

Membership in the Fund was to be held open to any country provided it would subscribe to the Articles of Agreement. These included commitments to observe rules of good conduct in respect to monetary policy, which would help realize the purposes enumerated above. For example, members agreed to establish an initial par value after World War II with the Fund's approval, to maintain and promote exchange stability, to maintain orderly exchange arrangements within specified margins for exchange transactions within their territories, not to alter the par value except to correct for a fundamental disequilibrium and then only with the Fund's concurrence except for minor adjustments of 10 percent or less of the original par value itself. Members also agreed to make their currencies convertible (at the end of a transition period anticipated to last five years) as defined by the Articles. Members were obliged to provide resources in order for the Fund to operate and to pay an initial subscription to the Fund equal to their quota, partly in domestic currency and partly in gold. Members were also committed to making necessary statistical data available for the operation of the Fund and to be bound by the Fund's decisions, including its interpretation of the Articles' provisions. Those decisions were to be taken by a weighted system of voting that gave proportionately greater power to members with large quotas. Management of day-to-day affairs of the Fund was to be the responsibility of a Board of Executive Directors operating in permanent session. In all respects, the conceptual framework and the mechanical operation of the Fund was far more in line with White's original plan for a stabilization fund, and there was very little resemblance to Keynes's clearing union proposals.

Over the course of the ensuing twenty months, almost all of the nations that had participated in the Bretton Woods Conference signed the Articles of Agreement and thereby joined the International Monetary Fund. An important question is why they did so; upon inspection, it is learned that reasons differed importantly depending upon the country.

The US Bretton Woods Agreement Act authorizing acceptance of both the Fund's and the Bank's Articles of Agreement was signed by the president on July 31, 1945. Passage by the Congress was made possible because of limitation in respect to the US financial commitment involved and the requirement that any future increase in US quota in the Fund (or the Bank) would necessitate congressional approval. There was no open-ended commitment on the part of the United States to provide credit to the Fund, a prime concern with the early Keynes proposal. Moreover, the system appeared to offer the stability of fixed rates while providing for smooth transition to a new configuration of exchange rates if so required. Finally, there appeared to be adequate safeguards against repetition of either the hyperinflation of the 1920s or the competitive exchange rate depreciations and trade and exchange controls that plagued countries in the 1930s. There would have been no IMF without US participation, and that basic fact allowed the United States to dictate, in effect, the broad workings, and to delimit the scope of, the postwar international monetary system to other countries.

The British joined the Fund and the Bank because of a number of negotiating concessions offered by the United States which made the original White plan more palatable: allowance for a period of transition (expected to last five years), provision for a facility by which countries could alter their exchange rates if they thought necessary, and ground rules for introducing exchange controls in the event US dollars became scarce. Also of great importance was the $3.75 billion US loan to Britain (the Anglo-American Financial Agreement of 1945) at near-concessional terms, plus another loan from Canada at about the same time, which pushed the total to around $5 billion. Those loans were made specifically to help Britain through an expectedly difficult period of reconstruction immediately after the war and in large part substituted for the overdraft facility Keynes and his colleagues were hoping to achieve in Keynes's clearing union proposal. The need for substantial postwar financial assistance for Britain had been recognized, but it was being provided on terms more clearly defined and acceptable to the conservative US Congress. By all accounts at that time, the British believed that the line of credit was sufficient and the transition period, which was expected to last five years, long enough to permit their economy to recover and at the same time allow the country to enter into obligations set forth in the Articles of Agreement.

The vast number of countries that attended the Bretton Woods Conference were developing or less developed countries. Their reasons for joining the Fund were substantially different from the arguments that led to either US or British acceptance of the Articles of Agreement. At that time many countries were interested in economic development; however, they had not lived with such ideas long enough to have a very good understanding of how development could be implemented or what conditions were necessary in order to pursue success-fully economic development. Accordingly, the Fund proposal, with its inherent equilibrium orientation and the attendant obligations, did not make it appear overly offensive to developing countries. (In later years, they would come to see how wrong their appraisal had been.) But what generated prime interest in developing countries was not the Fund but the Bank proposal; and in order to become members of the Bank, countries were obliged to join the Fund.

The purposes of the International Bank, as stated in the Articles of Agreement, were:

To assist in the reconstruction and development of territories of members. . . .
To promote private foreign investments by means of guarantees or participations in loans and other investments made by private investors; and when private capital is not available on reasonable terms, to supplement private investment by providing on suitable conditions, finance for production purposes out of its own capital, funds raised by it and its other resources.

Either directly from the Bank or indirectly as a result of its efforts, less developed countries (LDCs) envisaged that a great deal of money would come their way, thus assisting them instrumentally to promote their own economic development. Such expectations (which later proved overly optimistic) were more than sufficient to make up for any shortcomings entailed in the Fund proposal, and so the LDCs agreed to go along with the Bretton Woods proposals.

With their common objective of universal participation in mind, the United States and Britain clearly wanted the LDCs to become members of the Fund. The United States particularly was interested in having those countries abandon their multiple-currency clauses. In return, something had to be offered, and it was hoped that the International Bank would be able to attract funds to help finance development of their economies in which they were so understandably interested.

Other countries as well saw in the Bank an incentive for agreeing to the proposals put forth at Bretton Woods and thus to joining the Fund. The word *Reconstruction* was part of the title for the Bank and, as already mentioned, was part of the stated purpose of that institution. Thus, for a number of wartorn countries, quite apart from the LDCs, the Bank captured the public interest and imagination far more than did the Fund. For the United States, however, and for Great Britain, too, it was the Fund that commanded the bulk of attention.

This, therefore, recounts the spirit prevailing during the time of Bretton Woods and explains why proposals emanating from the conference were given their specific form. The Articles of Agreement of the International Monetary Fund were signed by the first twenty-nine members on December 27, 1945. When the Fund commenced operations in March of the following year, the number of members totaled thirty-nine. In time, all of the original attendees of Bretton Woods, with the exception of the USSR, joined the Fund.

3 The Record: Emerging Criticism

Reaction to the International Monetary Fund by informed observers has been varied over the quarter century of its operation. While a solid record of achievements has been compiled, there has also been a basis for criticism of the Fund and its activities. Such criticism may be categorized under two major headings. First, the Fund has not been adequate to deal with existing situations in the postwar period, either in the initial period up to the time of convertibility in Western Europe (that is, the end of 1958) or in the period thereafter. Second, the Fund has never worked in the ways originally intended, and this has caused excessive burdens of one sort or another to be placed on particular countries or blocs of countries. These two lines of criticism will be addressed in this chapter, but first, in order to set the stage, the principles according to which the Fund has operated will be described somewhat more fully.

Principles of Operation

At the outset, the first major task of the Fund concerned the determination of a system of exchange rate parities. This proved to be a very great challenge in view of disruptions to world trade and national economies stemming from World War II. Accordingly, it was decided that the Fund would accept exchange rates then existing but with the understanding that they could be altered.[1] Those initial rates were not looked upon as equilibrium rates but only as a basis upon which numerous adjustments would be made in accordance with the new procedures that would be applied by the Fund itself. Those procedures were twofold: one had to do with balance of payments assistance to countries suffering from temporary balance of payments difficulties; the other was addressed to circumstances under which exchange rate change owing to chronic balance of payments pressures would be permitted.

The fundamental wish of the Fund members and those who worked so hard to establish it was to promote stable exchange rates in a world free of exchange controls as regards current transactions. This was a goal impossible to achieve immediately because of existing controls that were a hangover from the war years. Provision was made in the Articles of Agreement of the Fund for a five-year period of transition to follow the beginning of exchange operations (in 1947). (In December 1946, thirty-two countries were formally assigned such initial par values.) It was hoped that such a period of time (which as matters turned out was far too short) would be sufficient for the restoration of free multilateral trade; if more time were needed, those IMF members still practicing controls would be obliged to consult with the Fund annually regarding their removal.

Even if wartime exchange restrictions were successfully eliminated, the Articles of Agreement stipulated that there might be other circumstances under which controls would be warranted. The first case was the so-called scarce currency clause, which provided that if a particular currency became scarce within the Fund's pool of currencies, the organization could either purchase fresh supplies of that currency with its gold holdings, or borrow, or could declare the currency to be scarce and then ration what remaining supply there was among needy members. By issuing a declaration of scarce currency, however, members were authorized to impose discriminating exchange controls against the particular currency. The second case dealt with the permissability of controls for curtailing undesirable capital movements, that is, large or sustained movements which if unsuppressed might lead to balance of payments problems and thus force countries to go to the Fund for assistance.

The second major task of the Fund pertained to providing assistance to member countries striving to maintain exchange rate stability in the absence of exchange controls. The premise of the Fund's founding fathers was that it would be preferable to give assistance to a country experiencing a short-run balance of payments deficit, either as a result of seasonal or cyclical factors, rather than to allow the country to give in to pressure by devaluing its currency or imposing exchange controls. Such assistance was to be provided in the following manner: When a member country needed a particular currency to make current international payments, and assuming its reserves and earnings of that currency were insufficient to meet those demands, that country became eligible to purchase that currency from the Fund by making additional deposits of its local currency. The nature of the transaction was technically more one of a sale than of a loan. A member that used the Fund's resources was under an obligation to repurchase its currency at a later date if its holding of gold and convertible currencies increased in the years pursuant to the purchase of foreign currency from the Fund. Interest charges such as would be applied against a loan accompanied sales of foreign currencies to members. The foreign exchange thus obtained was then used to alleviate the ongoing short-term pressures on the country's exchange rate or to replenish its depleted foreign exchange reserves. This kind of assistance was to be made available upon application to, and with the approval of, the Fund but only to assuage pressures that were temporary in nature and not regarded as having long-run significance. Limits to such assistance were as follows: purchases of foreign exchange in any one year must not exceed 25 percent of a member's quota nor could total purchases exceed 125 percent of a member's quota. The amount of each quota, which was determined by such factors as the size of a country's international trade, its reserves and its national income, determined a country's borrowing power in the Fund and also that country's voting power.

The third principal task of the Fund was to supervise changes in exchange rates when it had been determined that a member country was experiencing a major, chronic balance of payments deficit. Members were permitted to change their exchange rate, upward or downward, up to 10 percent of the original par value at their own discretion. Larger adjustments were upon the request of, and with the approval of, the Fund. The initiative to propose a change in par value lay solely with the country in question, not with the Fund or any other member country. Exchange rate adjustment was looked upon as a measure of last resort, one to be used only when it had become clear that a payments imbalance could not be corrected by making use of the financial resources of the Fund, by altering the exchange rate by no more than 10 percent or by implementation of some acceptable set of alternative domestic monetary and fiscal policies. The purpose of the Fund's supervision was to enable a particular member (or members) to alter its exchange rate so as to effect restoration of equilibrium in its balance of payments while at the same time preventing other members from following suit by changing their exchange rates and reducing the impact of the original action.

Regarding exchange rate changes, the Articles of Agreement state that the Fund "shall concur in a proposed change ... if it is satisfied that the change is necessary to correct a fundamental disequilibrium."[2] The term *fundamental disequilibrium* was never defined in the Articles and in fact has been a point of considerable dispute over the years. As good a definition as any was offered by Robert Triffin, who described it as,

a maladjustment in a country's economy so grave and persistent that the restoration or maintenance of satisfactory levels of domestic activity, employment, and incomes would prove incompatible with equilibrium in the balance of payments, if not accompanied by extraordinary measures of external defense, such as a change in the exchange rates, increased tariff or exchange protection, etc.[3]

Conditions that might be expected to lead to fundamental disequilibrium may be grouped in two categories: differential movements in growth rates or price levels between countries over an extended period of time, and the occurrence of structural changes in demand or supply of internationally traded goods. The first cause occurs because of different emphasis on the goals of growth, price stability, and high levels of domestic employment. While it was presumed at the time of the Bretton Woods Conference that all countries would pursue high-employment policies, differential rates of growth and price inflation have been recorded and in a number of instances have provided the rationale for exchange rate adjustment in the name of fundamental disequilibrium. Structural change, on the other hand, results from a shift in world demand—either toward or away from a country's exports—or a shift in a country's ability to supply goods for export which so affects a country's balance of trade that it leads to a disequilibrium in the overall balance of payments.

Inadequacy of the Fund

It has often been asserted that the Bretton Woods System never worked out in quite the way intended by the founding fathers. It is most assuredly true that the Fund came into being in a period plagued by great problems with which it was ill-suited to cope. The United States was powerful economically and financially, whereas other countries were weak, many near bankruptcy. Problems of recovery from the Second World War and problems of restoring free trade under a regime of fixed exchange rates and convertible currencies quickly proved to be far greater than first envisaged and were certainly beyond the scope of the Fund and the International Bank. This is the first criticism of the Fund and its initial activity (or inactivity) which merits further consideration.

Beginning in March 1947 the Fund was prepared to begin exchange transactions with members confronted by short-term balance of payments difficulties, to oversee and to pass judgment on exchange rate adjustments where the test of "fundamental disequilibrium" was met, and to pursue its objectives as outlined in the Articles of Agreement. One of those objectives was "to assist in the establishment of a multilateral system of payments and in the elimination of foreign exchange restrictions which hamper the growth of world trade." Recalling that a transition period of five years was spoken of in the Articles of Agreement and noting that the British-American Loan Agreement of 1945 stipulated that Great Britain should revert to full convertibility within one and one-half years after signing the agreement, it was to be expected that exchange controls would continue for a brief period. But when a number of years elapsed and still there was no dramatic shift to convertibility (Britain's convertibility of sterling was aborted after only a few months when its foreign exchange reserves had been used up), doubts were cast on the Fund's effectiveness in promoting removal of exchange restrictions. Those doubts were reinforced, moreover, by the surprisingly low volume of the Fund's currency transactions in the early years (that is, up to the mid-1950s) and by the fact that almost no use was made of the technique of exchange rate adjustments until the latter half of 1949—and all of this at a time of widespread balance of payments difficulties.

In response to such doubts and criticisms of the Fund, a number of rebuttals were offered. First, the officials of the Fund deemed it prudent that they exercise great caution in making resources available to members—on the one hand, because of concern that such resources would exacerbate the already severe inflationary pressures present in the world economy, and on the other hand, out of realization that the exercise of drawing rights on an automatic basis by members could quickly result in the exhaustion of the Fund's resources (of dollars and gold) and thereby lead to activation of the "scarce currency" clause entailing new restrictions. The Fund found itself on the horns of a dilemma since, by exercising close control over access to its resources, it left members with little alternative other than retaining their exchange restrictions, thereby frustrating one of the primary objectives of the Fund.

Second, it has been argued that US willingness to extend large-scale dollar aid, particularly to needy European countries, removed much of the pressure that would otherwise have befallen the Fund. The persistence of large balance of payments deficits in Europe and elsewhere arising out of postwar recovery and reconstruction needs was a paramount consideration behind the US decision to establish the Marshall Plan, which extended many billions in dollars to European nations during 1948-51. It was recognized that such tremendous financing could not be handled by the Fund or the World Bank and that the US government was the only possible source. It was presumed, moreover, that countries participating in Marshall Aid funds could satisfy their minimum dollar needs from proceeds of American loans and grants and that those same countries should resort to the Fund's facilities only in exceptional circumstances.[4] Proponents of this view argued that the Marshall Plan was necessary over and above all the resources that were given to the allied countries in the form of lend-lease, UNRRA help, and government loans, because of the great underestimation of their needs to achieve recovery.[5] Far from substituting for Bretton Woods institutions, therefore, the Marshall Plan was considered essential to create the environment in which those institutions including the Fund could ultimately fulfill their tasks.

Another line of argument used to absolve the Fund of direct responsibility for the failure to achieve basic objectives during the first decade of operation was that balance of payments deficits, by their very size and persistence, limited the use of the Fund's resources, which were intended to be made available to member countries experiencing *temporary*, not chronic, difficulties. Even so, exchange rate adjustment was seldom resorted to in the early years because a body of opinion held that because of lingering wartime distortions there was no pattern of rates likely to restore equilibrium. The Fund's view on this matter as stated in the *Annual Report* of 1948 was that countries devastated by war suffered from economic imbalances so fundamental that no exchange depreciation would permit them to achieve balance in international payments simultaneous with an acceptable level of imports. And "in countries where the primary cause of balance of payments deficits is the present limited export capacity, devaluation would not increase foreign exchange receipts, but would merely strengthen domestic inflationary forces."[6] With disequilibrium a fact of life for so many countries, no single country could safely move toward convertibility as long as others maintained the status quo. Indeed, countries had little option other than doing just that, since the Fund's resources were insufficient to support a move to convertibility by all countries simultaneously.

Not until some time later did the Fund adopt a more positive attitude toward exchange rate realignment.

In its own defense, the Fund advanced several other reasons why progress in removing exchange controls had been so slow. In the *Second Annual Report on Exchange Restrictions*, published in 1951, the Fund noted that some governments that had recorded strong gains in their foreign exchange positions were nonetheless reluctant to dispense with existing controls on the grounds that such gains might have been only temporary. Second, in a number of countries it was to the advantage of certain domestic interests to continue exchange control policies and the economic isolation they implied. Such forces acted as a brake on national governments wishing to comply with Fund objectives. Third, in the *Fourth Annual Report on Exchange Restrictions*, published in 1953, the Fund explained how several member countries viewed barriers to entering the US market as providing sufficient grounds for continuing exchange restrictions.[7] Finally, in the same report, the Fund stated that some member countries viewed continued reliance on exchange controls as more politically practicable than the alternative policy course of removing them and enforcing simultaneously more rigorous anti-inflationary measures.[8]

In all fairness, criticisms directed at the Fund's inadequately dealing with the postwar economic and financial circumstances in order to realize stated objectives are primarily aimed not at the Fund's performance as such, but instead are aimed more at the inappropriateness of the institution, whose scope and powers were set forth in the Articles, to deal with emerging problems. The Fund, as one of the two major institutions of the Bretton Woods system, was a novel experiment, launched in times of great optimism, apprehension, and uncertainty all at once, and was endowed with (as it quickly became clear) inadequate resources to meet the minimum needs of countries, a prerequisite to reestablishing free multilateral trade under fixed rates and convertible currencies. In hindsight, it comes as little surprise that the initial objectives were not achieved on schedule, and there is little basis for blaming the Fund's performance or that of any other institution then existing for the result.

A different kind of criticism began to be heard in the early 1950s. Doubts were raised over the desirability of the Fund's stated objective regarding removal of exchange restrictions for certain countries—namely, the less developed countries. At that particular time, interest and attention had begun to build up over what economic development was all about, what it meant and how to achieve it, using methods different from traditional recommendations that had failed in the past. The old atmosphere of complacency and resignation was giving way to a desire for change and to rising expectations.

One important argument to come out of the new discipline of economic development was that exchange control could indeed prove helpful to a less developed country as it strives to promote development. Similar to the classical economic argument favoring tariff protection in order to encourage growth of infant industries, some development economists put forth the argument that exchange control affords protection, by channeling scarce foreign exchange into high-priority areas and by curtailing competitive imports during a transition phase, and provides direction to economic development itself which contributes to the restructuring and increasing sophistication of ongoing economic activity.[9] According to Krause, "Once development is a reality, new forms of production are on hand as exchange control is removed, a situation which, *then*, permits the country to integrate into the internationalist trading order on an altered basis, hopefully to better advantage."[10] But because economic development is a process spanning many years, exchange controls ought to be retained for a considerable period of time.

According to the Articles of Agreement, which were drawn up before there was any great concern for, or understanding of, economic development, all member countries were presumed to desire free multilateral trade and therefore eager to remove as soon as possible exchange controls and other forms of discrimination. The less developed countries, however, were being caught up by a new, forceful desire to achieve development, and the policy recommendations emanating from the new body of thought were often at cross purposes with the objectives, indeed underlying philosophy, of the International Monetary Fund.

As matters have evolved, many LDCs practiced exchange controls into the 1960s, and many such countries still make use of them today. Since the Fund's authorities are obliged to work within the framework provided by the Articles of Agreement, they receive an annual "accounting" from these countries concerning their reasons for retaining exchange controls. The fact that an unwritten accord between the Fund and the LDCs has permitted these practices to continue does not dismiss the inappropriateness of the Fund's orientation to the specific needs and objectives of the LDCs.

The Fund's orientation, both as intended originally by the founding fathers and as it has functioned over the years, has been toward equilibrium. (It is this fundamental premise that the LDCs have found increasingly difficult to accept as they became development oriented.) Such an orientation may be found in the Fund's objective that member countries seek to maintain balance of payments equilibrium in the absence of exchange controls and in the presence of convertible currencies and fixed exchange rates. Should a disequilibrium situation arise for a particular country, then it is expected to pursue the necessary policies to restore equilibrium, borrowing from the Fund if it becomes necessary to correct a short-term problem, or adjusting the exchange rate if the disequilibrium is regarded as being more long-term in nature. Moreover, the Fund's resources consist of a fixed pool of currencies, and there has been no automatic provision for their augmentation, although on two occasions Fund members have voted to increase their quotas and thereby have augmented the Fund's resources.

Not only for the LDCs but for many developed economies, and indeed for the world economy as a whole, the equilibrium orientation of the Fund, with its implicit endorsement of the status quo, may be looked upon as inappropriate. When the Articles of Agreement were framed in 1944, it was expected that countries would follow high-employment policies. That has indeed been the case, with increasing success in recorded growth levels, although at a cost of some price stability. World trade and payments have multiplied many times over, and economic power among nations has been redistributed. The predominant themes of the post-World War II era have been growth and change. It may, therefore, be considered a mark of achievement that an equilibrium-oriented institution with such important responsibilities and notable achievements as the IMF was able to exhibit enough flexibility to endure as long as it has. That all of this proved possible was due in no small part to US policies, the US dollar, and to permissiveness of other nations, as we shall see later.

Out of the equilibrium cum status quo orientation of the Fund came another major charge, of inadequacy. The criticism was that the Fund's provision for international liquidity was unsatisfactory, both in composition and ability to insure its systematic growth over time in conjunction with an expanding world economy. Under the Bretton Woods Agreement, there were two sources of international reserves—gold and foreign currencies. The Fund was in a position to create neither but could lend from its fixed pool, which arose out of quotas contributed by member countries.

Although the Articles of Agreement made no provision for systematically increasing the Fund's resources, and therefore members' ability to borrow in time of need, negotiations within the Fund took place in 1958 and again in 1965 and resulted in a 50 percent and 25 percent increase, respectively, in members' quotas. Despite such increases, members' drawing rights were usually quite small in comparison to deficits experienced in their balance of payments. Accordingly, this cramped the Fund's task of helping member countries promote exchange rate stability in the face of short-term disequilibrium. Indeed, it was largely because of this that the General Arrangements to Borrow was formed in 1962 and bilateral currency swap agreements between countries were negotiated in order to deal with repeated crisis conditions of the mid- and latter 1960s. The GAB, as it is known, is a multilateral arrangement by which ten major countries agreed to make their currencies available to the Fund, which could in turn use the additional resources to help support a currency under speculative attack.

Robert Triffin in his famous book, *Gold and the Dollar Crisis* (1960), predicted the breakdown of the international monetary system established at Bretton Woods, precisely because of this failure of the Fund to provide for increases in monetary reserves appropriate to the maintenance of convertibility by major trading countries.[11] Triffin also indicated that another major source of monetary reserves, newly mined gold, had waned sharply, owing to increased industrial demand and demand by hoarders and speculators, and could not be counted on to take up the necessary slack. What happened, of course, was that official holdings of foreign exchange increased, the great proportion of which were US dollars.

To summarize this first line of criticism: the Fund was inadequate from the outset because it was not designed for, nor endowed with sufficient resources to deal with, existing monetary problems in the immediate postwar years; because it was an equilibrium-oriented institution which proved contrary to the evolving philosophy of a substantial bloc of member nations (the LDCs); and because it was a status quo institution with no provision for meeting requirements of additional monetary reserves within the context of a dynamic international economy.

Failure of the Fund to Function as Intended

The second major criticism of the International Monetary Fund was that it never really functioned in ways originally intended. Consequently, inequities were imposed upon specific countries or country blocs, and weaknesses of the system itself were allowed to fester into major problems.

As argued earlier, the Fund, which was launched at the beginning of the postwar period, was ill-equipped to deal effectively with the enormous problems besetting most members. Whereas a relatively short transitional period was envisaged—restoration of pound sterling convertibility in 1947 and convertibility by other currencies by 1951—removal of exchange controls proved a much slower and more arduous task. Not until 1958 did most European countries establish convertibility for their currencies; not until the Fund was in its twelfth year of operation could it focus on its primary task of maintaining convertibility rather than trying to restore it.

In a very real sense, the Fund took a back seat to the international financial operations of the United States during the 1940s and 1950s. During those years, the United States alone was in a position to, and did indeed, finance a huge transfer of real resources to various countries through gifts and loans. By dint of its unique position economically and financially, and through acceptance of the leadership role, the United States was the focal point of the international monetary system; the actions of this country were crucial to the functioning of the system and to the behavior of other countries. When other countries experienced balance of payments difficulties—frequently, if not chronically, the case in the early years—it was the United States which either took the lead in urging them to modify their policies or made supplementary funds available to them.

For example, the important devaluation of the pound sterling in 1949 was preceded first by a swing in official US and other countries' attitudes to the view that devaluation of some currencies would be in the interest of everyone, since more mileage could be gotten out of the newly launched Marshall Plan and recipient countries would be placed in a stronger competitive position to earn more dollars for themselves. Thereafter, American representatives held preliminary discussions in several European capitals with regard to the advisability of exchange rate adjustments. More formal meetings took place in Washington between British, Canadian, and American officials. All the while, the Fund was an interested bystander.[12]

It was during those early years that the dollar was reaffirmed as the leading world currency; it was used widely for current and capital transactions internationally; it was the currency that governments used to intervene in foreign exchange markets in order to support their exchange values as stipulated in the Fund Agreement; it was a reserve asset for governments which, unlike gold, could earn interest when idle. The US gold stock, which amounted to more than two-thirds of the world total, remained pretty much intact during the 1950s—a matter that continued to symbolize the imbalance of the international monetary system.

All the time the United States was assuming increasingly the role of banker. That role, for which neither the Fund nor any other institution was truly designed, became ever more important in the 1960s. By acting out that role, a means was stumbled upon by which international exchange rate adjustment could be deferred, and it was that development which exposed the vulnerability of the world monetary system and contributed ultimately to its collapse.

The important turning point in the postwar international monetary system and the US direction of it occurred at the end of the 1950s. Economic recovery of the European economies had been achieved, and their currencies were made convertible. Between 1958 and 1959, the US current account balance turned from surplus to deficit, and there also took place a drastic increase in net exports of private capital from the United States. While the United States would again experience current account surpluses, a long string in US basic balance of payments deficits had commenced. Beginning in 1949, there began to be recorded a string of US balance of payments deficits (unbroken with the single exception of 1957) as measured by the liquidity balance. That balance measures the change in the US liquidity position (consisting of net changes liquid liabilities to all foreigners, nonliquid liabilities to foreign official agencies, and official US reserve assets), and it indicates something as to the ability of US authorities to act in defense of the exchange value of the dollar.

The end of the 1950s also signaled a turning point in the sense that economic power which had become so concentrated in US hands began to shift back toward Europe and Japan. The redistribution of that power, along with the erosion of the US liquidity position, would mean eventually that the United States could no longer direct the international monetary system with the same authority, nor command the confidence of other nations, as it had during the 1940s and 1950s.

Two important ways in which the Bretton Woods system relied upon member countries to behave failed to materialize fully. One expectation was that countries could and indeed would manipulate domestic monetary and fiscal policies so as to eliminate temporary balance of payments disequilibria; the second was that when such disequilibria were diagnosed as chronic, adjustment of exchange rate parities would occur promptly. With regard to the first point, the mobility of international short-term capital movements has tended to limit the extent to which monetary policies could be altered in order to help correct a balance of payments disequilibrium. Less wieldy fiscal policies have not been particularly useful in combating short-term external problems; and for those few countries, such as Britain, which have achieved more flexible use of fiscal measures, undesirable effects with respect to business planning for domestic investment projects have been observed.

Beyond the shortcomings of standard policy instruments, most countries have experienced very considerable downward price rigidities since World War II. Rates of inflation have varied widely from country to country, but numerous institutional factors have stood in the way of governments' attempts to recoup lost competitive positions by reversing price movements. Moreover, strong political sentiment, virtually worldwide, favoring high-employment policies has made still more difficult government efforts to correct balance of payments disequilibria through changes in the domestic economic policy mix.

The second point concerns the fact that parity adjustment under the Fund has occurred surprisingly seldom, at least for industrial countries. In part, this has resulted from strong US leadership in negotiating various bilateral and multilateral agreements that make available to a particular country in balance of payments deficit very substantial amounts of foreign exchange with which to beat back speculative pressure manifesting itself in the foreign exchange market. Along with the availability of such foreign currencies, arrangements for which were made almost completely outside of the Fund, governments of most industrial countries viewed changes in exchange parities—up as well as down—as something akin to political catastrophe to be avoided at almost any cost, including "temporary" resort to trade and payments restrictions, which flew in the face of the original intentions of the Articles of Agreement. In a political sense, parity changes came to be viewed as a failure of past policies. (The reluctance of Britain to devalue during the recurring sterling crises of the mid-1960s is a prime case in point.) On both accounts, members of the Fund have willingly endured what might be termed chronically unrealistic exchange rates.

That short-term corrections of balance of payments disequilibria were more difficult to achieve than originally expected, and that parity adjustments were resorted to so seldom despite cases of obvious need, served as further testimony that the international monetary system was somehow failing to function as originally intended. While the Fund itself was equilibrium oriented, disequilibria were often papered over by actions both within and without the Fund's perview.

Both of these observed characteristics, the one of the system in general and the other more of the Fund in particular, were instilled by the leading members of the international economic community.

As the Fund evolved in the context just discussed, asymmetrical pressures became amplified. In the first place, it turned out that the pressures on deficit countries to resort to parity adjustment were greater than pressures on surplus countries, since in the case of the former, monetary reserves and lines of credit might become used up in defense of the parity exchange rate. Such could not happen for surplus countries so long as they were prepared to go on accumulating reserves through sales of domestic currency. Indeed, over the quarter century of the Fund's operation there were many more cases of devaluation than there were of revaluation.

A second asymmetrical feature of the Fund turned on those countries that experienced devaluation most frequently. It has been observed already that the large industrial countries resisted parity adjustment. As balance of payments disequilibria arose for them, the problems were diagnosed most often as short run in nature, which made them eligible to use their drawing rights at the Fund. Those countries were able to use the Fund's resources in their own defense.

For a large number of smaller countries, most of them in the less developed category, the Fund was able to work more in the manner for which it was originally designed. Through annual Fund consultations with those countries, the nature of individual balance of payments was analyzed and policy recom-- mendations were made to the particular governments. The Fund's resources were made available for short-run financing needs, but when the difficulty was judged to be chronic, as was so often the case, no resources were offered, and currency devaluation was recommended. In the general view of those countries, therefore, it was the industrial countries which were able to resort most frequently to the Fund's resources, while they were told to do without and to devalue their currencies. Sometimes in staff consultations with small countries or with LDCs, devaluation was suggested (with the blessing of the managing director) as the price of letting the country in question draw on the Fund. Officially, the Fund may not propose devaluation and generally in practice it waits for the country to act—especially if it is a big country. Every time the LDCs devalued they were of course able to absorb through imports a smaller amount of real resources per unit of domestic currency spent. This meant that their terms of trade worsened as a direct consequence of devaluation.

The sensitivity of the LDCs to this circumstance of worsening terms of trade was already very considerable for two reasons. First, the argument was widespread during the late 1950s and early 1960s that prices of primary products, which comprised the bulk of LDCs exports, tended to decline absolutely or to rise less rapidly than prices of manufactured products, which constituted the large part of developed country exports. This meant that quite apart from anything to do with the Fund, the terms of trade of LDCs were worsening and those of the industrial countries were improving.

Second, the high hopes that LDCs placed on the International Bank at the time of Bretton Woods were never fulfilled and in fact gave way to disillusion- ment as the years passed. The problem was that the World Bank did not have all that much money at its disposal, either in a direct sense or in the indirect sense of its borrowing capacity in foreign markets. A related problem was that the Bank was used initially to help finance reconstruction projects in Europe and later in Japan; funds available for development projects were further limited, and when they were available, it turned out that only certain projects (mainly public not private) could be considered.

Thus, the initial hopes for the World Bank, which had been a major justification for the decisions of LDCs to sign the Bretton Woods Agreement, petered out; and to make matters worse, the manner in which the Fund worked out was viewed as reinforcing the positions of the industrial countries while offering little to the LDC bloc.

Finally, the LDCs also came to regard the Fund as a rich man's club. Not only were the Fund's resources more readily available to its larger, richer members, but its Board of Directors, the important decision-making body, had no balanced representation of the smaller, poorer countries. (At least, that was what many representatives of those countries maintained.) Moreover, their small quotas in the Fund meant that the voices of those countries as voting members were small. And when the Fund was reorganized in 1959, the Fund's resources were increased without modification in formal wording of the Articles of Agreement, thereby precluding reflection of a more appropriate relationship between the Fund and the members in the LDC category, and without any apparent change in the Fund's basic philosophy. The Fund's unfriendly attitude toward the use of exchange controls, regarding which the LDCs saw rational and persuasive arguments, and the equilibrium orientation of the Fund's philosophy, as opposed to the LDCs' wish for change and development, showed no evidence of changing.[13] Not until 1963 as part of the Fund's decision on compensatory financing were LDC's quotas increased relative to those of industrial coun- tries.[14]

A third asymmetrical manner in which the Fund evolved directly concerned the United States. The US dollar became the numeraire of the Fund, with most currencies being defined in terms of dollars while the dollar itself was defined in terms of gold. All central banks except the US central bank used the dollar as the intervention currency, buying dollars when their own currency threatened to become dear relative to its official par value and selling dollars when the reverse applied. Governments were obliged to maintain their own exchange rate within 1 percent of par value, defined in terms of US dollars or gold; this meant that any two currencies could diverge by as much as 2 percent either side of par in relation to each other. The United States was obliged by US law (not the IMF Articles of Agreement) to buy and sell gold for monetary purposes at the fixed price of $35 per fine ounce.

As time passed and the Fund evolved, gold did not turn out to be the work-horse reserve asset of the system; instead, the dollar did. The supply of newly mined gold for monetary purposes never amounted to more than a trickle compared to the liquidity needs of the system, and since dollars were regarded as just as good as, if not better than, gold, dollars became the working asset of central banks. After the turning point in 1959, and with the accumulation of official US liabilities to foreign monetary authorities arising from US balance of payments deficits, the dollar became more than ever the most prevalent reserve asset of the system by virtue of its growth and acceptability.

The problems with this form of meeting world liquidity were fundamentally twofold. The mechanism was unsatisfactory because its operation was not clear-cut. On the one hand, the United States was required to run balance of payments deficits so as to just meet growing world liquidity needs. On the other hand, US trading partners were required to accept increasing amounts of dollars as monetary reserves in order to prevent their currencies from appreciating against the dollar, thus disobeying the rules of the Fund. This was fine as long as foreign central banks wished to accumulate more dollar reserves. But more difficulty was encountered as time went on with respect to volatile movements into or out of dollars and this posed new headaches for domestic monetary authorities abroad. The complicating factor was that US deficits arose for other reasons as well, namely, the decline in US competitive position vis-à-vis other nations and the United States role of financial intermediary for the rest of the world. Second, the viability of using a national currency as the primary world reserve asset was open to question—indeed, to a set of questions having to do with confidence.

The question of confidence arose gradually as US liabilities continued to grow in the 1960s. The magnitude of those liabilities was compared to the stock of US gold reserves, and once the former exceeded the latter, it became clear that should monetary authorities wish to convert all their dollars into other reserve assets—US gold or other foreign exchange reserves—the value of the dollar could not be sustained. If the value of the dollar (the most prevalent reserve asset) could not be counted on to maintain its value in relation to gold, reserve positions in the Fund, or other national currencies—that is to say, if convertibility of the dollar could no longer be fully guaranteed—then the threat of major monetary disturbances could not be ignored. To forestall this problem of confidence, US and foreign monetary officials concurred that the dollar must never be devalued. This was a complete turnabout in relative positions from the early postwar years and clarified the point that exchange rate adjustment as a means to solving balance of payments disequilibria, the most important method of correction offered under the Fund's rules, was not available to the United States. In a turnabout in positions, the initial US situation of unparalleled strength had become a position of weakness that threatened the stability of the monetary system itself.

The matter of confidence in the dollar surfaced in another way, too. International financial transactions have proliferated tremendously in the post-war years, far more than could ever have been imagined at the time of Bretton Woods. Such transactions have expanded naturally enough along with the growth of world trade; their expansion, however, has been magnified even more through relaxation of exchange controls in many countries, as a result of the great accumulation of wealth in the world generally, and because of the development of multinational business corporations with their widespread dealings in trade and investment. In view of the fact that private asset holders are very aware of the exchange value of their assets, and that under the Bretton Woods system exchange rate parities have been subject to infrequent but substantial adjustment, large shifts of private funds from one financial center to another have occurred, with only very small dealer costs and with the possibility for substantial windfall gains (or avoidance of losses) in the event that parity adjustment should indeed take place. This great mobility of international capital has afforded an important means of expression in recent years for those whose confidence in the value of the dollar has wavered. On such occasions the burden placed on the United States to take certain policy measures, even though perhaps quite inappropriate in relation to domestic economic conditions, has been very great.

An interesting sidenote is to be found in a line of argument advanced in 1966 by three well-known economists.[15] Building upon an idea propounded earlier,[16] they argued that the US deficits ought not to be regarded as representing balance of payments disequilibrium but instead that those deficits reflected the role of the United States as a world banker; that instead of being chastised for its deficits, the United States deserved the thanks of the world for performing an important service that neither the Fund nor any other body could do.

More specifically, the outflow of US capital and aid funds, which exceeded its current account surplus, filled two purposes. First, it supplied goods and services to the rest of the world; second, to the extent that US loans to foreigners were offset by foreigners investing their own money in liquid dollar assets, the US supplied financial intermediary services. US deficits, they argued, arose out of the second process, with the United States lending long and borrowing short.

These financial intermediation services, which the United States willingly supplied, were an important ingredient in ongoing economic growth outside the United States. Lack of confidence in the dollar reflected a failure to understand the implications of the intermediary function performed by the United States. Their recommendations were to create an international reserve asset to meet liquidity needs of the world but not to take measures that would restrict capital movements or otherwise interfere with international financial intermediation, which had proved instrumental in facilitating rapid world economic growth. Concern over the US "deficit" should not determine policy, because the deficit reflects the great strength of the US capital market and not a chronic weakness in a trade sense.

The conclusion that US deficits do not matter because of the US role of banker was contested by Edward Bernstein.[17] He asserted that no country or commercial bank could go on adding to its income-earning assets if its earnings (from net exports of goods and services) were insufficient to pay for those investments. Even after allowing for increases in foreign banking claims in the United States, reserves continued to decline. Most government officials and international financiers rejected the argument of Kindleberger, et al., and agreed with Bernstein, especially in view of the recurrence of exchange crises of the late 1960s and the eventual breakdown of the system in 1971-73.

The key currency school of thought, which originated with John Williams prior to the Bretton Woods Conference, only to fall on deaf ears, was revived around 1958. It will be recalled that the essence of the approach was that general stability of currencies is possible only when key currencies, namely the US dollar and the pound sterling, are stable and are in the correct relation to each other. Stability of key currencies depends on the pursuit of sound economic policies within those countries, and stability of lesser currencies depends upon the status of the key currencies. What is called for is not an international organization such as the Fund but close collaboration between major countries. The revival of this idea may have resulted from an awareness that the international monetary system was indeed swinging to the key currency approach and that more attention should therefore be focused on the international role of major economies and the need for sound policies within them to preclude serious international monetary disruptions.

As thinking unfolded, however, the revived discussion of key currencies led instead to new proposals for international monetary reform, many of which bore close resemblance to Keynes's earlier proposals for an international clearing union. There was the expression of a need for a new organization in the form of a world central bank which could reduce the crisis-prone feature, or vulnerability, of the international currency structure as major currencies encountered difficulties of one sort or another. Of these proposals, the Triffin plan and the Bernstein plans were among the most important (see Chapter 5). None of the proposals led to action, but they did serve as further evidence that the Fund was not evolving in ways originally intended.

In conclusion, the Fund never really had an opportunity to function in the manner originally conceived, first of all because it took so much longer to establish the international climate for which it was designed. During the period of reconstruction from war and economic recovery, the leadership role of the United States was firmly established and the groundwork was laid for monetary cooperation outside of the Fund; the dollar became the accepted world currency; and, importantly, a pattern of deciding a number of important monetary matters outside of the Fund's purview was begun. Added to the disadvantage of its slow start, the processes of balance of payments adjustment—concerning both short-term and long-term disequilibria—never worked as smoothly nor as quickly as initially envisaged. The Fund did work more or less along lines anticipated for smaller countries; besides the strong doubts raised as to the propriety of Fund's policy recommendations for such countries, and for the LDCs in particular, the fact that the Fund did not function similarly for the large industrial countries meant that equal treatment was not being meted out to all Fund members. Finally, the unexpected role played by the dollar as a reserve asset proved to be unsustainable for the system as a whole and for the Fund too, especially with the redistribution of economic power back toward Europe and Japan which began in the late 1950s.

4 The Record: Crisis

In spite of the determination of the founding fathers of the Bretton Woods system to avoid the mistakes of the past, in spite of the good intentions and best efforts of government officials, the set of circumstances that led first to recognized crisis conditions and ultimately to collapse of the international monetary system in 1971 possessed some striking parallels to the set of circumstances that resulted in the downfall of the pound exchange standard in September 1931.

On both occasions the currency of the country playing the dominant role in world trade—the key currency—established itself as the most popular means of settlement of international payments, as the unit of account for denominating contracts, as the official intervention vehicle for ensuring stable exchange rates, and as the international reserve asset. On both occasions, current account surpluses of many developed countries buoyed up effective demand and employment in their economies. In the 1930s this was done by means of competitive depreciation of currencies, whereas in the later 1960s it was achieved through inertia and unwillingness to appreciate currencies against an overvalued dollar. This left policy-makers in the more comfortable position of restraining rather than stimulating their economies.

The key currency country, however, bore the consequences of being world banker with an increasingly overvalued currency; those consequences included domestic unemployment problems and slower growth in productivity and real economic expansion, losses of domestic and international competitiveness stemming sometimes from monetary, not just real causes, and a steady drain of capital to foreign economies in response to artificially low production costs abroad as opposed to costs of home production. Because of the disequilibrated exchange rates, investment abroad appeared to promise higher rates of return than investment at home in the key currency country.

On both occasions, chronic balance of payments deficits of the key currency country caused erosion of its liquidity position and led to inconvertibility of the key currency, either de facto or de jure. The conflict between domestic economic policy requirements calling for expansion, and the balance of payments or external policy requirements calling for restrictive monetary and credit policies, was placed in sharper focus. Domestic needs, with their politically stronger imperatives, won a majority of the battles. Despite resort to protectionist measures, payments deficits increased exponentially. At that point, the gold-pound exchange standard came to an end; the gold-dollar exchange standard was allowed to flounder on, however, because of willingness on the part of foreign governments to absorb dollars flooding their markets by proportionately increasing the supply of domestic currency in circulation. Vast speculative movements of funds took place into the relatively strong currencies at a cost of very considerable price inflation in their economies. With no foreseeable way out of the dilemma, the United States, too, called a halt to the postwar dollar exchange standard on August 15, 1971.

Why did such a repetition of past mistakes happen? What can be done to prevent another dominant currency standard from presenting itself to the international community, ultimately causing chaos and disaster? These important questions are dealt with in subsequent chapters of this volume.

The present chapter addresses the question of how particular "crisis circumstances" evolved by the late 1960s. Reference will be made to the major criticisms of the Bretton Woods system, showing how they were relevant to laying bare the causes underlying the important crises that occurred with increasing intensity—crises that foretold the demise of the system.

An Overview

The Fund had been designed to remedy the defects of the international monetary system prevailing in earlier years. However, emerging criticism of the Fund suggested that the postwar international monetary system, quite unwittingly, was taking a different course, one that led to pitfalls encountered in an earlier period.

In the first place, the Fund provided a pool of international credit facilities upon which members could draw when confronted with balance of payments deficits. This feature was in response to the weakness of the gold exchange standard: once confronted with a shortage of monetary gold, demand for reserves was made up by increased holdings of national currencies (mainly the pound sterling), convertible into gold, and increased reliance on reserves borrowed from other countries.

Second, the Fund provided for carefully supervised adjustment of exchange rates under circumstances of fundamental disequilibrium, thereby acknowledging that there was a legitimate basis for such changes. At the same time, it was recognized that such changes could not be left to national authorities alone, since prior experience along those lines had led to beggar-thy-neighbor policies and to competitive devaluations designed to offset exchange rate changes by other countries.

Third, under the Articles of Agreement, members were allowed to use exchange controls or other techniques in order to combat destabilizing short-term money movements. Such transfers from country to country had been a key factor behind the upheaval of the 1930s and after. Convertibility of currencies and abolishment of controls under the Fund were applicable only to current account balance of payments transactions.

Fourth, the "scarce currency clause" in the Fund's Articles allowed members to discriminate in respect of commercial or exchange control policies against any member whose currency had been declared scarce in the Fund. The purpose here was to eliminate the deflationary bias of the gold standard, which forced deficit countries to adopt deflationary policies domestically but which did not force surplus countries to take the opposite course of reflationary actions. The scarce currency clause was of course aimed at the United States, which Britain and other countries feared might not supply funds sufficient to finance its expected payments surpluses. In fact, quite the opposite occurred and the scarce currency clause was never invoked. However, the memory still fresh in the minds of foreign monetary authorities was the propensity of the US to accumulate gold during the interwar period; their conclusion was that this had been partly responsible for resulting deflationary problems.

But for reasons quite beyond its control, the Fund was in many respects set outside the mainstream of postwar monetary developments. The nature of the postwar monetary disequilibrium, rooted as it was in ravages of World War II, and the magnitude of the problems of reconstruction and recovery included therein, was too much for the machinery and the resources of the Fund; accordingly, resolutions were sought elsewhere.

Embodied in the Fund's philosophy was the premise that all currencies were equal. The Fund was not designed to operate in a world where there were obvious disparities in currencies. But immediate requirements of Europe centered on large-scale financial and real economic assistance, and the United States was the only area capable of meeting those needs. Even the financial needs of those countries transcended by far the initial resources of the Fund, and so it could not even play a partial role in resolving the immediate postwar problems.

On the monetary side, therefore, a tremendous demand for dollars arose and a solution was found in the Marshall Plan. Dollars were provided in the form of loans and grants to finance dollar deficits. Real resources purchased from the United States were allocated between countries according to their needs. It was at that juncture that European countries developed international institutions to effect regional monetary cooperation and thus help resolve some of the problems arising out of various bilateral payments schemes. (These institutions were the Intra-European Payments Schemes, the European Payments Union and, after the end of the Marshall Plan, the European Monetary Agreement.) In all of these developments, which took place outside of the Fund, a record and tradition of monetary cooperation among a bloc of countries was building up.

An important development occurring simultaneously concerned the increasing extent to which the dollar was being used as an international reserve currency in place of gold. This, too, was something that evolved contrary to the original design of the Fund. While the Fund was predicated on the dollar being an important currency, the degree to which it assumed that role was probably not foreseen by the Bretton Woods architects. US balance of payments deficits were composed partly of dollar liabilities to foreigners and partly of US gold transferred to other countries. This ability to settle a large part of US deficits through accumulation of dollars by foreign individuals, businesses, commercial banks, and through purchases of dollars on the foreign exchange market by foreign central banks was what President de Gaulle in 1965 called an "exorbitant privilege."

For a time this was a real boon to the international economy. Such additions to world reserves clearly played an important role in facilitating the rapid growth in international trade and payments during the 1950s, growth that certainly would have been hampered otherwise because of the shortage of the stock of monetary gold and the meager additions of newly mined gold to that stock. According to Harry Johnson, "The emergence of the dollar as an international reserve currency has recreated the gold exchange standard of the 1920's, which broke down so disastrously in the 1930's, with all its inherent problems."[1]

Uppermost among the problems were the confidence problem, the long-run liquidity problem, and the adjustment problem. Those problems became increasingly acute after 1957, when the United States emerged as a country with chronic and substantial payments deficits. The same problems were made more severe as a result of a return to convertibility by most European currencies in 1958, which permitted increased capital mobility, and by clear resistance to exchange rate changes to correct balance of payments disequilibria on the part of monetary authorities of leading industrial countries. Resistance on the part of the United States was linked to the obligation not to devalue, which a reserve currency country is assumed to have vis-à-vis its creditors. Resistance on the part of European countries in surplus was associated with the 1949 devaluations, which appeared later to be disturbing and unnecessarily large, and with the idea, which the United States had expounded in an earlier period, that payments deficits arising from domestic inflationary circumstances must be resolved through currency depreciation of the deficit country—not currency appreciation of the surplus country.[2] The upshot was that by 1960 the international monetary system had become characterized by rigid exchange rates and the occasional recurrence of destabilizing capital movements for which effective controls were not devised. Both developments threatened the viability of the system. In both respects, it was a system not at all in accordance with the intentions of the Fund's founding fathers.

The state in which the international monetary system found itself in 1960 corresponded to what Robert Triffin called "Act Two" of the three-act drama of evolution and inevitable deterioration of the dominant currency standard.[3] In Act Two, economic, social and political problems emerge. Growing dollar deficits after 1957 resulted for reasons already enumerated above, and the dollar changed from an undervalued to an overvalued currency with important economic sectors in the United States feeling the continuing pinch on their market shares as a result of shifts in demand in home and foreign markets.

During the 1960s, governments, often collectively, responded to financial crises, but it was always too little and too late. The need for coming to grips with the fundamental problems was not met. Until mid-1963, primary attention was given to strengthening the reserve currency system—not the role of the Fund. The United States consistently regarded its payments deficits as a short-run phenomenon, insisted that the dollar was sound, and called upon other countries to lend their support. Under the direction of Robert Roosa, then Undersecretary of the US Treasury for Monetary Affairs, a variety of ad hoc arrangements with European countries were established. These included currency swaps, prepayments on loans dating back to the war, and issuance of medium-term securities denominated in foreign currencies (the so-called Roosa bonds). Arrangements were undertaken to improve cosmetically the US balance of payments, to finance US deficits without jeopardizing US gold reserves, which had already dwindled substantially from their postwar peak. Europeans collaborated, knowing full well that continued operation of the international monetary system lay in the balance.

A second and lesser important line of evolution of the international monetary system during the first half of the 1960s had to do with strengthening the role of the Fund. An increase in quotas had been agreed upon in 1959, and another increase would be forthcoming in 1965. Beyond that, standby credit facilities for countries in payments difficulties were conceived of and arranged for without any modification of the Articles of Agreement being required. In 1962 agreement was reached concerning the General Arrangements to Borrow. This provided the Fund with an increased stock of currencies which could be sold to members in need. Resort to the GAB, however, was at the discretion of the countries supplying the currencies, a stipulation that reflected European interest in maintaining control in their own hands and not relinquishing it to the Fund. The Fund was drawn into a more general review of the monetary system in 1963 as parallel, high-level investigations by the International Monetary Fund and the Group of Ten were set in motion to consider the outlook for the functioning of the system and its probable liquidity needs for the future.

After the middle of 1963, the United States ceased to adhere to the position that US deficits were temporary. This was presumably because opportunities for further resort to ad hoc arrangements had been exhausted and because new evidence indicated US deficits were likely to be chronic and not a fleeting phenomenon.[4] Foreign countries were reluctant to accumulate more dollars and instead during 1964-67 converted the entirety of their current foreign exchange reserve gains (about $4.4 billion) and some of their previously accumulated foreign exchange holdings into gold and gold-guaranteed claims on the IMF.[5]

In another important respect, the demise of the Bretton Woods system and the dollar exchange standard was hastened by the emergence of inflation in the

United States after 1965. Inflationary conditions resulted as a direct consequence of the buildup in the Vietnam War, which was superimposed on an economy already approaching full-employment output. As an international reserve asset, the dollar ceased to offer a reference point of stable, real purchasing power that could serve as indicator for exchange rate adjustments.[6] For John Williams's key currency approach, the stepped-up rate of inflation in the US—the primary key currency country—would also have loomed as an ill omen, unsustainable for very long without serious disruptions to the system.

By 1967 crisis conditions had arisen and the need for some kind of reform of the international monetary system was clear. Significant steps in that direction were taken in 1967, when agreement was reached at the annual IMF Meeting in Rio de Janeiro concerning the creation of a new international reserve asset (special drawing rights, or SDRs); and in 1968, when the London gold pool was closed and the United States, in accordance with the international agreement to establish a two-tier gold market, ceased to buy or sell gold at the official price of $35 per ounce except on a limited basis to other monetary authorities. This plan was announced March 18, 1968, after a meeting in Washington which included governors of the central banks of the United States, United Kingdom, Belgium, Germany, Italy, the Netherlands, and Switzerland—countries that were members of the gold pool. The purpose of the plan was to protect the international monetary system from further gold speculation. These developments, however, by themselves were woefully insufficient, and crisis conditions escalated dramatically during the ensuing three years.

The 1960 Gold Crisis

The gold crisis of 1960 marks the beginning of problems for the US dollar. That and important crises occurring thereafter will be reviewed so as to set forth the sequence in which crisis circumstances of the late 1960s came into being.

The price of gold took a dramatic jump on the London gold market, the world's largest, on October 20, 1960. Whereas the price had never before exceeded $35.15 per ounce, the price went up to over $40 per ounce on that date. To informed observers, this development came as no great surprise, since US gold sales, net, and increases in dollar liabilities had been occurring for over ten years and had taken a sharp turn for the worse during the most recent three-year period. But government officials who had steadfastly maintained that all was well and that there was no need for concern were jolted from their complacency. The extent to which officials were caught off guard by the rise in the price of gold just after the conclusion of the Annual IMF Meeting in Washington was captured in the comment of a Treasury official: "We are watching it closely. We are wondering just what has happened."[7]

The sudden and, for many, unexpected events in the London gold market created widespread concern, which was viewed as an adverse reflection on the strength of the dollar. Following conversations with officials of the Bank of England, the US Treasury publicly reaffirmed its policy of willingness to sell gold to monetary authorities at its legally fixed price of $35 per ounce and indicated it had no criticism of stabilizing operations in the London gold market by British authorities. This was interpreted to mean that the Bank of England could replenish from the US Treasury any gold it sold on the London market.

Behind the scenes, it was decided that monetary stability would be served best if the gold price were maintained at the official level. To that end, an agreement to establish the London gold pool, consisting of eight central banks (the seven central banks of the countries mentioned above plus the central bank of France), was made in February 1961. According to that agreement, purchases or sales in the private gold market were to be made in fixed proportions by the eight participating central banks as conditions warranted. The purpose was to iron out fluctuations between private demand for, and the supply of, newly mined gold. The London gold pool worked well—and anonymously—until several years later when instead of buying gold on balance it became a net seller on a large scale.

More generally, the events in London during 1960 touched off a fresh appraisal of the US balance of payments situation and the international monetary system. Several actions were taken by the outgoing Eisenhower administration late in 1960 in order to demonstrate US determination to defend the dollar. On February 6, 1961, President Kennedy's statement on the "Balance of Payments and Gold" injected a new urgency and sense of importance to achieving overall equilibrium in US international payments, and proposed a program consisting of measures to improve domestic monetary arrangements, to strengthen international cooperation in economic and monetary policy, and to correct the persisting balance of payments deficit.[8] All the while, however, it was held that defense expenditures and aid to LDCs should not be jeopardized by balance of payments considerations.

Within the Congress, the Joint Economic Committee commenced efforts to educate all concerned on sundry aspects of the international monetary problem and the US balance of payments deficits. A Subcommittee on International Exchange and Payments was established, with the Honorable Henry S. Reuss as chairman, to study "International Financial Arrangements." Congress was in fact ahead of the administration in pressing forward its investigation of the broad issues of international monetary reform and tended to regard as inadequate the patchwork and palliative measures adopted by the administration during 1961-63.

Academicians took to the forefront in their general advocacy of revolutionary reforms of what they saw as an outdated, crisis-prone international monetary system. Their ideas were aired in congressional hearings in the early 1960s and were given lengthier attention in the professional literature.[9] In one way or another, much of the controversy and attention generated over the international monetary system and the problem of US payments deficit was touched off by the 1960 gold crisis and the implications of that event.

The Pound Sterling Crises

The pound sterling endured four serious, costly crises between 1964 and 1968 before it was finally devalued on November 18, 1967. Those crises were in fact the culmination of long and deep-seated problems, both domestic and foreign, against which Britain had held out. War debts, the responsibility of operating a reserve currency (primarily for sterling area countries), an economy in which productivity could not seem to increase pari passu with labor's ability to push up wages, increasing dependence on foreign energy sources rather than domestic coal resources—all of these considerations came to bear in 1963-64.

Both the balance of payments and domestic economic conditions suggested that sterling was seriously overvalued and ought to be devalued. Yet that policy course was denied largely as a consequence of British political choice in hopes that protective measures, borrowing from the Fund, multilateral currency support operations, a wage freeze, and underutilization of the domestic economy would buy sufficient time for adjustment to occur by a "natural," competitive realignment of prices and costs.

At the time, currency adjustment of any sort was widely viewed as something to be avoided at any cost by leaders of industrial countries. This was all the more true for devaluation, and it was nearly unthinkable that a reserve currency country such as Britain—a key currency country—would take such a major step with all its political ramifications. Nevertheless, for private businessmen and exchange market operators the compelling evidence, which pointed to a fundamental disequilibrium of sterling and the inability of the British Government to correct the problem by other means, led them to take positions against the unthinkable—a devaluation of sterling.

Throughout the sterling crises, the US played an important role, both in the narrow sense of helping to muster together funds to defend the sterling parity and in the broader sense of encouraging the British to seek adjustment by means other than by devaluation. The Federal Reserve provided dollars on a swap basis directly to the Bank of England, which in turn used them to defend against speculative attacks on the pound. The swap line with the Fed was first set at $500 million and then increased to $1000 million in September 1964. Other short-term credit facilities with European central banks and with the Bank of Canada were obtained. $1000 million in standby credits from the Fund in August 1964 were used also to defend the sterling parity. On November 25, 1964, it was announced that a $3000 million credit package provided by eleven countries and the Bank for International Settlements was at the disposal of the

Bank of England. By the end of November, net drawings by the Bank of England on its various short-term credit facilities amounted to $1200 million, of which the Federal Reserve was responsible for $675 million.[10] The bulk of those borrowings were repaid early in the new year, 1965, as the speculation ceased and there was some strengthening in the British trade account.

The sterling crises of June-August 1965 and June-July 1966 involved increasingly heavier speculative attacks on sterling. Accordingly, further resort to swap lines and multilateral credit facilities was made in order to defend the parity—$1300 million during the second crisis and $1800 million during the third. After each attack, the bulk of the borrowings were repaid.

The finale in the series of sterling crises commenced in April 1967. Export growth petered out and imports rose far more rapidly than predicted. Other adverse factors included the relatively slow growth of world trade and production, the Six Day War in the Middle East (which led to the closing of the Suez Canal and resulted in higher-cost oil imports, and the serious dock strikes in September). Despite increasing talk of devaluation, the government was reluctant to capitulate, partly because of the political costs of admitting defeat of policies pursued for more than three years at great economic sacrifice to the nation in terms of reduced growth and high unemployment, and partly because of the burden of outstanding foreign debts ($904 million to various central banks due to be repaid by the end of 1967 and $1523 million owed to the Fund and due by the end of 1971).[11] Sterling, however, was under almost continuous pressure, pressure that reached unprecedented proportions in the week before sterling was devalued from $2.80 to $2.40, or by 14.3 percent, on November 18. In the final days of defense, the Bank of England purchased some $1000 million from the foreign exchange market at the $2.80 rate. When speculators later went to repurchase sterling, they obtained windfall profits at the expense of the British government.

The British experience with its balance of payments problems and ultimately with devaluation afforded three important lessons. First was the lesson of how costly inept handling by government officials could be. Two days before devaluation was publicly announced, the chancellor of the exchequer responding to questions in Parliament all but tipped his hand about the Cabinet decision already made favoring devaluation. Yet the foreign exchange market remained open for another day, allowing speculators to sell sterling against dollars and thus make sure profits. Then the prime minister implied in his official statement that devaluation itself would solve the problem; only later was it made clear to the public that more deflationary measures would be required in order to correct the payments deficit and to compensate for the adverse effect of devaluation on the terms of trade (reduced foreign exchange earnings for a given amount of exports and higher foreign exchange costs for a given amount of imports). Moreover, there was a delay of several months before the government decided upon and announced deflationary measures necessary to make devaluation effective. This time lapse caused adverse speculation abroad about the viability of the $2.40 sterling rate. Finally, the mix of deflationary measures that were finally announced (especially reduced private consumption to be achieved by increasing indirect taxes) touched off a sustained consumer spending spree during the time remaining prior to their adoption.

The second lesson went largely unlearned because of the gold crisis of 1968 and other exchange market pressures (one of which is treated below) which prevented the sterling devaluation from working itself out in relative calm. It has already been indicated that according to the original conception of the Fund and the operation of the international monetary system, exchange rates ought to be adjusted in orderly fashion by international agreement in cases of "fundamental disequilibrium." The way the Fund and the system functioned during the 1950s and 1960s, that philosophy appeared to have been largely abandoned, particularly by large industrial countries, and was replaced by the view that exchange rates were more fixed in relation to each other. This was not something that evolved out of conscious rational decisions of governments but out of a spontaneous reaction to events and increasing dependence on key currencies.

As a case in point, the devaluations of 1949, which occurred before the Fund was operating in the intended environment of convertible currencies, left the impression that a country of standing such as Britain would have to devalue by more than necessary in order to convince others that such action would not be repeated soon again, and that because of the magnitude of devaluation by the major currency, other lesser currencies would also change their rates in an offsetting manner with unpredictable results. For example, the sterling devaluation in 1949 amounted to 30.6 percent but, because of other devaluations, resulted in an improved competitive position as measured on a trade-weighted basis of only about 8 percent. It was in this inadvertent manner that exchange rate adjustment, the only truly reliable mechanism of adjustment available to the system, came to be viewed as something to be avoided at all costs. In place of that mechanism, governments relied on interventions in international trade and payments and on domestic policies aimed at influencing prices and wages to effect international relative price adjustment.

The positive feature of the 1967 sterling devaluation was that it occurred in close cooperation between leading central banks, and as a result of international agreement, it provoked no serious retaliatory exchange rate changes. The 1967 sterling devaluation of 14.3 percent also resulted in an approximate 8 percent improvement in Britain's competitive position. In short, it was an adjustment much more like that conceived of by the framers of the Bretton Woods Agreement. Had not the sterling devaluation been clouded over by speculative exchange rate and gold crises immediately afterward, it might have led government officials back toward the original intentions of the Fund and the Bretton Woods System in much the same spontaneous, intuitive manner that earlier had led them in another direction.

The third lesson of the British experience was the increasingly important role that short-term capital movements had come to play. Much speculative attention was attracted to exchange markets during the recurrent sterling crises, and as events unfolded it was clear that a growing amount of liquid funds stood ready to take a position in the market when speculative profits appeared in the offing. The profits that did in fact result from the eventual devaluation confirmed the judgment of speculators, and their hunger for more contributed to growing instability of international financial markets.

The Canadian Dollar Crisis

This crisis occurred during January-March 1968, right on the heels of the sterling devaluation but not as a consequence of it. The Canadian dollar crisis resulted not out of weakness in the domestic economy nor out of any threat to the competitive position of the country compared to the United States, which was and is Canada's major trading partner. Instead, the crisis developed out of speculator opinion that the new US balance of payments policy, which was announced January 1, 1968,[12] and entailed mandatory restrictions on foreign direct investment, might impede or stop the flow of capital from the United States to Canada. If so, it was believed that the Canadian economy and the Canadian dollar would be seriously weakened.

Despite explicit assurances from US Treasury Secretary Fowler that the US program would not present difficulties for Canada or other countries such as the United Kingdom and Australia which were heavily dependent upon US capital markets, speculators took positions against the Canadian dollar. This forced the Bank of Canada to enter the foreign exchange market to purchase the excess supply of Canadian dollars (by selling part of its foreign exchange reserves and drawing upon its swap arrangements with the United States) and thereby maintain the parity exchange rate within the agreed support limits. The Bank used about $310 million of its reserves in January alone. In February, announcement was made of a $426 million Canadian drawing from the Fund but this, rather than stabilizing the market, caused adverse reaction and more private selling of Canadian currency. The crisis was resolved early in March when Canada was granted complete exemption from the US balance of payments program. In return, Canada promised that the US balance of payments would not suffer as a result of the exemption and that the government would enforce measures to prevent Canada from becoming a conduit through which funds from the United States could pass through to foreign countries and thereby frustrate US attempts to deal with its payments imbalance arising on capital account.

Lawrence Krause has identified two important lessons emanating from the Canadian dollar crisis.[13] First, governments of the United States and Canada were made aware of the great interdependence of their capital markets, a reputation of the popular but mistaken assumption of national sovereignty for either country on economic and financial matters of common interest. Second, the fragile state of the international monetary system was laid bare to observers all over the world. No currency, it was thought, could be completely safe from speculative attack if one seemingly as secure as the Canadian dollar were vulnerable. Moreover, the standard institutional form of international cooperation—a drawing from the IMF—was wholly inadequate before a concerted speculative attack.

The 1968 Gold Crisis

By the end of 1967 symptoms of an unhealthy international monetary order had become more widespread in comparison with those of just a few years before during the 1960 gold crisis, or even compared to symptoms prevailing in 1964 when the sterling crises began in earnest. The adverse balance of payments effects of the Vietnam War and of inflation within the US economy associated with the war buildup had blossomed and were arousing the ire of European countries; General de Gaulle had initiated an all-out campaign against reserve currencies, specifically against the dollar, and in favor of gold; moreover, the private gold demand for nonmonetary uses exceeded newly supplied gold (both from current production and from Russian gold sales) for the first time in 1966, which meant that the gold pool switched from its former position of net buyer to net seller. During 1967, net official sales of monetary gold rose sharply to $1580 million compared to $45 million in 1966.

Net sales of gold by central banks constituted a fundamental sign of a "turn for the worse" for the monetary system, for gold had become the most important reserve asset of the system by virtue of its increasing scarcity relative to foreign exchange reserves ever since the beginning of the 1960s. If the central banks were continually forced to sell gold to maintain the official price of $35 per ounce, then continued expansion of international trade, itself requiring growth of world liquidity, could occur only if other reserve assets—foreign exchange and IMF borrowing facilities—increased at an ever more rapid pace. Coexistence of different reserve assets required, however, that the exchange value between them remain fixed; but this was asking almost too much if those different reserve assets constituting world liquidity did not expand in roughly equal proportion over time.

Official gold sales, therefore, were ominous on several counts: First, such sales exacerbated the general liquidity problem, that is, the shortage or threatened shortage of international liquidity; second, if allowed to continue, gold sales would further upset the balance between reserve assets coexisting together and would threaten the fixed price relationship between them, which could only mean international financial chaos and ultimate collapse of the system; third, in countries where gold trading was legal, purchases and sales of gold by the gold pool had domestic monetary consequences similar to open market operations in government securities.[14] The problem was that discretion lay with the public and not the central bank. Compensatory actions were available to the domestic central bank but only through intervention in domestic financial markets. Excessive gold transactions—either sales or purchases—in such countries consequently posed potential problems for executing domestic monetary policy.

As it was, the gold market was a very good environment for speculators. Purchases could be made on small cash margins, and there was no downward risk since the $35 per ounce price was supported by the gold pool. Between November 1967 and mid-March 1968, approximately $3000 million of official gold was sold on the market, with the "gold rush" becoming especially acute during March 11-13.

The immediate cause of the gold crisis was the growing belief that the dollar had become overvalued and that, like the pound sterling, it would soon have to be devalued. Since the value of the dollar was defined in terms of gold, this led speculators to express their preference for gold. Devaluation would mean a rise in the price of gold (and in some fashion as well, although less clear before the event, an increase in the value of other currencies relative to the dollar). Many US experts argued at the time that a dollar devaluation (that is, against gold) would likely be fruitless, since other currencies might also change their gold price proportionately and therefore maintain their currencies' exchange rates relative to the dollar. Such an outcome would be a welcome gift to private and official holders of gold, but unlike the sterling devaluation would offer no possible improvement in the US payments imbalance. Partly for this reason, but also because of the long-standing US political commitment to the fixed dollar-gold price, US officials insisted the existing value of the dollar would be maintained.

At the request of the United States, the London gold pool suspended operations on March 14 (private trading was stopped as well) and members of the gold pool (except France, which had resigned some time before) convened hastily in Washington to discuss their next move. At the conclusion of the conference, a joint statement was issued proclaiming the "two-tier" gold market. Central banks agreed not to buy or sell gold to private individuals, thereby freeing the price in private markets and allowing it to seek its own level according to daily supply and demand. Monetary gold held by governments was to be kept as part of international reserves and could continue to be traded between central banks but only at the official price. The plan was endorsed by other central banks and by the IMF.

The significance of the two-tier gold market, which in fact functioned smoothly, was that gold had been demonetized because gold circulating among central banks at an arbitrary price unrelated to the private market was only a unit of account.[15] Economists proclaimed that whereas the world was formerly on the dollar exchange standard, it was thenceforth on the dollar standard. In Professor Triffin's view, inconvertibility of the dollar, the key currency of the monetary system, meant that the dollar was transformed into an "uncontrollable instrument of world wide inflation" and that the US had become "exempted from any international adjustment mechanism."[16]

Summary

Crisis circumstances within the international monetary system had emerged indeed by 1968. The financial crises reviewed above, which were not the only ones that occurred but which were important in typifying evolution of the generally recognized crisis conditions, reveal how far the Bretton Woods system had drifted away from its initial conception as a consequence of US dominance and emergence of the dollar standard. While the world financial community was becoming increasingly dependent upon the dollar and upon the United States as world banker, the transfer of real economic power was taking place in the opposite direction, that is, from the United States toward European countries and Japan. With the passage of time, therefore, the ability of the United States to direct the international monetary system as it had done before—and was increasingly being asked to do—was being eroded.

The three long-recognized problems of the dollar exchange standard became ever more manifest; the liquidity problem having to do with the deterioration of the liabilities: assets ratio of the key currency, and, stemming therefrom, the loss of confidence in continuing convertibility of the key currency into gold; the general confidence problem associated in the official sense with the growing gap between desired and actually obtainable composition of reserve assets, and in a private sense with the speculative shifts of short-term capital between financial centers; and the adjustment problem.

Nevertheless, government responses to these problems were not forthcoming or were inadequate to the needs. Part of the explanation for this may be found in the increasing national jealousies of the key currency country on the one hand and the non-key currencies on the other. For the United States, the evolving situation was seen more and more as one of unacceptable responsibility, while for other countries, the US position appeared to be one of "exorbitant privilege" for one or another set of reasons. Jealousies were by no means limited to economic-financial matters but spilled over into political areas, too. Jealousy, inertia, stubbornness, pleas of special circumstances, and future uncertainty blocked any concerted grappling with fundamental problems.

In simplest terms, the recognition of crisis circumstances in 1968 centered on two points: first, the growing overvaluation of the US dollar, permitted both by continuing failure of the nonreserve, undervalued currencies to take some sort of action to appreciate their currencies and by failure of adopted patchwork measures (in the form of interferences with free conduct of economic transactions and restraints on wages and prices) to cause the required relative price adjustments; second, the mushrooming volume of speculative funds capable of swift transfer from one financial center to another, seemingly impervious to governmental control.

Part III:
Movement to Reform

5 Events of 1968-72

This chapter sets the stage for subsequent chapters addressed to problems and issues of particular countries or blocs. The ever increasing ills of the Bretton Woods system occurring after the recognition of crisis circumstances in 1968 are related, followed by a recounting of the sorts of measures that governments adopted in order to deal with those ills. Then, important examples of the many proposals for monetary reform offered by the academic community are grouped into three main categories and presented in brief. Finally, two key conferences occurring in 1972, the third United Nations Conference on Trade and Development and the Annual Fund-Bank Meeting, are reviewed for their impact on the monetary reform discussions now under way.

Crisis Conditions and Destabilizing Capital Movements

Pursuant to the emergence of generally recognized crisis conditions during late 1967 and early 1968, the tempo of hectic foreign exchange market activity in leading financial centers escalated; intensified movements of short-term capital were presented to governments as an increasingly troublesome and most difficult problem with which to deal. These capital movements across the foreign exchanges, sometimes amounting to very large sums of even a few billion dollars, were capable of occurring within a surprisingly short span of time—a few days or weeks. This section briefly recounts those critical high points occurring in the four years prior to the demise of the Bretton Woods system.

From May 1968 through October of the following year, there were recurrent periods of heavy speculation concerning possible devaluation of the French franc and revaluation of the German deutschemark. Difficulties surrounding the French franc had their roots in the domestic disturbances, economic, political, and social in nature, which took place during May and June 1968. The major disruption was a nationwide strike by large sectors of the labor force over issues of alleged inequity and persistent structural economic imbalances. Leaders of government and industry finally caved in and granted a very large wage increase in order to restore order. Following those dramatic events, it was only a matter of time before resulting price increases on wide ranges of products led to erosion of France's international competitive position. That erosion was manifested first by a deteriorating balance of trade and the emergence of balance of payments deficits, and before long by mounting uncertainty in exchange markets that the franc parity rate could be maintained.

In Germany, where inflation in the postwar period had been an anathema both to government and the general public, the practice had developed whereby strict measures were enforced as soon as there appeared to be firm evidence of overheating within the economy. So disastrous had been the German experience with hyperinflation during the 1920s and 1930s, that only secondary regard was given to matters of general employment. The preoccupation German policy-makers revealed in favor of price stability caused the DM during the 1960s to become overvalued relative to other currencies, whose countries' governments had demonstrated a greater tolerance of price inflation either by design or out of inability to achieve stability.

The strong external position of Germany therefore contrasted increasingly with the worsening external position of France during the latter half of 1968 and early 1969. In view of the two countries' close economic interdependence, ensuing discussions with the European Community and the Group of Ten were directed to considerations of exchange rate changes for both currencies; but because domestic political difficulties faced both countries' governments, no exchange rate adjustments were made until the second half of 1969.

In the interim, the French franc sustained two major crises at a cost of some $3.7 billion in reserves, and resort had to be made as well as to harsh exchange controls and a number of trade restrictions. In August 1969 the French franc was devalued by 11.1 percent. Germany, as a result of speculation over the possible revaluation of its currency, was forced to purchase $8.6 billion (increasing its foreign exchange reserves by a like amount) between the end of August 1969 and the end of September 1969. Following a nearly four-week-long "float" of the DM, a 9.3 percent revaluation was announced October 24.

The French franc and DM crises of 1969 were severe for their time, a conclusion supported both by the large magnitudes of speculative capital movements involved and the resulting changes in the official reserve levels, and by the fact that at one point foreign exchange markets were closed officially for one week to let matters cool off and to allow international conferences to decide how best to restore calm. Moreover, the crises involving the two currencies further exposed the nature and depth of the adjustment problem inherent in the Bretton Woods system. Finally, the float of the DM was important, for it was the first departure by a major industrial country from the fixed exchange rate system of the Fund.

A second high point during 1969-70 was recorded as a result of the very large movements of short-term capital between financial centers, both between European financial centers and between Europe and the United States, in response to changes in interest rates. Facilitating these capital movements was the ever expanding Eurodollar market. Eurodollar deposits are dollar-denominated commercial bank liabilities outside the United States. The Eurodollar market has its center in London, where Eurodollars are loaned and invested. Other financial centers where substantial amounts of Eurodollars are on deposit include those in continental Europe, in Canada, and in Japan. Although the exact magnitude of the deposits in the Eurodollar market is unknown, their rapid growth over time has been well established. The Bank for International Settlements has estimated the volume of the market to have increased from approximately $9 billion in 1964 to $26 billion in 1968 to $97 billion in 1972.

During the "credit crunch" occurring in US financial markets in 1969, short-term interest rates rose above the ceiling imposed by Regulation Q, which fixes the maximum interest rates member banks of the Federal Reserve System may pay on time deposits. As a result, US commercial banks' ability to attract new deposits from domestic money markets was impeded, and so they resorted to Eurodollar borrowing through their foreign branches. Such borrowing increased precipitously, and for the year as a whole an inflow amounting to $8.7 billion of foreign private liquid funds was recorded. Such a large borrowing of Eurodollars forced up overseas interest rates to record high levels. In June 1969, Eurodollar interest rates exceeded 11 percent and stayed at about that level for the remainder of the year. The sources of funds included liquid funds in European domestic money and capital markets which were switched into dollars on the foreign exchange market and then loaned to American branch banks. In a real sense, many of the dollars came from European central banks' holdings of dollar reserves which they would have gained otherwise during the course of the year through their intervention in exchange markets to support the dollar.

Needless to say, the ability of commercial banks and private individuals to undertake such actions was upsetting to the pursuit of domestic monetary policy not only in the United States but also in many European countries from whence the funds came. At the time, there was also occurring a process of circular flow, which enabled individuals to take advantage of existing interest rate differentials that resulted from Regulation Q. Private dollars moved from the United States to the Eurodollar market and then back again through foreign branches of US banks. It was this process which created such a divergence in two standard measures of the balance of payments—the liquidity balance and the official settlements balance.

The passing of the US economic boom in 1970 brought about a reduction in demand pressures in markets for goods and services; presently, the Federal Reserve introduced easier monetary policy, and interest rates in the United States began to come down. In Europe, however, demand pressures remained very strong during the year and financial conditions continued to tighten. Accordingly, substantial net outflows of private liquid capital from the United States took place. For 1970 as a whole, this outflow amounted to $6.2 billion, and this was a major factor explaining the shift in US official transactions balance from plus $2.7 billion in 1969 to minus $9.8 billion in 1970. As US dollar borrowings were repaid, foreign central banks entered the exchange market to mop up excess dollars and thereby maintain exchange rates within agreed support points. US liquid liabilities to foreign official agencies rose by $7.6 billion during 1970 after having declined by $0.5 billion the previous year. In effect, this was a reversal of 1969 activities as US banks repaid their costly borrowings from foreign branches, borrowings that changing conditions in the United States made no longer necessary.

While these large movements of liquid funds were handled smoothly by exchange markets during the two-year period, the potential destabilizing power of volatile short-term capital was recognized, including the extent to which such capital movements could interfere with pursuit of domestic monetary objectives. Some countries, including Japan, Belgium, and France, did attempt to block such transfers but with only partially successful results. Most other countries lacked the administrative machinery or political will—or both—to enforce the kinds of regulations necessary to curtail such movements.

The next high point was the one that finally fractured the international monetary system—the 1971 international financial crisis. Early in the year a convergence of views was taking place in regard to the previous international monetary system. First, there was the view that the dollar had long been overvalued, perhaps throughout the decade of the 1960s, that the situation was proving less and less sustainable all the time, and that soon some fundamental corrective exchange rate adjustments would have to be taken. Second, it was believed that the poor wage-price-productivity performance of the US economy between 1965 and 1969 had severely damaged the US international competitive position, that this was evident in the steadily declining US trade surplus in recent years (including the small $2.1 billion surplus recorded in 1970 when recessionary conditions prevailed in the United States and boom conditions existed elsewhere), and that with a resumption of strong US economic growth in 1971, a balance of trade deficit could quite easily arise for the first time in this century. This would mean only one thing: much larger overall payments deficits for the United States. Third, in early 1971, evidence was continuing to appear that developments in the realm of monetary policy in the United States and abroad were a basis in themselves for large, disequilibrating capital movements between financial centers.

Adverse developments in the US trade balance did in fact appear, and this gave greater impetus to expectations that a change in the value of the dollar might soon occur. Beginning in May, two massive movements of dollars began; one was a stepped up outflow of liquid funds from US residents to residents of other countries, the other a massive conversion of dollar funds held by banks and businesses abroad into other currencies. The tide of those capital flows was so serious that exchange markets were closed by international agreement during May 5-9, 1971. Some hastily arranged meetings took place among finance ministers of the leading countries during those days. Then, on May 10 it was announced that the deutschemark and Dutch guilder would be allowed to float and that the Swiss franc would be revalued. Nevertheless, exchange market pressure and general anticipation of imminent, momentous decisions continued to build.

On August 15, President Nixon announced a new and bold set of economic policies to be pursued by the United States.[1] There were two basic objectives: to correct the overvalued dollar and reestablish US competitiveness in international markets; and to reform the international monetary system in order to ease the no longer sustainable burdens placed upon the United States. Beginning August 16, convertibility of the dollar into gold or other reserve assets including SDRs was suspended as were exchange rate guarantees, which had been offered previously to central banks of foreign countries for any drawings made on the currency swap agreements. In effect, the dollar was left to float on the world's foreign exchange markets.

The dramatic initiative of the United States touched off intense bilateral and multilateral negotiations. There was a great deal of pressure for an early and favorable settlement, applied first by the United States and then by other leading countries. But a breakthrough did not appear until the Group of Ten meeting in Rome, November 30-December 1. Then on December 18 at the Smithsonian Institution in Washington, D.C., agreement was reached among the same Group of Ten countries to realign exchange rates and to widen the bands (from 1 percent to 2¼ percent either side of parity) within which central banks would permit exchange rates to move. Economic experts and political leaders hailed the Smithsonian Agreement as a great achievement in international monetary relations. The more arduous task of framing a new system for international monetary exchange and cooperation was called for in the agreement and has been under way ever since.

The Smithsonian Agreement was at best an interim agreement designed to patch up the infirmities of the old Bretton Woods system until a new system or fundamental reform of the old one could be agreed upon and implemented. Even for that limited purpose, however, the agreement was soon found wanting. Very suddenly in June 1972, only six months later, a crisis erupted involving the pound sterling. Approximately $2.5 billion in British reserves were spent defending the new central rate for sterling during the days of June 16-22. Then, to the surprise of many observers, Her Majesty's Government announced on June 23 that the pound would be allowed to float. Exchange market pressure against the dollar reappeared in July 1972, but for the moment there was no further unraveling of the Smithsonian Agreement.

In the third week of January 1973 there began to unfold a succession of developments whose origins were in Europe. Great speculative pressures were brought to bear, first in one financial center and then another, with the result that the Swiss franc was floated as was the Italian lira (the latter only for financial transactions). Those capitulations were insufficient to restore confidence, and an even greater run on the dollar took place in the first nine days of

February. There were more secret negotiations between high-level policy-makers of leading countries, at the end of which it was announced on February 12 that the dollar had been devalued for the second time in less than fourteen months. Revaluation of four leading European currencies occurred the following day, as well as the announcement by Italy and Japan of their unilateral decisions to float their currencies. But these developments did not suffice to relieve the pervasive speculative fever against the dollar, which reintensified at the beginning of March. Official exchange market operations were suspended from March 2 until March 16, after which it was agreed that all leading countries would permit their currencies to float against the dollar—a state of affairs that continues today.

A number of factors combined to make the Smithsonian Agreement unsustainable. Inconvertibility of the dollar made foreign central banks reluctant to purchase large amounts of dollars in the foreign exchange market, which it turned out was necessary in order to support the newly agreed configuration of exchange rates. While that reluctance was expected and understandable, it was also expected that improvement in the US trade position and balance of payments would become apparent rather soon, perhaps in the latter half of 1972. That improvement failed to occur for several reasons. First, there was the lag in business cycle conditions abroad compared to the United States, which not only made for sustained US import demand but also for sluggish foreign demand for US exports. Second, the effects of the first dollar devaluation and revaluations of other currencies were absorbed in varying degrees by commercial traders all over the world, which minimized the real impact of the exchange rate realignment. Third, there was miscalculation based on uncertainty and overestimation of the impact of the Smithsonian Agreement in the short term and over the medium term. As a result of all these factors, the patience and willingness of foreign governments to go on supporting the dollar gave way in the face of massive speculator anticipation that they would do just that. And they did.

Measures Adopted to Deal with Crisis Conditions

By and large, measures resorted to by governments to combat the crisis conditions that had arisen by 1967-68 were measures of patchwork variety designed either to help finance payments deficits or to suppress or paper over apparent trouble spots in one or another sectors of the balance of payments. In one or two instances, governments were able to concur on matters that changed part of the framework of the international monetary system. For example, the special drawing rights (SDRs) did indeed address one of the fundamental problems of the international monetary system. The decision to set up the two-tier gold market and in effect to demonetize gold was another instance in which governments agreed to a contingency plan that altered the format of the Bretton Woods system as it had been known up to that time. But progress along those lines, which was not only painfully slow but was also incomplete, did not go sufficiently far to divert the postwar international monetary system from its course of deterioration and ultimate demise.

Consider first the agreement to establish the two-tier gold market and the decision to create SDRs, the two being importantly intertwined. In September 1967 members of the Fund convening at their annual meeting in Rio de Janeiro agreed to establish a new reserve facility to meet the need for supplements to existing international reserve assets. Provision was made for regularly creating special drawing rights (SDRs) by the Fund which would be accepted by member countries as reserves and would be used henceforth in international settlements. Allocations of SDRs was based upon the size of member countries' quotas in the Fund. Unlike other credit facilities available at the Fund, SDRs were intended to provide a permanent addition to international reserves.

On two counts, SDRs represented a very significant development in the evolution of the international monetary system. Until the advent of SDRs, the growth of international reserve assets had depended upon newly mined gold that found its way into central bank hands and upon balance of payments deficits of reserve currency countries. But as Robert Triffin had been warning since the late 1950s, annual additions of gold to monetary reserves were on the wane because of rising private industrial demand and because of gold purchases for other private uses, including hoarding. The price of gold simply was not high enough to stimulate the mining of enough new gold to supply growing private demand and still have enough left over to meet the world's growing liquidity needs. The other source of reserve assets, payments deficits of reserve currency countries, mainly the United States and Britain, had proven unreliable, since the presence or absence of such deficits, as well as their magnitudes, were determined by a number of other important factors, not just changes in the optimum level of world liquidity. The decision to create SDRs was therefore the first decision to rationally and systematically add to world reserves and thus satisfy growing demand in the face of expanding world trade and payments.

The other unique feature of SDRs was that they were created on paper; their value as a reserve asset rested on the obligation of Fund members to accept them in exchange for any convertible currency. SDRs possessed no value as a commodity, unlike gold or silver. Resort to such a form of reserve asset, sometimes called "paper gold," was a step forward in rationalizing the world's monetary system and making it more sophisticated.

The regretful aspect of the decision to create SDRs (which indeed represented a major step forward in overcoming the liquidity problem) was that it took so long to reach. Negotiations were begun in 1963; agreement was reached in 1967; and then only in 1970, after ratification by IMF members, was the first allocation made. By that time, the fate of the Bretton Woods system was already sealed and the recognized crisis conditions were far advanced. The other shortcoming of the decision to create SDRs was that it did not go far enough; that is, there were incomplete answers as to the relationships between SDRs, gold, dollars, and sterling, the role each would be assigned in future reserve creation, and the problem of vulnerability of the system to massive shifts in preference from one reserve asset to another.

The other advance in the development of the international monetary system during the crisis period 1968-72 was the establishment of the two-tier gold market. The decision was hastily arrived at in Washington during a meeting of central bank governors representingthe gold pool. (It may be recalled that the meeting was convened in order to deal with the massive speculation against the dollar and in favor of gold which took place in the London gold market following the sterling devaluation.) By isolating the private gold market from official sector of the international monetary system, and through the agreement among central banks neither to buy nor to sell gold to private dealers, the official monetary gold stock became frozen at the existing level, which was about $40 billion held by all noncommunist countries, the IMF, the Bank for International Settlements, and the European Fund. The clear implication was that future growth in monetary reserves would have to come from other sources, namely, new allocations of SDRs.

Had not the decision already been made to create a new reserve asset, the problem confronting central bankers meeting in Washington in March 1968 would have been much more difficult. For without SDRs, central bankers faced with growing liquidity needs would have been in a fix, since they would have had to rely solely on the dollar, which was under speculative attack. Fortunately, they did not find themselves in that awkward position. Members of the gold pool were able to argue rationally and logically that the existing stock of monetary gold was sufficient, that in view of the establishment of the SDR reserve facility it was no longer necessary to buy gold from the private market, and that the future orderly growth of monetary reserves could be assured by isolating the private gold market from monetary gold stock and relying solely on SDRs.

Unfortunately, however, the logic underlying the "new gold standard" was not permitted to proceed to its conclusion. As government officials were soon to learn, opportunities for private speculation still abounded after closing the gold pool, and it was just such speculation which could influence incentives for a central bank to shift between existing reserve assets. The monetary gold stock was fixed, but stocks of other monetary reserves besides gold and SDRs, chiefly dollars, remained variable. And with ever mounting dollar deficits and the still existing national commitments to support parity exchange rates, foreign central banks were forced to add billions of dollars to their monetary reserves in 1969 and again in 1971 before the Bretton Woods system finally collapsed.

Thus, the move to the two-tier gold market, by itself a logical step forward in the development of the international monetary system, was offset by bearish dollar speculation. The only possible way to avoid what happened would have been for central banks to agree to fix their stock of dollar reserves as well as their stock of gold reserves and to require future US payments deficits to be financed by drawing down US reserves (resort to IMF drawing rights or gold sales) or dollar devaluation. Only by such action could the double step to the two-tier gold market and to full reliance on SDRs to supply future liquidity needs have been achieved successfully.

Other measures resorted to by governments during the recognized crisis conditions were addressed to visible manifestations of fundamental problems. They were stopgap measures designed to suppress an imbalance. One type of measure was designed to directly affect capital movements. The US balance of payments program of 1968 was a case in point. Included therein was a mandatory program to restrain US direct investment abroad and to require larger remittances of foreign earnings from past investments. Foreign lending by banks and other financial institutions was curtailed through enforcement of tighter regulations under the Federal Reserve Voluntary Foreign Credit Restraint Program. The administration also proposed, but Congress did not approve, that "nonessential travel outside the Western Hemisphere" be discouraged by a tax on tourism. And foreign exchange costs of maintaining US forces in Europe were to be reduced by seeking compensating payments from allies. None of these measures, except possibly the last one, offered any curative effects for the US balance of payments deficits. Once the selective controls were removed, the outflows or expenditures would in all likelihood have resumed or increased. In the meantime, there was no certainty that plugging a few holes in the dam would prevent water from seeping out faster somewhere else.

The kind of corner into which the US painted itself in regard to official efforts to control capital movements was aptly demonstrated by the interest equalization tax. First imposed in 1963 as a "temporary" measure to stem foreign portfolio investments by Americans, the IET is still in force ten years afterward. Foreign demand for US capital was not deterred, however, and found other means of being met, such as lending by US banks. But that development required that controls be imposed there, too. While each new control was aimed at some handpicked item in the balance of payments, and while a measure of success could be proclaimed for each one, it is very doubtful that the fundamental purpose of suppressing the overall US payments deficit was achieved for more than a few months, or even at all.

A basically different type of measure designed to offset international flows of liquid capital concerned a number of arrangements for short- and medium-term official financing and other forms of cooperation among national monetary authorities as well as between those authorities and such institutions as the Fund, the Bank for International Settlements, and the Organization for Economic Cooperation and Development. Included in this category of measures were drawings from the Fund, use of BIS member currencies, sales of US government securities to foreign central banks holding large amounts of dollar reserves, and swap lines among central banks wherein provision was made to extend credit to a given central bank in order to help it defend its currency against speculative attack. (The swap lines and credit packages used prior to 1967 devaluation of sterling are cases in point.) While these steps proved helpful in overcoming balance of payments difficulties arising from large international capital movements, there was no satisfactory way to offset problems posed for domestic monetary management by those movements.

Subsidiary to this category of policy actions were official interventions in the foreign exchange market. Such actions were taken to reduce incentives for interest rate arbitrage[2] or to roll back purely speculative purchases or sales of a particular currency. From time to time, official intervention was resorted to by a number of central banks, including the United States.

To summarize, during the period of recognized crisis conditions, several leading industrial countries were in balance of payments surplus, with the surpluses of Germany and Japan being the largest of all; in contrast, the United States found itself in a chronic and ever worsening deficit position. Most countries pursued with varying intensity and success measures to suppress what appeared to be particular problem points with the balance of payments. For each country, the nature of measures employed was often quite different and depended upon special characteristics of domestic financial institutions and philosophical attitudes of the private business sector and society in general. Thus, what Japan could and did do to try and hold down its surplus differed from what Germany decided to do and was by no means the reverse of what the United States was capable of attempting. A common theme found in the policy actions of all countries, however, was the revealed preference for selective, stopgap measures of the cosmetic variety rather than for measures designed to meet head on and to cure the fundamental problems of disequilibrium.

Reforms Proposed But Never Activated

Most national governments, including the United States, the International Monetary Fund, and the Group of Ten, insisted that the Bretton Woods system of fixed, but not unalterably fixed, exchange rate was working well despite evidence to the contrary: the often repeated crises of confidence, chronic US payments deficits, growing political tensions between the United States and Europe, and increasing resort to quantitative controls which undercut often expressed government preferences favoring increased freedom for international trade and payments. Not until August 15, 1971, was it conceded that such difficulties were manifestations of fundamental problems within the system itself. A great number of international economic experts and such prestigious bodies as the Joint Economic Committee of Congress had spoken out for years, some for more than a decade, in favor of comprehensive reform of the Bretton Woods system. In time, study and discussion of the international monetary system led to the identification of the three fundamental problems: the liquidity problem, the confidence problem, and the adjustment problem. Proposals for reform, of which there were almost as many varieties as there were authors, were designed to resolve one or more of these problems. For purposes of simplification, the more serious proposals may be grouped into three basic categories.

Closure of the gold pool and the agreement to issue special drawing rights went a long way toward resolving the liquidity problem. With those steps taken, a mechanism had been devised to expand the stock of international liquidity in an orderly, rational manner. The long-standing concern that a liquidity shortage might arise had ended, although the potential problem (soon to be realized) of too much liquidity as a result of excessive US dollar deficits still existed. Along with that aspect of the liquidity problem, there remained the confidence and adjustment problems.

One group of proposals was concerned primarily with the liquidity and confidence problems. Included in this group were the Triffin plan, the Bernstein plans, and the Despres plan. The Triffin plan was first set forth in his book, *Gold and the Dollar Crisis*, published in 1960, although its origins lay both with Keynes's preBretton Woods proposal for an international clearing union and with Triffin's own experience as mastermind of the European Payments Union. To resolve the confidence problem, Triffin proposed that there be an international central bank empowered to create credit for use by national central banks.[3] Deposits would entail a gold guarantee, would be fully transferable into gold or any national currency, and would earn some specified rate of interest. Balance of payments deficits would be financed by means of loans from the bank, although such loans rather than being automatic would be made at the discretion of the bank. The deposit-creating powers of the international central bank might be contained to some maximum rate of yearly increase so as to avoid the kind of criticism directed earlier at Keynes's plan for a clearing union, that if improperly used, it could lend an inflationary bias to the world economy. The only real limit, however, would be the willingness of members in the bank to accept the bank's "money" (which Triffin called *consols*).

In order to convert from the existing system to the one he was proposing, the United States and other key currency countries would have to bar the use of their currencies for use as monetary reserves by others. Member countries of the International Central Bank would then have to transfer some portion of their foreign exchange holdings and gold to the International Central Bank in exchange for deposits. Over time, according to Triffin, the bank could liquidate the foreign exchange holdings, and the resulting proceeds could be reinvested in less developed countries.

Bernstein offered at least four proposals for monetary reform during the mid-1960s, each one offering a slight variation on the others.[4] In essence, Bernstein suggested that all countries place all of their reserve assets (gold, foreign exchange, SDRs) in a deposit account at the Fund called the Reserve Settlement Account. The deposits would be denominated in reserve units, the total amount for any country depending upon the value of reserves at the time of deposit, not on the composition. Countries would retain reversionary rights to gold, foreign exchange, and SDRs so deposited.

In the case of a deficit country, its account of reserve units would be drawn down and the RUs would be converted into the desired currency to be used for purposes of exchange market intervention. A surplus country acquiring currency through exchange market intervention would convert the excess amount of its working balances into RUs. Only RUs would be used in international settlements. A deficit country drawing down its RU account would involve pro rata use of its reserve assets in the proportions in which they were deposited by the same country in the Reserve Settlement Account. And for a surplus country, its RU account would increase by acquisition of a claim in gold, foreign exchange, or SDRs in the proportions that deficit countries' RU accounts were composed.

Upon establishment of the Reserve Settlement Account, the amount of foreign exchange reserves would become a fixed fiduciary issue that could not be increased but which might be decreased through retirement and replacement with special issues of SDRs at a later point in time. The foreign exchange remaining in the RSA would carry a gold guarantee and would be invested in special securities bearing some rate of interest. Growth of aggregate monetary reserves in the future would come about only through regular issues of SDRs, since there would be no further increase in the monetary gold stock and since the level of foreign exchange reserves would have been fixed.

The Despres proposal was a proposal for a dollar standard.[5] The first central postulate was that the dollar was actually better than gold, that the desire for gold rested on the fact of its unlimited convertibility into dollars. The dollar was the predominant international currency as well as being a national currency. The second postulate was that the United States as the world financial center had been confronted by a banking problem first and foremost, not a balance of payments problem. The banking problem stemmed from an inflated demand for gold, which itself resulted from US gold policy. In order to assuage the problem, a genuine change in prevailing asset preferences would have to be effected, a change that increased the desire for dollars and reduced that for gold. Only the United States could effect this change; it could not be achieved by international negotiation to create a new reserve asset. Accordingly, the United States should strictly limit the amount of gold it was ready to buy at the fixed price, while continuing its past willingness to sell gold without limit at the statutory price.

The fixed relationship between gold and the dollar would continue, but the convertibility of gold into dollars would be cut off and credit would be substituted for that amount of monetary gold made redundant by quota limitations. Adoption of Despres's proposal would cause a shift in asset preferences from gold to dollars and would eliminate the weakness impairing the United States from performing its banking role. In effect, a dollar reserve system would be created.

Each of these three proposals would eradicate the confidence problem with respect to foreign dollar holdings, since convertibility into any other reserve asset would no longer be at the holder's discretion. In the Triffin and Bernstein plans, changes in international liquidity would be determined rationally and systematically, independent of US payments deficits, deficits of any other country, or world gold production. In the Despres plan, international liquidity, which would be dollar denominated, would be tied to US deficits, and therefore the stock of liquidity could conceivably be subject to considerable variation. Nevertheless, all three proposals purport to resolve the liquidity problem, although one might have reservations as to how satisfactorily that might be achieved in the Despres proposal. (It would depend on one's confidence in the US fulfilling smoothly its world banker role. And since 1968 events were not such as to increase that confidence.) Finally, for all three proposals, the adjustment problem would remain and the mechanism used would be the same as the adjustable peg of the Bretton Woods system.

A second set of proposals was concerned specifically with the adjustment problem. Many of the best minds within the economics profession were drawn into lively discussions and debates that took place during the late 1960s over matters of limited exchange rate flexibility. Interest in the proposals for limited flexibility derived from realization during the crisis circumstances beginning in 1967-68 that the adjustable peg mechanism—fixed, but not unalterably fixed, exchange rates—had worked poorly indeed, and that in failing to resolve smoothly existing balance of payments disequilibrium, it had actually intensified weaknesses inherent in the reserve currency system.

The major weakness stemmed from the fact that the combination of fixed rates, convertible currencies, and autonomous national economic policy proved to be incompatible with each other over time. Divergencies in national economic policies caused the pattern of fixed exchange rates, initially in equilibrium, to fall into disequilibrium. Disequilibrium exchange rates gave wrong signals to international trade and capital flows and to domestic production in the countries concerned. Growing external and internal tensions led to insistence that devaluations of deficit currencies and revaluations of surplus currencies take place. When such adjustments become unavoidable and in fact occurred, there were severe shocks in those market economies where wrong price signals had led to misallocation of resources.[6]

Proposals concerning greater exchange rate flexibility fell into two broad categories. One had to do with so-called wider bands, according to which exchange rates would be allowed to fluctuate within a wider range, or band, than the narrow margins around par values permitted in the Fund Articles of

Agreement. (Recall that the width of the band was widened by the Smithsonian Agreement of December 1971, from 1 percent to 2.25 percent either side of parity. Many band proposals suggest a width twice as great as the Smithsonian band, or even more.) Not a new idea, the concept of widening the margins between the gold-points under the gold system originated with Robert Torrens in the early nineteenth century.

Band proposals generally suggest that exchange rates be allowed to vary around fixed par values and within predetermined support points. Exchange rates are free in the sense that they may rise or fall between the support points, yet they are fixed in the sense that they are attached to the parity as a point of reference. An intervention currency is a necessary part of band proposals, for once the exchange rate reaches the upper support point, the monetary authorities must buy the intervention currency in unlimited amounts; the converse holds when the exchange rate reaches the lower support point. In general, relatively smaller amounts of reserves are necessary to support relatively wider bands. The basic argument favoring wider bands is that by permitting exchange rate variations to perform their market functions, real adjustments necessitated by divergent national economic performances and policies would be smoothly and immediately initiated, not postponed until some later date.

A question that arises with the band proposals is: What distinguishes the wider band from the adjustable peg when the exchange rate presses against one or the other support point? If such circumstances prevail for very long, monetary authorities must expend or accumulate large amounts of the intervention currency in order to avoid discrete exchange rate adjustment (i.e., a change of parity either through devaluation or revaluation). The answer is that basically there is nothing to distinguish the two situations. The virtue of the wider band is that it permits more scope for the market mechanism to function; but once the string has run out and the exchange rate can move in but one direction because of official intervention, the same shortcomings characterizing the adjustable peg apply.

This leads to the second category of limited exchange flexibility proposals, which includes the "gliding parity," "sliding parity," and "crawling peg."[7] The common denominator among such proposals is the idea that small and frequent changes in exchange rate parity should be substituted for large and infrequent changes that occur under the adjustable peg mechanism. There are two advantages to the gliding parity proposals. The first is that exchange rate adjustment at any point in time is very small and consequently, destablizing capital movements will not likely become large and unmanageable. The expected rate of return from speculation would be low because of the smallness of exchange rate adjustment at any one time; moreover, changes in national short-term interest rates could offset the incentive for interest arbitrage. The second is that the gliding parity would allow for continuous adjustments through time so as to correct for the kind of disparities emanating from different national monetary policies which cannot be successfully handled alone by the wider band.[8]

Some advocates of limited exchange rate flexibility have propounded plans which offer a combination of both a wider band and gliding parity. Such proposals are called "movable band" proposals.

In any case, greater but still limited exchange flexibility won widespread endorsement of leading experts in recent years. Partial evidence of this was to be seen in the June 1969 press release announcing publication of *The Bürgenstock Papers*, which resulted from a two-week conference of thirty-eight experts in international finance convened at Bürgenstock near Lucerne, Switzerland.[9] The press release stated:

After reviewing the recent experience of the international monetary system, the participants recognized that structural changes in international supply and demand and in capital movements, as well as divergent rates of economic growth, differences in economic objectives and policies, and varying trends in prices and costs among nations would from time to time call for changes in the exchange rates of particular currencies. There was a consensus that such changes when appropriate should take place sooner, and, thus, generally be smaller and more frequent, than during the past two decades.

Further evidence was forthcoming in the IMF Report on *The Role of Exchange Rates in the Adjustment of International Payments*.[10] In that report, the Fund proved it could be the greatest champion and defender of the existing international system in which it played such an integral role. At the same time, willingness was expressed to make concessions that came close to the sort of changes proposed by the majority of participants at the Bürgenstock Conference, that is to say, "both widening the range (or band) within which exchange rates may respond to market forces and permitting a more continuous and gradual adjustment of parities."[11] Slowly but surely, people were coming round to the view that such proposals could offer an acceptable resolution of the adjustment problem.

A third set of proposals purported to offer resolution of all three fundamental problems confronting the international monetary system. Three examples of such proposals are set forth here. The first advocates return to the gold standard and has long been a position favored by the French but by very few others.[12] It is contended that in order to return to the classic gold standard, governments of leading industrial countries would need to agree first of all to freeze their holdings of foreign exchange, such as dollars and sterling, and second, would have to concur on a substantial increase in the official gold price so that foreign exchange liabilities of reserve currency countries could be liquidated. The increase in the gold price, furthermore, would have to be great enough to meet anticipated liquidity needs for the next several years and thus to prevent the possibility of destabilizing capital movements in anticipation of early need for a further change in the gold price. If such steps were taken, international settlements in gold alone could be restored without fear of deficit countries going broke. Widespread opposition to this proposal in many quarters, especially in the United States, has all but ruled out serious consideration of such a plan. This opposition is based upon a wish to downgrade not upgrade the role of gold in the monetary system, and upon great politico-economic reluctance to expose countries to the harsh adjustment process of the gold standard.

A second proposal in this category lies at the opposite end of the spectrum from the first and involves institution of freely flexible exchange rates.[13] According to that proposal, prices of foreign currencies would be determined freely in foreign exchange markets by demand and supply on a daily basis. There would be no intervention in exchange markets either by national monetary authorities or by any international body, and thus there would be no need for international reserves. The full arsenal of monetary and fiscal policies would be directed toward achieving domestic economic goals such as price stability, high employment levels, and optimum economic growth. The balance of payments would be maintained as a result of freely adjusting exchange rates which would constantly seek that rate at which exchange markets were just cleared and no excess demand or supply remained.

Advocates of flexible exchange rates have contended that long-run structural adjustments in the balance of payments would take place in response to appropriate changes in relative prices, incomes, and costs, and that the behavior of private speculators would tend to be stabilizing in the sense that it would give support to currencies facing short-term pressure and would hasten changes in other currencies' exchange rates which were found to be in real or fundamental disequilibrium. Very considerable controversy has been generated in the economic literature over both contentions, leading advocates of freely flexible rates to modify their proposals to include some ground rules for intervention by either national or supranational authorities. Even so, this proposal for reform, endorsed so widely by the economics profession, was never considered seriously at the political level. The present circumstance of floating rates in 1973 comes close to, but is still significantly different from, a freely flexible rate system because governments are intervening in exchange markets from time to time but are doing so according to no common set of ground rules. The fact that balance of payments deficits and surpluses still abound is evidence that exchange rates are not being freely determined.

A number of other proposals for reform offering solutions to the three basic problems were circulated at the end of the 1960s and beginning of the 1970s. By and large, they were far less drastic, more pragmatic, than either of the two proposals discussed above; many of them incorporated changes already achieved in the IMF system such as special drawing rights as an international reserve currency. One example of these proposals is that pronounced by Lawrence

Krause.[14] In his proposal, all par values would be specified in terms of SDRs, not dollars or gold. There would be wider bands within which exchange rates could fluctuate, including an inner band within which monetary authorities would be precluded from intervening at all. Gold, dollars, and other foreign exchange reserves would be consolidated and replaced with SDRs; profits from demonitizing gold would be used for aid to less developed countries. Interest earning SDRs would become the only reserve asset of the reformed system, but US dollars would still be used for purposes of intervention. (The current limitation on the SDR interest rate would be removed.) Finally, the institutional role of the Fund would be strengthened, and interpretation of present rules, particularly in respect of fundamental disequilibrium, would be changed in order to effect smaller, more frequent, and less traumatic changes in exchange parities and thereby achieve needed adjustments in competitive positions.

During the recognized crisis conditions beginning in 1968, the already keen interest of economists in the realm of international monetary reform was redoubled. Discussion and debate ensued around the various proposals contained in the above three categories. To the extent that a trend could be observed, it seemed to be toward proposals, or combinations of proposals, which met head on all the recognized weaknesses of the Bretton Woods system and which tended to build upon the present system and its institutional framework, rather than toward proposals which would have scrapped all that which had existed before in order to begin anew.

Further Developments

Two conferences took place during 1972 which very likely will have an important impact on the movement to reform. The first to occur was the United Nations Conference on Trade and Development, held in Santiago, Chile, in April. This was the third such conference involving all UN members to be convened since 1964; in each case, the focus has been on the pressing problems of world trade and development. UNCTAD was established in the early 1960s in answer to rising expectations within LDCs for a greater say in international economic matters. The purpose of placing the organization within the United Nations was to provide a forum in which developing countries could make known and discuss their opinions and views on important economic issues with developed countries. UNCTAD III was especially important in shedding light on major economic problems relating to monetary reform as seen by the LDCs, and in helping to classify what their main thoughts were concerning those problems.

There were three matters of major concern at UNCTAD III. Most important, and the one of direct relevance to monetary reform, concerned the question of special drawing rights and their future role in world trade and development.[15] The Fund's procedure for disbursing SDRs into the international monetary order has been determined by the size of each member country's quota within the Fund. Accordingly, developed countries received about 75 percent of each SDR allocation. From the viewpoint of the LDCs, long subject to persistent liquidity crises which inhibited their pursuit of economic development, such a procedure was of dubious merit.

In response to the problem of LDCs being recipients of only incidental SDR allocation, the idea promoted at the conference was that in the future, SDR allocations should be "linked" somehow to the provision of international development assistance. The link proposal did not originate at UNCTAD III but had been bandied about some years previously during the arduous discussions within the Fund and elsewhere which preceded the SDR Agreement in Rio de Janeiro in 1967. While the question of the link between SDRs and development assistance was repulsed successfully by developed countries at that time, discussions at UNCTAD III made clear the fact that the issue is still very much alive in the minds of LDCs and that it is one that will most probably give increasing importance to in future negotiations.

The second important conference to occur in 1972 was the Annual Meeting of the Governors of the International Monetary Fund and the World Bank, convened in Washington, D.C., in September. It was the first such meeting to be held after the Smithsonian Agreement of the previous December, and it was the first one to look ahead toward negotiations dealing with monetary reform itself. It was a meeting held in a new spirit of hope and expectation. Some countries made positive statements on the problems to be considered in monetary reform; others that had taken adamant stands in the past on one or another of the issues made conciliatory statements. But there was a resounding silence as far as industrial countries were concerned on the question of the link between SDRs and international development assistance. It was doubtful, however, that such silence would or could be maintained for long once negotiations got under way. Thus, while it was apparent that there were clear-cut differences of opinion as to the appropriate measures to be taken in the reform process, it appeared that those differences could ultimately be reconciled. A realistic timetable, it was believed, could look forward to the 1974 Annual Fund-Bank Meeting for achieving agreement on a new system with ratification of that agreement by member countries in the following year.

Issues and Blocs: I

Many informed observers have asserted that the United States enjoyed an "enormous privilege" as the key currency country during the era of the Bretton Woods system. The United States never quite saw matters in the same light, and in fact, US policy-makers were frequently made aware of the costs of being the world's banker and possessor of the key currency, costs that by mid-1971 had grown intolerable.[1] Costs in the sense that the United States was limited in its choice of tools which could be used to adjust the balance of payments. What were left were inefficient policy tools which worked poorly or not at all. The cost in an economic sense has been a reduced rate of growth in output and a lower level of employment.[2]

The US interests in monetary reform lie in creation of a system that will apportion more equably rights and obligations to all members. Most important is the establishment of a new, smoothly functioning international monetary system based on par values of exchange. In order to accomplish this, a strong adjustment procedure is needed which will be applied to all currencies—including the dollar—as balance of payments imbalances arise, and before they are allowed to cause international crises of major disruptive proportions. According to the US view, it was the adjustment process of the Bretton Woods system which never worked properly and was the fundamental cause of the system's demise. Any new system, therefore, must not be allowed to suffer from such a defect.

Although the adjustment mechanism commands the primary interest of the United States, other issues are also deemed to be very important. Some of these include the role of the dollar and other reserve currencies, the roles of gold and of SDRs, the matter of the SDR-AID link, consolidation of outstanding official liabilities based on national currencies and the question of currency convertibility. US views toward these issues will be addressed in this chapter. In order to set the stage, however, it is important to be aware of the overall thrust of the US position, and to realize that rather than offering anything new or daring, what the United States is really after is a better means of carrying on its previous and still ongoing political-economic role of world leader. Complexities of the present day and changes in the world power structure are likely to make this a much more difficult task than the one that confronted the United States at Bretton Woods.

The Thrust of US Objectives on Reform

One enlightening way to approach the question of overall thrust of US objectives is to recall first that the positions taken by earlier US administrations concerning balance of payments questions during the 1960s differed fundamentally from positions taken more recently by the present Nixon administration. Earlier administrations placed great significance and value on maintaining the fixed relationship between gold and the dollar. Not only was the value of the dollar regarded as sacrosanct, but also there was a body of opinion at the policy-making level which regarded changes in the value of other major currencies such as the pound sterling as likely to pose direct or indirect problems for the dollar. Such exchange rate changes were therefore to be avoided if at all possible. In addition to such general feelings about resort to exchange rate adjustment as a means of dealing with balance of payments disequilibria, there was less concern generally with the US international competitive position and relatively little interest was shown in ways to strengthen the current account of the US balance of payments. American officials, moreover, were sensitive to other nations' concerns about their own payments positions and did not press hard on their authorities to pursue necessarily harsh corrective measures. In order to deal with US balance of payments deficits during the 1960s, the US officials resorted to various capital account restrictions to reduce the magnitude of overall payments deficits, concocted schemes with other countries incurring payments surpluses to help finance those US deficits, helped to arrange for credit packages and to provide a network of swap facilities both of which could be used to roll back periodic speculative exchange market pressures.

The attitudes of the present administration contrast quite sharply on all of these matters. High-level officials in the Council of Economic Advisers, in the US Treasury and elsewhere have clear philosophical inclinations toward more market-like solutions concerning problems arising in the external sector as well as the domestic sector. A more tolerant attitude within the administration toward resort to exchange rate adjustment can be traced back to the summer of 1969. Although actual use of that market mechanism did not occur for the dollar until the latter half of 1971, it was used with much greater frequency by other major currencies during 1969-71, presumably with the blessing of the US government.

Interest and concern was also expressed from 1969 on by the Nixon administration over the international competitive position and the US current account balance. Various measures, including the DISC (Domestic International Sales Corporation), export promotion programs, and provision of easier terms and conditions for financing US exports were discussed, and many were implemented for the purpose of augmenting US exports. While a general aversion was expressed by US officials regarding existing controls on capital account transactions of the US balance of payments, it was recognized that they could hardly be removed immediately in view of the then still weak overall US payments position. Interest in their removal at the earliest possible date was repeatedly expressed, however, by US officials. In fact, in early 1973 it was announced that the existing controls on US capital transactions, including those administered through the Voluntary Foreign Credit Restraint program of the Federal Reserve, the interest equalization tax, and the Commerce Department's Foreign Direct Investment Controls, would be removed by the end of 1974.

Actions taken on August 15, 1971, under what was known as President Nixon's New Economic Program, represented the clearest break with earlier administration approaches to balance of payments problems. During the currency crisis that ensued, the United States appeared to pressure other countries to appreciate their currencies against the dollar and thus to implement corrective measures the United States deemed necessary. Furthermore, improvement in US exporters' ability to gain access to foreign markets (and thus to increase US sales abroad), more equitable sharing among the United States and its allies of the military burden in Europe and elsewhere and in providing aid to underdeveloped countries, all became very important concerns of the United States in its negotiations with foreign countries, and all were said to be related to the monetary questions that centered on exchange rate realignment. Clearly, US officials had taken off the kid gloves in dealing with problems of the external sector and negotiating their resolutions with other governments.

These essentially different philosophical attitudes exhibited by ranking officials of the Nixon administration and evidenced in a number of recent policy actions are having an important and observable impact on US thinking regarding reform of the international monetary system. While these aspects of US reform proposals will be discussed in more detail below, it is also important to be mindful of the fact that both present and past US officials with responsibility in the international financial area overlap on certain fundamental matters and, accordingly, that important themes of the past are to be found in present thinking.

A key feature of the US external sector is its substantial size in relation to the rest of the world's trade and payments, yet its very small size compared to US domestic economic activity. US trade constitutes approximately 17 percent of total world trade (excluding communist countries) and US exports comprise only about 4 percent of US GNP. No other single country has as great an impact on world trade as the United States; no other industrial country of any consequence has such a small external sector in relation to its domestic sector. Only India among all the other members of the Fund has a smaller percentage of GNP in exports of goods; the percentage for Mexico is only slightly higher than the US percentage. The weighted average of Fund members, the United States excluded, shows merchandise exports to be about 15 percent of GNP or about four times as great as the US proportion.[3] These two facts have caused even small changes in US economic activity to have a relatively large impact on foreign economies and, consequently, have led other governments to voice complaints to the United States when their economies have been adversely affected in any way as a result of such changes. While US officials have expressed sympathy over this matter, they have never attached a high priority to the balance of payments from a policy-making point of view precisely because of its relatively small size in relation to the rest of the economy. This has been especially true when domestic economic conditions required one set of financial policies and the external sector required a conflicting set. In such instances, the US balance of payments clearly came off second best.

These relationships are a fact of life for any US government, and as long as they persist it is a very good bet that any US administration will continue to give a low secondary priority to balance of payments considerations in relation to domestic policy needs. Accordingly, as far as international monetary reform is concerned, it is very much in US interests to have a system imposed upon it which does not require the free pursuit of domestic economic policies to be jeopardized or to be seriously compromised whenever a balance of payments imbalance arises.

A second important area of overlap between past and present attitudes of US officials concerns freedom to pursue foreign policy objectives. During the 1950s and 1960s, US administrations were relatively free from any balance of payments constraints to pursue various objectives related to the political-military area. In certain instances, ways were found to alleviate some of the foreign exchange costs involved in pursuit of such objectives, but there is no evidence that the overall thrust of the objectives were ever compromised because of chronic US balance of payments difficulties.

The Nixon administration has taken some clear initiatives that indicate that the scope, the form, and the substance of US commitments throughout the world are currently being revised and scaled down somewhat; there are indications that this movement will in all likelihood continue throughout the second Nixon administration. All of this suggests that the relative balance of payments costs incurred through pursuit of revised objectives relating to US commitments will diminish. Nevertheless, as long as this country continues to bear critical global responsibilities, no administration is going to participate in any kind of international monetary system that might jeopardize its freedom to pursue its political-military role because of balance of payments considerations. In other words, US interests dictate that any monetary system be flexible enough so as not to constrain a carrying out of the US leadership role.

Under the Bretton Woods system, those interests were served by the United States being able, in the face of continuing payments deficits, to accumulate dollar liabilities to foreigners, rather than having to exhaust its supply of gold and foreign exchange reserves or to devalue the dollar repeatedly. While that kind of liberty cannot be expected in any new monetary system currently under consideration, it can be expected that the United States will press hard for an agreement that will allow, through means acceptable to other countries, the same ends to be attained—the maintenance of a key US world role without interference from balance of payments considerations.

The US Role in Monetary Reform: 1944 vs. 1973

The present setting and circumstances surrounding monetary reform discussions contrast markedly with those prevailing immediately prior to and during the Bretton Woods Conference. In that earlier era, the United States and Britain were the major parties negotiating a new international monetary system, one which in many important respects was without precedent. Because of the novelty of the system envisaged, there were important presentational problems vis-à-vis the public, the Congress, and the Allied Nations which had to be taken into account. On the other hand, disruptions to trade and economic activity resulting from World War II meant that the monetary architects were in many respects starting afresh rather than modifying or patching up an ongoing system.

Now, in 1973, while the relative weight and influence of the United States are still great, there is no comparison to the earlier period. The redistribution of economic power toward Europe and Japan, the awakening and then assertion of interests by less developed countries, make the outcome of current negotiations much more likely to reflect compromise by all sides. It is very unlikely that any outcome of the current negotiations will reflect US interests and desires to the extent that the outcome of Bretton Woods did.

In addition to all that this implies regarding the complexities and intricacies of the multilateral negotiations taking place within the Committee of Twenty, it must be recognized that all the while international commerce and payments are ongoing and that there are all sorts of influences affecting what might be referred to as the present "system," or better, "nonsystem." Those influences include periodic disturbances or crises which take the time, try the patience, and affect the thinking of the very individuals who are involved with constructing a new monetary system. Another set of influences has to do with current trends in the international area which affect the present but which also have an impact, direct or indirect, on any future monetary system. Included here would be the substantial monetary reserve gains of Middle East oil-producing countries, the financial behavior of multinational corporations, the matter of European monetary union, and the new round of international trade negotiations scheduled to begin in September 1973, under the auspices of the General Agreement on Tariffs and Trade. While much uncertainty and speculation surround these issues, their course over the years to come must also be of concern to today's monetary architects as they negotiate a system that will be relevant to the international financial scene for some years to come.

The complexities of today's international finance and economy and the growing interrelatedness between nations of the world have led the United States to the position that there must be a common point of departure, a common philosophy for negotiations concerning monetary reform and trade reform. During the 1971 monetary crisis, reforming the monetary order was regarded by the United States as very much interrelated with progress in negotiating freer world trade. This approach made sense in some quarters, but European leaders by and large took the view that the two areas were separate areas of specialization and that negotiations should go forward in the Committee of Twenty on monetary matters and in the GATT on trade matters. There appeared to be concern on the part of leading Europeans that the United States might hold out on a monetary agreement until Europe made substantial concessions on the trade side.

Whether or not this was ever in the minds of the US officials, any idea of somehow linking the trade and monetary areas together has been quietly abandoned, and negotiations are to proceed at their own pace in the respective forums. Although the conception of a broad philosophical link between trade and monetary reform is probably sound and no doubt important in the current world setting compared to the much simpler set of conditions prevailing during Bretton Woods, there was always the practical problem of keeping the agenda for discussion narrow enough so that an accord could be negotiated and agreed upon within a reasonable period of time. Possibly more than anything else, this explains why negotiations are proceeding separately along present lines. The Smithsonian Agreement of December 1971 underscored the need for prompt monetary reform, and certainly all countries involved in reform discussions have stressed the importance of reaching an accord on monetary reform at an early date, with some countries stressing the critical time factor more than others.

US Views on Monetary Reform

In his speech before the 1972 Annual Fund-Bank Meeting in Washington, Treasury Secretary Shultz called attention to a number of principles underlying monetary reform which then commanded widespread support. Among those principles, he cited "the need for clear disciplines and standards of behavior to guide the international adjustment process. . . . a crucial gap in the Bretton Woods system." The other principles to which Secretary Shultz referred were: first, mutual interest in encouraging freer trade of goods and services and freer capital movements to developing countries; second, the need to develop a common code of conduct which would protect and strengthen a free, open international economic order; third, the need for clear disciplines and process; fourth, the right of national governments to choose among alternative adjustment instruments; fifth, the need to build into monetary reform incentives for trade liberalization; sixth, the basic need of major countries to pursue sound policies to promote domestic growth and price stability. But in the US view, provision of a smoothly working adjustment mechanism that can and will prevent the buildup of large reserves by any single country is the most important requirement of the present monetary reform.

The United States believes that failure of the adjustment mechanism to work properly in the past was fundamental to the chronic international financial problems that confronted this country and ultimately caused the demise of the Bretton Woods system. In the face of balance of payments imbalances, the United States was precluded from devaluing the dollar because of its special role as the chief reserve currency country and because there were no assurances that a dollar devaluation against gold would not be offset by other countries deciding to devalue their currencies against the dollar by an equal amount. This at any rate was the prevailing US view. On the other hand, adjustment being a two-sided process, countries experiencing balance of payments surpluses (and therefore accumulating foreign exchange reserves) failed to appreciate the value of their currencies to the extent necessary to eradicate the existing payments imbalances and thus reestablish international monetary order. The first currency to be appreciated in value was the German mark in 1961, but that country's payments surpluses persisted and soon increased. This failure in the adjustment process led to the buildup of short-term dollar liabilities that took on very large proportions in relation to US gold reserves. Because of that increasingly lopsided relationship, the dollar was de facto inconvertible from 1968 on and was declared inconvertible de jure by the president of the United States on August 15, 1971. Thereupon one of the key pillars of the Bretton Woods system was removed and the fate of the system itself was sealed.

Having identified the shortcomings of the previous adjustment mechanism and the ultimate consequences that flowed therefrom as far as international monetary order was concerned, and having cited the common vital interests of all participating nations, the United States has offered what it believes to be a comprehensive, coherent plan for monetary reform based upon effective and symmetrical incentives for balance of payments adjustment.[4]

The US proposal recognizes that most countries wish to maintain a fixed point of reference for their currencies. This in turn entails a willingness to support those fixed points of reference by assuring convertibility of currencies into other international assets. In conformity with present official US attitudes which particularly favor more active use of the exchange rate adjustment, the US proposal calls for a sufficiently wide margin of fluctuation around the central or par value of exchange, in order to dampen incentives for short-term capital movements and to ease transition when changes become desirable. At the same time, the US plan recognizes the possibility of legitimate need for countries to float their currencies. If floating should occur for more than a brief transitional period, however, there should, in the US view, be strong international surveillance to assure consistency of action by the country or countries in question with the basic requirements of a cooperative monetary order.

With respect to international reserves, the United States would like to get out of the reserve currency business, a feeling no doubt based on past experiences, which today leave the United States with some $90 billion in short-term liabilities to foreigners and which, ever since mid-1971, have caused the value of the dollar to be an open question in every currency crisis regardless of origin or cause. The United States would like to see the IMF special drawing rights facility (SDRs) increased in importance to become the formal numeraire of the system and the major primary international reserve asset. A gradual transition is envisaged during which the role of gold would be diminished and foreign currency holdings might be exchanged into a special issue of SDRs at the option of the holder.[a] The US proposal for monetary reform put forth by Secretary Shultz was not specific as to how this might best be achieved.

Based on the premise of a system of national currencies linked together by central or par values of exchange and convertible into other international assets, the US plan proposes and endorses a strong, effective balance of payments adjustment process. In conjunction with all that has been laid bare concerning the adjustment problem, the United States desires a mechanism that performs without discrimination for surplus and deficit countries alike, a mechanism that performs smoothly without triggering large destabilizing international capital flows. In conjunction with philosophical inclinations of US officials, the US proposal places great importance on exchange rate changes as one of a variety of policy responses to affect balance of payments adjustment.

According to US thinking, what was wrong with the Bretton Woods adjustment system as it evolved was that excessive reliance was placed upon subjective judgment regarding the need for adjustment, that there was no strict international surveillance or threat of sanctions by which persistent refusal on the part of any country to take fundamental adjustment measures could be overturned in the interests of international monetary order and durability of the prevailing system.

Thus, the US current proposal turns to objective indicators—specifically, the level and trend of each country's foreign exchange reserves—to guide the adjustment process. The argument here is that in a system of fixed exchange rates and convertible currencies, there is a close relationship between balance of payments disequilibria and reserve changes. Therefore, persistent movements of a country's reserves in one direction or another is an unambiguous, comprehensive, and readily available indicator of an emerging disequilibrium.

Adjustment may occur through the use of orthodox monetary or fiscal policies or through the use of exchange rate adjustment or some combination of them. The use of direct restraints may occur only in exceptional circumstances and for a limited period of time; but if used they should be general and nondiscriminatory. The US proposal leaves up to each individual country the

[a]The importance of this last suggestion concerning consolidation will be dealt with again below and at greater length in the following chapter.

decision of how to effect the necessary balance of payments adjustment. If, however, adjustment is not realized within some reasonable time period, international sanctions in the form of withdrawing various privileges would be invoked. But what the United States desires most is a system in which countries would willingly take corrective actions presumed necessary on the basis of objective indicators and would do so before ultimate sanctions would be invoked.[5]

The balance of payments adjustment process that the US proposes has its parallel in domestic monetary policy. There has been a long-standing debate over the issue of whether application of certain decision rules can or cannot result in a better timed, more appropriate domestic monetary policy than the use of discretionary action which draws heavily on judgment of experts.[6] Many economists with philosophical inclinations similar to those holding key positions in the Nixon administration have argued in favor of rules vs. authority, while other economists more closely identified with past Democratic administrations have voiced sentiment in favor of discretionary monetary policy management. The US proposal on the adjustment process comes very close to endorsing the "rules" approach to balance of payments adjustment. In a recent Treasury paper, "Quantitative Indicators From the Point of View of the Overall Operation of the System," released June 15, 1973, this idea is made quite clear.

In our view, quantitative indicators would play a central role in assuming that the adjustment mechanism contained an equivalent degree of certainty ("certainty" in the sense that there needs to be a strong presumption that adjustment actions will be taken by surplus and deficit countries alike, though not "automatically" in the sense that a particular country must undertake a particular exchange rate or other adjustment action when a particular indicator point is reached).
    Indicators would:
        —call attention to emerging disequilibrium;
        —suggest which nation or nations should adjust to correct such disequilibrium;
        —assure that prompt and effective adjustment actions are taken;
        —induce international pressures on countries refusing to correct large and persistent disequilibria.

The US proposal on monetary reform takes a strong stand against the use of capital and other balance of payments controls. The adjustment process should be directed toward encouraging freer trade and more open capital markets. What is sought is a movement away from controls, which stifle the free flow of international investment. This feature of the US proposal is entirely consistent with the philosophical views of the Nixon administration, which favor operation of free markets without interference of controls. More than that, it takes into account the insurmountable task, at least as far as the United States is concerned, of administering any sort of comprehensive system of capital or exchange controls. It would be quite beyond the capability of present institutions and bureaucracy, as well as being offensive philosophically to both public and private officials.

With respect to trade controls, the United States believes they should be permitted temporarily in extreme cases on balance of payments grounds and should be in the form of surcharges or across-the-board taxes rather than quotas. Concerning capital controls, Secretary Shultz has said they "should not be allowed to become a means of maintaining a chronically undervalued currency. No country should be forced to use controls in lieu of other, more basic, adjustment measures."[7]

The US proposal for a new comprehensive set of monetary rules entails important institutional implications. The International Monetary Fund as guardian of the new rules would be endowed with greater authority than the Fund enjoyed and exercised under the Bretton Woods system. This would be true by virtue of the explicitness of the rules themselves. At the same time, the Fund would have less discretionary authority than before; there would be much less opportunity for judgmental override in any particular situation. What the United States is saying to be true in its own case, and what the United States is asserting about other members of the Fund, is that it is easier to "bite the bullet" on politically distasteful policy measures presumed appropriate by an international body administering a pre-agreed set of rules to deal with given international monetary conditions, than it is to accept the same policy measures recommended by the same international body that is exercising discretionary authority.

Finally, the United States monetary reform proposal asserts that in view of the close interrelationships between trade and payments, the new role of the Fund "will not be effectively discharged without harmonizing the rules of the IMF and the GATT and achieving a close working relationship."[8] While conceding the propriety of monetary negotiations taking place within the Committee of Twenty separate from and at a pace independent of the detailed trade negotiations opening under the GATT in September 1973, Secretary Shultz again made clear that the United States regards reform of the monetary and trading system to be part of the greater overall project of improving the international economic order. He stressed the comprehensiveness of the US approach to these matters and the common philosophical point of reference when he stated that the monetary and trade negotiations needed "to be supplemented by negotiations to achieve greater equity and conformity with respect to the use of subsidies and fiscal or administrative pressures on trade and investment transactions. Improper practices in these areas distort trade and investment relationships as surely as do trade barriers and currency disequilibrium."[9]

Reactions to the US Proposals

One immediate reaction to the US monetary reform proposal concerned the irony that US attitudes on the international monetary system had turned around between the time of Bretton Woods and the current period. In 1944 the United States largely rejected the Keynes plan and endorsed the quite different White plan; present US proposals as first put forth by Secretary Shultz in 1972 reveal broad acceptance of the principles Keynes propounded in his international clearing union plan. Some examples will illustrate key points of similarity in the two plans.

In 1943, Keynes stressed the need for a system that would allow, indeed encourage, full employment and a vibrant domestic economy. In his IMF address, Secretary Shultz stated: "Any stable and well functioning system must rest on sound policies to promote domestic growth and price stability."

On the question of a reserve mechanism, Keynes had said in 1943: "We need a quantum international currency which [is not] determined by the technical progress of the gold industry . . . but is governed by the actual current requirements of world commerce, and is also capable of deliberate expansion [or] contraction." On the same point, Shultz indicated: "We contemplate that SDRs would . . . become the formal numeraire [standard of value] of the system. Changes in the amount of SDRs in the system as a whole will be required periodically to meet the aggregate demand for reserves. [This does] not imply restoration of a gold-based system. The rigidities of such a system, subject to the uncertainties of gold production . . . cannot meet the needs of today."

And on the balance of payments adjustment process, Keynes said: "We need a system possessed of an internal stabilizing mechanism by which pressure is exercised on any country whose balance of payments with the rest of the world is departing from equilibrium in *either direction*, so as to prevent movements which must create for its neighbors an equal but opposite balance." This was the way Shultz put it in 1972: "Sight has too often been lost of the fact that adjustment is inherently a two-sided process—that for the world as a whole, every surplus is matched by a deficit. Any effort to develop a balanced monetary system must recognize that simple fact. . . . Effective and symmetrical incentives for adjustment are essential to a lasting system."

Reactions on the part of industrial countries to the US monetary reform proposal have shown widespread and considerable reservations over the balance of payments adjustment mechanism. Specifically, there is concern that the US plan goes too far in its tolerance of floating currencies and its dependence on exchange rate flexibility. (The major exception to this concern is Canada, which would like to see floating made entirely legitimate.) The United States is clearly the leading advocate of such flexibility, but most other leading nations adhering to more traditional views believe there must be a greater degree of exchange rate fixity, that resort must be made to other policy measures, both domestic and external, to correct balance of payments disequilibria. While the use of an exchange rate adjustment mechanism is regarded as a critical part of any monetary reform, many European countries, Japan, and some other nations such as Australia believe that resort to exchange rate adjustment should come considerably later after other less drastic measures have been tried and found wanting.

In part, this foreign sentiment may be traced to a slightly different concept of balance of payments discipline, that countries should be held accountable for shortcomings in pursuit of basic economic goals and not be allowed to slip away too quickly or too easily by adjusting their exchange rates. Another consideration is that many foreign industrial countries have sizable external sectors relative to their domestic sector; as indicated earlier, this is true for virtually every industrial country when compared to the US economy. For such countries, alteration of their respective exchange rates by any given amount will amount to a sudden and often more painful measure than for the United States, because of the relatively great impacts on domestic price structures and consequently on the allocation of resources. Accordingly, governments of those countries much prefer to try to achieve the necessary adjustment through more gradual, less harsh means.

A third related consideration is that, for planning purposes, many countries prefer more stable exchange rates to greater flexibility. This is true whether the planning relates to industrial development of a domestic industry likely to be involved significantly in foreign sales or one likely to be faced with foreign competition for domestic markets, or whether the planning relates to some foreign investment project. In all such concerns, banking interests that provide large amounts of financing are known to favor greater rather than less fixity of exchange rates.

Another concern of foreign nations voiced about the proposed adjustment mechanism has to do with the role of reserve indicators and the degree of automaticity implied in their use. Certainly the most novel feature of the US plan is the suggestion that reserve data be used as an objective indicator to determine the need and location of requirements for adjustment in the system. Other developed countries have been skeptical that reserve indicators could be relied upon to give consistently the correct information that officials would be trying to elicit from them. Instead, it has been suggested that there should be a number of objective indicators (with reserve indicators offered by the United States as one type), economic forecasts, and other evaluations and that the sum total of information from all sources be used as evidence on which recommendations for action might be based.

There is strong resistance in foreign quarters to the idea that reserve indicators or any other indicators be used for inducing global policy action or inducing graduated pressures by the international community. What the objections boil down to is an aversion by foreign officials to becoming locked into a straitjacket of rules based upon presumptive indicators which would leave little if any room for alternative discretionary action deemed appropriate in view of prevailing circumstances in any particular case. There is widespread support for using the indicators for initiating consultations.

A general difference of opinion exists concerning the use of capital controls. The US reform proposal and other recent statements by the Nixon administration have quite clearly expressed a preference for removal of capital controls and for open capital markets. In Europe, the tide has been in favor of more rather than fewer controls. In Japan, exchange controls have been used for many years with official confidence and private acquiescence in order to deal with a variety of unwanted international capital movements. More than Japan, European countries appear convinced that if exchange rate pressures are great enough, then controls on capital accounts will not work. There are simply too many possibilities for multinational corporations to shift funds from one center to another. Yet, a general feeling can be discerned among those countries that if they were to do nothing in the way of capital controls, they would be more exposed and perhaps more likely to be pushed in directions they did not wish to proceed—for instance, early exchange rate adjustment or a fundamental change in domestic monetary policy. In all these feelings, there are strong political and emotional elements; the economic arguments are conceded to be less persuasive. The sharpest difference of opinion between the US and foreign officials centers on controls of short-term capital movements.

The US interest in reducing the role of gold and attaching much greater importance to SDRs has widespread support in other leading countries. There is a broad consensus that the new monetary order should be based on an international paper asset, carefully designed to command confidence, new amounts of which would be created and injected into the system as total liquidity needs increased over time. While the French have argued for years in favor of the disciplinary characteristics that gold entailed as the centerpiece of international monetary systems of the past, and therefore have often advocated some kind of return to a gold-based system, they too have expressed optimism that SDRs could be tailored to include the characteristics of gold they found desirable.

What is at heart here, particularly for the French but in general for Europeans and Japanese, is a desire to create a more decentralized international monetary order, one that is much less dominated by the United States and by the dollar than the Bretton Woods system turned out to be. For the United States, the purpose in proposing SDRs as the primary international reserve asset rather than gold, the dollar, or other national currencies is to create a more sophisticated, more controllable monetary order which does not place upon the United States or any other country unique obligations that may not be sustainable. This does not mean, however, that the United States would willingly and in all instances relinquish its ability to create dollar liabilities so as to pursue high-priority foreign policy objectives; for there might be a time in the future when, in order to fulfill its role as world leader, such resort might again become essential. These conflicting motivations, therefore, have led both the United States and other industrial countries to support a greater role for SDRs; it is the existence of such conflicting motivations which accounts for tedious, lengthy negotiations on how the common objective is to be achieved.

With respect to the US proposal that currencies be convertible into other international assets, there again is strong support among other countries. As the next chapter shows, the matters of convertibility and consolidation of dollar liabilities are the central issues as far as Europeans are concerned, just as the adjustment mechanism has been shown to be the central concern of the United States. While convertibility and consolidation represent the bait the United States holds out to other nations in order to get agreement on what it deems to be a strong, workable balance of payments adjustment process, the two issues are of great interest to the United States. With the level of short-term dollar liabilities to foreign official institutions at $70.7 billion ($92 billion to all foreigners) and with a US Treasury bill rate currently around 8 percent, terms and conditions of any consolidation agreement will have a significant bearing on government interest payments as part of the national budget and on the US balance of payments. For negotiating purposes, however, the consolidation-convertibility issues appear to be given secondary importance.

Other Major Issues of US Interest

Implicit in the Shultz proposal on monetary reform is the US scenario of how its balance of payments may be brought back into equilibrium. The scenario was explicitly stated by officials during the 1971 monetary crisis, and since then there has been nothing to indicate a change in thinking. The scenario is that the US current account must swing from a 1972 deficit of $8.3 billion to a position of substantial surplus which cannot only cover an expected long-term capital account deficit of $5 to $6 billion annually but which can also allow the United States to run an overall balance of payments surplus for some extended period of time. The overall surplus is necessary to lend some counterbalance to the many years of US payments deficits, to help shrink the outstanding level of dollar liabilities, and generally to restore the dollar to a sound place in the international monetary order. Given the philosophical and administrative arguments against capital controls, and recognizing the US commitment along with other industrial countries in the Development Assistance Committee of the OECD to provide 1 percent of its GNP in the form of development assistance to LDCs, a substantial deficit on long-term capital account is envisaged (although it needs to be stated that US officials anticipate no net capital flows from the United States to developed countries—only to LDCs). Given the magnitude of the so-called dollar overhang and the very large interest payments to foreigners entailed therein, no substantial surplus is expected in the service account. (Interest earnings and repatriated profits from past US investment abroad, which at one time were expected to grow rapidly and cause a large surplus to appear in the services account, are now more or less offset by the huge interest payments to foreigners on outstanding short-term liabilities.) Therefore, the United States maintains that the only alternative is to realize a substantial US trade surplus.

Foreign developed countries are most eager for the United States to set its balance of payments in order and do not appear averse to the prospect of US balance of payments surpluses in the future. However, there is concern and objection over the manner in which the United States proposes to achieve the mutually desired result. Without continuing controls on long-term capital account, let alone the question of enforcing stronger controls than have been in effect during recent years, Europeans are concerned that the past capital outflow in the form of direct investment may continue or even increase; that politically sensitive circumstances of the 1960s may somehow reappear where substantial amounts of US direct investment take place; and that on account of that investment (sometimes characterized as the United States systematically buying up choice European firms) Europeans will be forced to sustain sharp increases in their trade deficits with the United States to offset it and thereby realize the desired US balance of payments surplus. Not only are they reluctant to lose direct ownership of key industries—although as a matter of principle US investment is viewed as a good thing—but they are specially concerned as to the domestic economic implications of any sudden change in their global trade balance. This concern is real and understandable in view of the prominent positions maintained by external sectors of those countries with respect to total economic activity.

Europeans deny that this attitude belies a mercantilist philosophy on their part. They defend their position because of the adverse domestic economic impact implied by any sharp change in their global trade balance, and on other grounds as well. For example, the Common Agricultural Policy of the Common Market, has long been a subject of US attack because it allegedly protects less efficient European agricultural interests from US competition and imports. Europeans defend the policy on the grounds that a social problem exists: 15 percent of the total population still is employed in agricultural pursuits, and their interests require at least partial protection. It is maintained, moreover, that even if the CAP were abolished and if the above-mentioned social obligations to European agricultural producers were removed, there would still be a real question of US ability to meet demand consistently, for there is no guarantee that the United States is willing or able to export foodstuffs to foreigners on a long-term, dependable basis. (In mind here are the US export controls imposed in mid-1973 because of constricted domestic supply of a variety of foodstuffs.)

The Europeans are not arguing that they should continue running overall balance of payments surpluses in the future simultaneously with the US attempts to restore balance of payments equilibrium. In fact, for some nations such as Germany and Switzerland where chronic payments surpluses have been identified as the prime cause of domestic inflationary ills, deficits might provide some welcome relief. They are expressing concern over adverse structural shifts that would possibly result from acceding to the US analysis that the main ingredient for balance of payments improvement is restoration of substantial US trade surpluses. Instead, Europeans would much prefer the United States to hold down its capital accounts deficits; if successful, this would relieve the need of such a large improvement in the US trade account.

Another important issue is the SDR-AID link, a matter of great interest to the less developed countries (see Chapter 8). The United States has consistently and steadfastly opposed any form of link between the issuance of international reserve assets and the provision of aid to developing economies. A prime US concern has been that establishing credibility and acceptance of SDRs is a delicate matter which will take time to accomplish; to burden the main policy objective, which is to introduce SDRs into the international monetary system at a pace that coincides with growing liquidity needs, with a second policy objective, which is to transfer real resources from developed to underdeveloped countries, would overburden the one mechanism for issuing new liquidity with a twofold policy objective (with the possibility of conflicts arising between them) and would ultimately jeopardize the reliability of SDRs. It is suspected that the pressures to create more SDRs to meet LDCs' needs relating to development finance will run ahead of growth in world liquidity needs, that an inflationary mechanism of substantial and possibly very damaging proportions may be created if a link proposal is in fact enacted.

The United States advances a second argument against the link: legislatures in general, and the US Congress in particular, might not approve it anyway, because to do so would mean the surrender of their authority to approve or disapprove the amount of AID funds given bilaterally or to multilateral institutions and to approve or disapprve programs or projects for which the funds would be used. A third US reservation on the link is that even if it were somehow enacted, AID funds now given bilaterally or through multilateral institutions by developed countries might wither away, the legislatures or the Congress arguing that LDCs were already receiving financial assistance in the form of SDRs via the link. Thus, rather than providing additional international development assistance to LDCs, the link might only be a substitute for fund transfers now taking place through other means. After considerable discussion and careful consideration of the many forms of the link proposal that have been advanced, the United States remains the leading antagonist on the issue.

As already discussed, Secretary Shultz's monetary reform proposal called for a system based on fixed but adjustable exchange rates with national currencies convertible into other international assets, a system incorporating symmetrical exchange rate adjustment (including the right to pursue freely domestic economic objectives) with equal rights and obligations for all members, a system promoting freer trade and open capital markets. In the most general sense, this solution to correct currency problems is referred to as a one-world solution or the international option.[10] Philosophically, the inclination of the United States has long been in favor of such an outcome; for only within that context can the world's resources be optimally allocated and used most effectively to the benefit of all countries.

The United States would indeed regard it as a failure of present negotiations if instead of such an outcome the world began to split up into regional economic units based on regional currencies, especially if trade creation within regions took place at the expense of trade diversion between regions. The US dollar was the dominant, most important currency of international use during the quarter century after World War II, just as the pound sterling enjoyed the same if not greater position of prominence during the nineteenth century and very early years of this century. While the key currency role, first for the pound sterling, and then for the dollar, was created neither by default nor design, the United States hopes that a more rational, ultimately more durable and symmetrical monetary system can now be negotiated and agreed upon by all participants. While the dollar will no doubt continue to be a currency of international prominence for some time to come, it could assume a substantially different, less important role in the kind of system the United States has put forth.

Finally, on the matter of official exchange market intervention to support an existing exchange rate structure, an obligation of all member governments under any convertible currency system based on fixed but adjustable exchange rates, the United States favors multicurrency intervention such as now occurs within the European Common Market. This position itself strongly implies a more equal sharing of obligations among leading members of a new system than resulted under the Bretton Woods system, where the dollar was the predominant intervention currency. The United States would therefore like to see a much diminished key currency role assumed by the dollar in the future. The United States, however, would not wish for a world containing a few financial blocs that could cause trade and commerce to become inward looking.

7

Issues and Blocs: II

Other developed countries, principally those of Western Europe, Australia, Britain, and Japan, have keen vested interests in reform of the world's monetary system. All have shared in and benefited from the economic prosperity prevailing generally since World War II. Western Europe and Japan in particular have been recipients of economic power redistributed from the United States over the past two decades. Illustrations of this shift in economic power may be cited. In 1950, the US accounted for 50 percent of the world's GNP; by 1970, that share had declined to 30 percent. In 1950, the US produced 76 percent of the world's automobiles; by 1971, the proportion had fallen to 30 percent. In 1950, the US produced 46 percent of the world's steel; that percentage was down to 20 percent two decades later. In 1950, the US held some 50 percent of the world's monetary reserves; the figure today is 8 percent. On the other hand, the nine Common Market countries (including Britain) today control 40 percent of the world's monetary reserves and Japan, which was near bankruptcy in 1950, now has 15 percent of the total. Any new international monetary system must reflect this shift in its form and substance as compared to the evolved Bretton Woods system, which was so uniquely directed by the United States.

An Overview of the Key Issues

Out of that redistribution of economic power, and the financial wealth that has gone with it, are born some of the major issues of monetary reform for the developed countries. Still other major issues are carried over from the past, including some emanating from the harsh lessons learned during the 1930s.

Uppermost in the minds of almost all developed countries outside of the United States is the issue of convertibility. A new system is desired which will be based on fixed but adjustable exchange rates with national currencies convertible into international reserve assets. A closely related issue has to do with consolidation of the billions of US dollar (and also pound sterling) liabilities held by these countries. A third issue ranking high on all countries' list of priorities concerns international liquidity and controlling its creation in the future so that it may not become a dangerous inflationary force as in the past. These and other issues of major interest to developed countries which command considerable attention in the reform negotiations will be discussed in this chapter.

As for the fundamentally different approaches toward monetary reform taken on the one hand by the United States, with central concern placed upon the balance of payments adjusted process, and on the other hand by most other developed countries, with central focus on convertibility, a few comments may be germane at the outset. First, the fact that all other industrial countries' economies are substantially more open than is the US economy (in the sense that greater shares of total economic activity derive from foreign trade) was mentioned in the preceding chapter. In a number of ways this makes for heightened sensitivity over changes in external economic conditions and devotion of greater priority on the part of governments to see that adversity is quelled in the least possible disturbing manner. Hence, there is greater preference for continuity of an existing rate structure, for required adjustment to be achieved by other, more gradual means than exchange rate changes, and for enforcement of convertibility into primary international assets as a disciplinary measure and to ensure order. For the United States, however, exchange rate adjustment is viewed as the expedient way to effect payments adjustment (and still maintain a given foreign policy stance) since it allows for greater freedom to pursue domestic financial policies deemed appropriate.

Second, there is the conjecture over the increasing problem of inflation in recent years. Developed country officials generally, and Europeans in particular, argue that financing US deficits confronted them with problems of unwanted monetary expansion—in some cases, virtual paralysis of monetary policy because of the magnitude of dollars pouring into domestic financial institutions and converted into local currency. To avert repetition of this serious inflationary source in the future, convertible currencies and tight asset settlement of payments deficits would prevent balance of payments imbalances on the part of any country from reaching the disturbing proportions of the past. (Americans contend on the other hand that their prices have been relatively stable over the years. Moreover, the presence of a large US current account surplus until 1968 if anything exerted a deflationary influence. US current account deficits in 1968 and 1969 were small by any standard, and it was not until 1971 and 1972 that those deficits became large.

Third, while personalities and philosophical inclinations have led some key US officials to embrace the market mechanism with its ability to function effectively in the present-day context, more traditional banking and governmental inclinations prevail in other developed countries. There, the efficiency of the market mechanism is more suspect. Not only is there a preference for more fixity of exchange rates, but various market interference by government are accepted as necessary, and the tide is running in favor of still greater resort to them.

In Search of a Common European Position

Before turning to a more detailed examination of the issues, a brief comment should be made regarding the cooperative spirit on matters of monetary reform demonstrated by members of the European Common Market. In contrast to matters of politico-economic concern internal to the EC, over which there have been frequent instances of conflict and discord slowing progress toward economic union, Europeans have been able to get together over a common set of objectives concerning the ultimate shape of a reformed monetary system. They have done so, in fact, with greater speed and to a higher degree than was anticipated by other countries, including the United States. It should be stated, however, that when it comes down to practical matters of how to implement generally agreed principles, European unity frequently tends to disappear. In the following exposition, some of the significant divergences of EC members' positions on important matters of reform will be noted.

The evolvement of a common European position on major issues could have an important bearing on the outcome of monetary reform negotiations. While the EC is a body of nine sovereign nations, they are nonetheless united under a charter which itself lends a cohesiveness to their views and actions with respect to the rest of the world. Especially since member countries have already displayed some ability to develop a unified position on the monetary reform issues, the EC represents a critical counterweight to the United States in the actual negotiations. The enlarged EC has replaced the United States as pre-eminent world trading power; the combined GNP of its members is three-quarters of the US GNP; its official reserves composed of gold, foreign currencies, and SDRs are three and one-half times as great as reserves of the United States. In a comparative sense, the counterweight the EC poses to the United States in 1973 is far greater than the counterweight posed by Britain in 1943, a nation then close to bankruptcy and facing the enormous task of postwar reconstruction. Accordingly, the views of the EC on particular issues may be reflected to a considerable degree in any ultimate monetary accord.

The EC and the Issues of Monetary Reform

At a July 1972 meeting of the EC finance ministers, announcement was made of a wide measure of agreement on eight major objectives to be pursued in monetary reform discussions. While very general, these eight objectives represent a format for further discussion of EC thinking on key issues. (The issue of central importance to the EC—convertibility—is dealt with at greater length in the section immediately following.) The eight objectives are:

1. The new international monetary system should continue to be based or fixed but adjustable parities;
2. It should be designed to reestablish a general convertibility of currencies;
3. Provision must be made for the effective international regulation of the supply of world liquidity;
4. It should secure the necessary adjustment in balance of payments of participating countries;

5. It must have regard to the need to reduce the destabilizing effects of short-term capital flows;

6. There should be a principle of equal rights and obligations for all countries;

7. The interests of developing countries must be regarded;

8. Such a system is in no way incompatible with the progressive achievement of economic and monetary union of the enlarged EC.

European affinity for fixed but adjustable parities of exchange is widespread and is much more enthusiastic than the US attitude. In the March 27, 1973 communique of the Committee of Twenty, it was stated that "in the reformed system the exchange rate regime should remain based *on stable but adjustable* par values."[1] While the Europeans emphasize the word *stable* or *fixed*, the Americans frequently underscore the term *adjustable*. On this issue there is a considerable gap in views.

The European rationale for greater fixity of exchange rates, a cause led by the French and supported in the main by other countries, is that frequent changes are likely to be disruptive to the development of world trade. Since European countries are trading nations—some to a very considerable degree of their total economic activity—official exchange market intervention should be used to support fixed parities as short-term balance of payments disequilibria arise. Moreover, other policy measures on the domestic side should be used to correct the causes of disequilibrium, and other means should be employed if necessary (for instance, measures to control disequilibriating international capital movements). Only as a later resort, and then if deemed appropriate, should exchange rate adjustment occur.

There is wide concurrence in Europe that a better adjustment mechanism is needed in a new system than prevailed under the Bretton Woods system. There is more of a balance, however, as between the importance of internal or domestic adjustment and external adjustment. The Dutch and the French, for example, still feel the concept of "fundamental disequilibrium" has relevance in determining whether or not exchange rate adjustment should take place. The reference to that term, the source of so much controversy during the past quarter century, is just another bit of evidence that Europeans are looking more toward a carry-over from the past on the matter of fixed exchange rates and balance of payments adjustment, than they are looking for any new or daring approach.

As to the operation of the adjustment mechanism, a potential contribution of objective indicators is recognized, but their use would be much more circumscribed in that they would only give rise to consultations or negotiations—not to a presumption that policy actions up to or including exchange rate adjustment should be implemented. Europeans are most leery of any reference to sanctions that might be applied according to the US plan.

Countering the US proposal that the adjustment mechanism be based on a set of rules that would be applied objectively and would afford little room for discretionary action, the Europeans suggest that the consultation process be strengthened. The United States has expressed willingness to have a more active, stronger consultation process. However, the United States would prefer to give greater weight to objective indicators and in consultations to see if there was any reason why presumptive actions based on the indicators should not be followed. On the other hand, European nations would hold consultations without any initial presumption that policy actions were required. For example, a high-level board, similar to the IMF Executive Board, might be convened on a quarterly basis to discuss problems of apparent balance of payments disequilibrium and to discuss the circumstances of each country on the basis of indicators and other considerations. It is maintained that a better consultation process could make up for shortcomings of the previous system with respect to the adjustment process while at the same time avoiding the surrender of national sovereignty and discretionary action implicit in the US plan.

Regarding intervention to maintain an existing pattern of exchange rates, Europeans believe countries should maintain working levels of various foreign currencies and that intervention should take place on a multicurrency rather than a single-currency basis. This would preserve greater symmetry, which everyone desires to be built in to the new system. Multicurrency intervention would in effect result in a more decentralized system than prevailed when the dollar was used almost exclusively as the intervention currency. Here, again, is a feature that Europeans would like to see become a part of the future monetary order, and, indeed, the United States, too, favors multicurrency intervention to support parity exchange rates.

Convertibility of national currencies into primary international assets is the central concern of Europeans. Before convertibility can be realistically restored there must be agreement on a plan to consolidate the billions of dollar liabilities outstanding which, since April 15, 1971, have de jure as well as de facto been inconvertible into gold or other US reserve holdings. The two issues are therefore very closely related and will be discussed in greater detail in the section immediately following. The important point as far as Europeans are concerned is to establish a greater degree of discipline than existed before. Settlement of balance of payments imbalances should take place in the form of primary international assets, not national currencies. Foreign currencies should be convertible into international assets. While other nations might agree to make credit available to a deficit country, this should by no means become a regular practice nor should it continue indefinitely in any case.

The great emphasis which European countries place on convertibility is in part a desire to carry over that which appeared to work well in an earlier period, namely, characteristics prevailing during the gold standard. The other and probably the major part of the explanation lies in the experience of the 1960s and beginning of the 1970s when official reserves in the form of dollars grew far more rapidly than any other recognized asset; concomitantly, the dollar reserves became decreasingly convertible by virtue of their weight in the total pool of international liquidity. Any concerted effort to convert them into other reserve assets would have resulted in default by the United States, which no longer had an adequate supply of gold and other reserves to cover its dollar liabilities, and collapse of the system, which rested to an important extent on the fixed relationship between the value of gold and the US dollar. It is a possible repetition of such past events that European countries want to avoid under a reformed monetary system.

As for the characteristics of international liquidity, most European countries (and other developed countries too) endorse the general suggestion that special drawing rights be modified, be made the numeraire of the system against which all currencies would be valued, and become the major international reserve asset. This presupposes a diminishing role for gold and for reserve currencies in the form of national currencies. The ultimate question about gold is a political matter. Because of the great discrepancy between the official dollar price of gold ($42 per fine ounce) and the free market price (more than $100 at the time of writing), several European countries believe there should be no official gold price in the future and that its relationship with SDRs should be severed—in effect, gold should be demonetized.

In contrast to that view, France believes the new system will need characteristics that gold has provided in the past: first, the exertion of discipline on countries in deficit; second, the enduring confidence and trust it has commanded worldwide for decades. While France has softened considerably its early opposition to SDRs in the mid-1960s, her leaders maintain that international assets must have wide acceptance if a system of asset settlement is to work successfully.

Underlying France's traditionally strong endorsement for gold and its prominent placement in any international monetary system is her strong sponsorship of national sovereignty. The French believe that the world is not likely to become so unified that gold as a reserve asset will become totally obsolete. Possession of gold in the past during times of war was something for which there was no substitute. Possibly more significant in the present-day context is the growing potential of trade with communist nations. Known to be financially conservative and to have settled past trade payments on the basis of gold, those countries, particularly the USSR, have sizable stocks of gold. Monetary architects will have to give more than just passing thought to how to make the future system flexible and attractive to various communist nations so that, as political hurdles continue to be overcome, trade between East and West may indeed flourish and may even be facilitated further owing to a system in which there is provision for payments to or from nonmembers in mutually acceptable assets.

The extent to which the role of reserve currencies is diminished and that of SDRs increases depends to a very considerable extent on the manner in which

SDRs are defined in relation to other currencies and how attractive they become as an investment compared to other instruments (such as US Treasury bills or Eurocurrency deposits). The greater the confidence in SDRs and the higher their interest rate, the greater would be the inducement to move out of reserve currencies and into SDRs. (Initially, since their inception, SDRs yielded an almost insignificant 1.5 percent rate of interest.) The more this occurs the better are the prospects for controlling the future increases in international liquidity through orderly SDR creation and allocation. How to value SDRs and what rate of interest should be assigned to them are not simple issues to resolve. For if the SDR is made much more attractive than other substitute instruments (US Treasury bills or Eurodollar deposits) then countries will be reluctant to part with them or otherwise use them in settlement of their payments imbalances.

European thinking on this issue varies, but several countries, such as Britain, Germany, and the Netherlands, favor governments holding only working levels of various reserve currencies for purposes of exchange market intervention; the bulk of each country's reserves would be placed in primary assets, or, in other words, in SDRs. Other countries, such as Italy, would prefer to retain a somewhat wider degree of choice as to how their monetary reserves might be held at any given time.

Despite some variation in country positions on these matters, there is strong agreement that future liquidity creation must be effectively regulated. More than the United States and more than other developed countries, EC nations, led by Germany, have been deeply concerned by the international transmission of inflation. One necessary means of insuring a better performance in the future is to prevent the explosion of world liquidity, such as occurred in the early 1970s, when countries' reserves in the form of gold, SDRs, reserve positions in the Fund, and foreign exchange reserves increased from $78 billion at the start of 1970 to $176 billion in March 1973. Of the total, foreign exchange reserves, mainly dollar reserves, increased from $32 billion to $115 billion directly in consequence of US payments deficits. Lesser factors accounting for the approximate trebling of foreign exchange reserves included reserve creation in the Eurocurrency market and diversification of currency reserves. If SDRs were established as the primary international reserve asset and if the Fund, with approval of its members, were responsible for new SDR issues, new liquidity creation could be controlled with levels commensurate with world needs.

The European approach toward dealing with destabilizing short-term capital movements is to use controls in various forms. France, Belgium, and Italy are among the countries that have resorted in the recent past to a two-tier foreign exchange market in which the rate for financial or all noncommercial transitions is allowed to float and the commercial exchange rate is pegged officially and supported in the normal fashion. Other countries have resorted to an all-out float. All countries have taken steps to reinforce exchange controls and domestic banking regulations pertaining to short-term capital inflows. For example, extra high reserve requirements are imposed on bank deposits placed by foreigners. While there is the general conviction that such controls are decreasingly effective as exchange pressures increase, the presence of controls places governments in a less exposed position than if they pursued the US prescription of open capital markets.

Beyond the general consensus favoring short-term capital controls, very little has developed concerning how to specifically deal with the problem in the future. This applies also to the question of whether controls should be placed on outward or inward disequilibrating capital movements—or both. As Dr. Otmar Emminger put it in June 1973,

We know now all the questions involved, but I doubt whether we know much about the really practicable answers. No panacea has as yet been found for dealing with this crucial problem [of disequilibrating capital flows] in a future system. So we may have to continue in the pragmatic manner which has evolved under the pressures of crises until world-wide payments equilibrium and restored confidence in all major currencies have removed the problem from the critical list.[2]

Europeans are in accord with the United States that a new monetary system must exhibit symmetrical rights and obligations for all members. They concur that surplus countries, just as deficit countries, must be responsible for pursuing effective balance of payments adjustment. Different views arise not over the matter of symmetry but over the ways in which it is to be built in to a new system.

Europeans exhibit more concern and sympathy to the interests of developing countries than does the United States. Germany notwithstanding, the view is that some form of link between the issuance of special drawing rights and the provision of development finance could be devised which would not jeopardize the monetary system generally nor confidence in SDRs. Recognizing that the chief issue for LDCs is the link proposal, most Europeans seem willing to accommodate in some manner or other. There is also support for better commodity stabilization agreements which would assure LDCs of a more steady stream of foreign exchange earnings over time.

Italy has been among the most vocal of European nations favoring the SDR-AID link and has lent its support for such a scheme since 1968. Their view, now that amendments to the Fund's Articles of Agreement are likely, is that SDRs should not be allocated directly to LDCs without any precondition (the position favored by LDCs and by some EC countries favorably disposed toward the link), but indirectly through international institutions such as the World Bank, the Asian Development Bank, the Inter-American Development Bank, and the African Development Bank. This would insure proper use of funds, and it would retain for developed countries a say in the manner in which allocations were made. Italy's inclination toward the link is based on the idea that money creation is associated with the transfer of resources both domestically and internationally, and on the value judgment that benefits for creating international liquidity should accrue to LDCs. There is no technical reason why this method should be any better or worse than another method.

The attitude of most other European countries has been to take a wait-and-see posture on the link while expressing the opinion that it might be possible for some form of the proposal to accommodate LDCs' interests and developed countries reservations. This amounts to support for the link with some qualifications. The exception to this attitude is Germany, which has sided with the United States in strong opposition to any link in a reformed monetary system, although recent evidence suggests that German opposition to the link in principle may be weakening. Germany's main concern with the link, as with other major issues of reform, is that it may give rise to worldwide inflation. Especially if aid channeled to LDCs via SDRs is aid additional to what is being provided already through bilateral and multilateral institutions; then LDCs' demand for goods and services produced in industrialized countries will rise proportionately, thus adding further demand-pull inflationary pressures. Recall the recent experiences of Germany and Switzerland with inflation, and the immigrant labor that has been absorbed into the domestic labor force to meet rising demand.

The EC's final principle position on monetary reform is that there must be no conflict with their intentions to bring about economic and monetary union.[3] A most complex goal to be achieved by 1980, according to the Werner Report,[4] the union would be characterized by the following features: first, either a single currency or rigidly fixed exchange rates of member's currencies; second, complete liberalization of all capital movements within the area; third, a common central banking system similar to the Federal Reserve System; fourth, a common budgetary policy; fifth, centralization of responsibility for general economic policy decisions, standardization of national economic policy instruments, and ongoing consultations among member states at the community level.

Of interest here is the fact that the present stage of Europe's efforts to establish a union includes a so-called snake arrangement, whereby member countries have agreed to maintain their exchange rates within a band 2¼ percent of each other. This is done through multicurrency intervention, not on the basis of intervention using one currency such as the dollar, with provision for settlement of accumulated foreign exchange balances among members. While this currency arrangement binds European countries together, the EC and other participants are floating jointly against the rest of the world, including the US dollar. Denmark, Norway, and Sweden are also participating in the current snake arrangement, also known as the "common float." For the time being, Italy and Britain are not members of the snake arrangement and are permitting their currencies to float in relation to all currencies including other EC currencies. It is hoped by other EC members and by officials of Britain and Italy that they will be able to rejoin the present monetary arrangement as soon as possible and will work actively with other countries to realize the common objectives as outlined.

Just as the EC is interested in insuring that monetary reform does not interfere with efforts to establish economic and monetary union, the rest of the world is just as interested in seeing that the Common Market does not become restrictionist and thus does not seriously erode prospects for a one-world solution to monetary reform. It was to this point that Secretary Shultz addressed himself during the 1972 Fund-Bank Meeting: "We also visualize . . . that countries in the process of forming a monetary union–with the higher degree of political and economic integration that that implies–may want to maintain narrower bands among themselves, and should be allowed to do so." Thus, as Europe continues along the path toward its objective of forming a union, there is no inherent reason or basis for conflict with the other objective of reaching accord on international monetary reconstruction which employs the internationalist option or one-world solution, rather than a solution based upon a few financial blocs.

Convertibility: The Major Issue for the EC

As stated at the outset of this chapter, the center of attention with respect to monetary reform as far as Western Europe and certain other developed countries have been concerned is the issue of convertibility. Three reasons were offered in explanation for this focus of attention: the relatively high degree to which the economies of those nations depend on foreign trade and payments for their livelihood; the concern at least within European countries over the growing severity of inflation and its relation to the international monetary system, and the personalities and philosophical inclinations of foreign officials involved with monetary reform. Two further comments may be made in order to set the stage for European thinking on the convertibility issue.

Earlier in this volume reference was made to General de Gaulle's remark in 1965 that the United States enjoyed an "exorbitant privilege" in view of the dollar's role in the international monetary system. What he referred to was the US's ability to encounter balance of payments deficits and to pay for them with US dollars, that is with domestic currency, rather than with gold or other foreign exchange assets as all other nations were obliged to do. In conjunction with that privilege, economists define *seigniorage* to be the value that derives from the right to issue money. In the case of reserve currency countries, this has meant the real resources the United States (and the United Kingdom in an earlier period) were able to import and never pay for, thanks to its ability to finance deficits by printing US dollars. European interest in convertibility is tailored to prevent that kind of exorbitant privilege from befalling the United States, any other country, or any bloc of countries in the future.

The second comment has to do with the so-called n-currency principle in international payments adjustment. According to the principle, in a system of n commodities or n currencies, there can be only $n-1$ relative prices with one commodity or currency serving as the numeraire. As the Bretton Woods system evolved, the US dollar became the numeraire currency. As such, the dollar's position was asymmetrical with respect to positions of other currencies. Other currencies were defined in terms of the dollar; the dollar was used as the intervention currency; it became ultimately the major store of value as an increasing proportion of international reserve assets were held in dollars or in interest-bearing short-term dollar instruments.

Some important consequences followed as a result of the dollar being the nth currency in the international monetary system. The consequence of prime interest here is that the United States was the pacesetter for world inflation. Since the external sector of the US economy is very small relative to the domestic sector, monetary and fiscal policies of this country are influenced very little, if at all, by balance of payments considerations.[5] What balance of payments influences there are or whatever exchange rate changes occur tend to be normally minor and can be offset by changes in US domestic policies.

For other countries with proportionately larger external economic sectors these considerations did not apply. That is to say, balance of payments considerations have had considerable impact in the determination of domestic macroeconomic policies. Moreover, since other countries were accustomed to pegging their currencies to the US dollar, the numeraire of the system, they passively accepted the US rate of inflation as a base. That was true regardless of the US inflation rate, whether it was zero, positive, or negative, as long as exchange rates were fixed to the dollar and currencies remained convertible. Only by changing their parities or by floating could other countries extricate themsevles from the backwash of US domestic price activity.[6]

The consequences of these described relationships prevailing under the Bretton Woods system were not a problem as long as US wage and price inflation were low. Beginning in 1965 and thereafter, the rate of inflation in North America began to rise as a consequence of the strains imposed by the Vietnam War buildup and of macroeconomic policies beginning in 1966.[7] The response was a rise in the general level of world prices which in turn was a very significant cause of even greater wage and price increases in countries outside of North America.[8]

The upshot of all this is that the Europeans came to understand, both through observation and through bitter experience, that the Bretton Woods system had ceased to serve their economic well-being or to function in a manner that accorded with their new-found collective economic strength in relation to the United States. Herin lies the explanation for their overriding interest in designing a new monetary system based upon an international currency, in which the international currency serves as the numeraire and the position of individual national currencies in relation to it is symmetrical, in which national currencies are convertible into the international currency. The objectives are to enforce balance of payments discipline on all sovereign nations and to prevent any single country or bloc from imposing upon the rest of the world an unacceptable rate of change in general prices.

Among EC members, Italy is perhaps the leading spokesman on the convertibility issue and is the one that has enunciated most frequently European positions and proposals. There is strong support from all other EC members, however, many of whom have made substantive contributions of their own to the thinking on the subject. The essence of the proposal set forth by the Italians is that balance of payments imbalances should be regularly and fully settled by the transfer of primary international assets from deficit countries to surplus countries. Asset settlement in primary reserves (which means international currency such as SDRs or any other recognized assets other than national currencies) should not take place bilaterally as was supposed to have occurred under the Bretton Woods system. This type of settlement was subject to serious political problems; there was domestic criticism whether or not payments surpluses were redeemed in gold from the United States. In the end, the system simply did not work. Accordingly, Italy proposes that settlement be on a multilateral basis through the International Monetary Fund with the Fund performing the bookkeeping role of determining what is owed to whom. If convertibility along these lines were made part of the future monetary system, so that members were obliged to settle their payment imbalances in the prescribed fashion through an international agency, it is contended that the political problems of the past would be removed, that discipline would be enforced fairly and impartially on all members, that the growth of international liquidity over time would be controlled and decided upon by the collective membership taking into account net global requirements.

The question arises, of course, as to how the world would get from its present state to one in which pursuit of convertibility by all countries could be practically carried out. The Italians offer as part and parcel of their convertibility proposal a way to resolve the problem of the dollar overhang. This overhang consists of the huge imbalance between the $70.7 billion held as official reserves by foreign governments and the limited supply of primary international assets which the United States itself holds as backing against its liquid liabilities.[9] (A similar but less awesome overhang persists in the case of sterling liabilities and it is a question for monetary architects whether or not to handle the dollar and sterling overhang as a single issue of consolidation or whether the sterling problem might be handled separately by members of the European Economic Community.)

In order to handle the dollar overhang, it is suggested that the Fund provide a facility whereby holders of reserves in the form of national currencies would be free to convert them into SDRs. The former reserve currency countries would be obliged to redeem their respective currencies for primary assets to the extent that the Fund determined that any "basic" deficit in their balance of payments existed. This refers to the so-called basic balance, which is the credit or debit balance arrived at by summing merchandise trade balance, the services or invisibles account balance, unilateral transfers, and the long-term capital account balance. To that extent, former reserve currency countries would be immediately responsible only for future deficits—not for all past deficits. As for the reserve currency absorbed by the Fund, the former reserve centers would assume long-term liabilities to the Fund, would pay interest on them, and would be allowed to amortize or to pay off those long-term liabilities as "basic" surpluses in their balance of payments were incurred.

The proposed Fund substitution facility and the attractiveness of SDRs would have to be made alluring enough so that countries that presently hold substantial amounts of national currencies (mainly dollars) as reserves would wish to convert them—or part of them—into SDRs. This might be done by offering higher rates of interest on SDRs, rates more in line with interest rates paid on ninety-day US Treasury bills. It is also suggested that SDRs be given properties more closely resembling currency than credit. This might be accomplished in part by removing the reconstitution rule pertaining to SDRs. According to the present reconstitution requirement, each country must have held on average for a stipulated period (say five years) a minimum 30 percent of SDRs issued to it during the time of allocation. If the minimum average balance is less than 30 percent, then the country pays a nominal rate of interest on that amount to the Fund. If the average balance for the period exceeds 100 percent, then the country receives the nominal interest payment from the Fund.

Another suggestion the Italians offer is a gentleman's agreement obliging countries with more than $1 billion worth of reserves held in national currencies to convert at least 10 percent of their holdings into SDRs. If this still did not significantly reduce the overhang problem, then SDRs might have to be made still more attractive.

In essence, the Italian proposal for consolidation is that it be handled flexibly and more or less voluntarily through the Fund, thus avoiding political embarrassment. Ultimately, the objective would be to reduce official reserves held in the form of dollars or other key currencies to levels that would just suffice as working balances to be used for purposes of official exchange market intervention.

The matter of consolidating national currency liabilities of the reserve centers runs head on into the interests of certain developed countries such as Japan and Canada and almost all LDCs. For those countries, placing the bulk of their reserves in highly liquid instruments of key currency countries, for example, in US Treasury bills or in US commercial bank or Eurodollar deposits, affords them not only a good rate of return; it also establishes a valuable financial relationship between the foreign central bank and the central bank or commercial banks of the key currency country. In the latter case, this usually affords the foreign country a line of credit to which it would not otherwise have access. For this reason, the substitution of SDRs for existing holdings of reserve currencies will have to be made relatively attractive, or perhaps other alternatives will have to be sought in order to compensate for financial relationships sacrificed in the name of consolidation. As far as the United States is concerned, the ultimate question is how to amortize consolidated dollar liabilities and how to ensure that once consolidation occurs there is not a reverse movement back into dollars or other national currencies—in other words, how to prevent against false funding or only temporary consolidation.

As for the strong European attachment to early restoration of convertibility and the central desire that convertibility be the mainstay of any reformed monetary system, there are two questions which can only be posed at this stage. First, as the United States views the issue, the presumption of those who pursue convertibility and argue for a tight asset settlement system at more or less fixed exchange rates is to discipline the United States or any other country from the outside, to assure that there is resort to effective restraining domestic financial policies before payments deficits become so large or so long-lasting as to have serious repercussions on foreign economies. US officials express some doubts as to whether or not a tight asset settlement arrangement would indeed be workable. If the volume of reserves were too low to finance payments imbalances and thus to sustain stable exchange rates for the dollar or other leading currencies, then resort would have to be made to floating exchange rates. The concern is how to effect the right balance between the level of world liquidity, the desire to impose balance of payments discipline, and yet maintain relatively stable exchange rates. The question is whether or not the US Congress or the administration, in view of the small size of this country's external sector, would willingly become a part of and adhere to such an international monetary system. It would, in short, be a system requiring more surrender of national sovereignty—particularly with respect to domestic economic policy making—than has ever occurred before.

The second question is that if a tight asset settlement scheme were instituted, might it not be necessary to have some provision to finance international capital flows? A proposal made in anticipation of this question is to establish a third "window" at the Fund, in addition to or supplementary to the drawing rights facilities already in existence, which would be similar to the discount window of the Federal Reserve System (to which member commercial banks may turn to borrow funds temporarily to meet a temporary liquidity shortage). But this poses another question as to whether an international decision-making mechanism, with the inherent necessity for careful, stylized procedures, could react fast enough to provide financing or this sort. A more technical question is that if a multilateral swap facility or a third window facility were established within the Fund, and if financing were denominated in SDRs, who would bear the risk in the event of exchange rate adjustment?

Resolution of the twin issues of consolidation and convertibility poses a very considerable challenge to monetary architects. It is clear, however, that Europeans attach primary importance to them and have already formulated in their own minds what kind of resolution is in their interests.

Other Developed Countries and the
Issues of Monetary Reform

The roles to be assumed and played by other developed countries in monetary reform are subsidiary to those roles of the United States or of Europe. Some countries, the Scandinavian countries, Austria, and Switzerland for example, are closely related in an economic sense with EC countries, and their views on monetary reform tend to be quite similar to those already outlined above. Other developed countries identify more closely with US views on reform. Nevertheless, monetary reform is of great interest and importance to them and the issues of paramount concern will be touched upon in brief.

Japan is probably the single most important country in the reform discussions outside of the United States and Europe. Only in very recent years has Japan emerged on the world scene as a major economic power posing a formidable challenge to technological and industrial superiority of Western countries. On the issues of monetary reconstruction, Japan has adopted a moderate, conservative stance; above all, she takes a flexible, pragmatic attitude.

From Japan's viewpoint, the Bretton Woods system worked well, but considerable revision and overhaul are necessary in order to make it workable and responsive to present requirements. In the main, Japanese interests appear more closely associated with those of Europe than the United States, although Japan sees its present role as being an informal arbiter between the United States and Europe. Japan has a clear preference for fixed exchange rates. Some suggest this preference results from the fact that the great bulk of her international trade and payments continue to be denominated in foreign currencies. Alternatively, the preference for fixed rates may be rooted in past habits and practices which proved so successful for Japanese traders. Neither objective indicators to reveal which currencies should be adjusted, nor frequent resort to exchange rate changes have particular appeal among Japanese officials. Japan has great confidence in its exchange control system and believes that other countries including the United States would do well to adopt tighter measures to deal with disequilibriating capital movements.

Japan's positions on issues of consolidation, convertibility, and asset settlement closely parallel those of Europe. In short, Japan thinks that all countries in surplus or in deficit should be subject to the same kind of disciplinary forces.

On the matter of the SDR-AID link, Japan has moved from a position of strong endorsement of US opposition to a stance of showing considerable sympathy for the idea. At the 1972 UNCTAD meeting in Santiago, the Japanese representative, Kichi Aichi (now finance minister) expressed a willingness on the part of his country to study the link proposal with an open mind. Not to be compromised, however, is the overriding need to establish confidence in SDRs and facilitate their becoming the numeraire and main reserve asset of the future.

Somewhat surprisingly, Japan has taken a calm attitude with respect to its high proportion of reserve holdings in the form of billions of US dollars. There is no question but what close ties to the dollar and to the US economy generally have been in Japan's interest and that those ties have served Japan well. Moreover, the strong and continuing political-military ties with the United States imply close allegiance with the dollar. Nevertheless, Japan sees the future monetary system as one based more solidly on an international currency such as SDRs rather than national currencies or key currencies. In fact, the experience of Britain and the United States make Japanese officials most reluctant to permit the yen to become an international reserve currency.

Canada is another developed country with important interests in the outcome of monetary reform but one which has a less dominant role to play than other leading countries. Canada takes a more balanced stance between domestic and external considerations than many countries. She is Keynesian in the sense of being concerned with domestic unemployment; but trade and payments are an important part of total economic activity, too. In respect of her balance of payments considerations, relations with the United States are of overwhelming importance. This is true for both trade and investment.

Largely because of its unique ties with the US economy and financial markets, Canada has on two extended occasions chosen to float its currency in order to protect itself from speculative pressures. The float of the Canadian dollar has resulted in a remarkably stable exchange rate over the years, thanks in part to a responsive domestic monetary policy which has been adjusted over time to keep in close tune with US monetary developments. Canada is the only developed country with extensive experience in floating its currency. She continues to have faith in that policy alternative and would like to have a reformed monetary system look upon floating or managed floating as a dignified, equally respectable alternative to fixed parities.

Canada's position on currency floating is consistent with her position on other issues. She is leery of adjustment mechanisms that would rely on objective indicators or would make provision for international sanctions. Her approach in these matters is close to that of Europe. As for consolidation and asset settlement, Canada has sided with those countries that feel a need for wider freedom of choice as to the composition of its reserves. While believing SDRs should become the main asset of the system over time, Canada sees no need to rush it into such a role.

Canada takes positions similar to those of the United States on the issues of capital controls and the SDR-AID link. Controls especially between the United

States and Canada are believed useless and are not attractive otherwise to Canada, although she concedes that capital controls may be fine for other countries. While not so adamant as the United States (or Germany in the past) in opposing the link, Canada believes that crucial monetary characteristics of SDRs could become imperiled. Instead, Canada prefers to give more aid to LDCs through traditional bilateral and multilateral channels.

All developed countries, including Japan, Canada, and others, strongly favor a one-world international monetary system. Resort to financial and economic blocs would in most instances be politically unpleasant and in some cases could threaten or at least undermine economic well-being. The major and no doubt decisive issues for developed countries are those that have been spelled out already in contrasting positions being embraced by the United States and by Europe. Essentially, each country wants to be able to have its cake and to be able to eat it as well.

A Note on Britain's Role in Monetary Reform

In the current period, Britain's role with respect to reforming the international monetary system differs considerably from what it was in 1943 and thereafter up to and including the Bretton Woods Conference; a couple of themes, however, are common to both occasions.

In the earlier period, Keynes came forward on behalf of the British Treasury with a comprehensive, elegantly conceived and refined plan for an international clearing union. This brought forth a US response known as the White plan, and bilateral discussions with the United States were set in motion which ultimately led to the Bretton Woods Conference and establishment of the Bretton Woods system.

Again in 1971, when almost all other monetary officials including US officials were preoccupied with the immediate currency crisis, British Chancellor of the Exchequer Barber put forth the broad outlines of monetary reform necessary to ensure smooth operation of a future system.[10] In short, he proposed that the SDRs be so modified as to become the numeraire of the system, in terms of which parities would be expressed and in relation to which currencies would be revalued or devalued. He suggested SDRs should become the main asset in which countries hold their reserves with currency holdings largely confined to working balances. Third, he suggested there would be need for arrangements to provide for the controlled creation of adequate, but not excessive, world liquidity without reliance on the deficit position of any country. Barber stated that a system along such lines "should provide for, and indeed promote, appropriate adjustment by all countries—those in surplus as well as those in deficit—in order to maintain equilibrium, and so avoid one of the unsatisfactory features of the present system."[11] While there was nothing earthshaking or exceedingly novel in his suggestions (they in fact bore strong similarity to previous suggestions, including Keynes's) Britain had again gone on record as the country out in front, prodding others to join in the momentous task of monetary reform.

In the current period, just as before, Britain's economy is one whose external sector is large; accordingly, she has particularly strong vested interests in the outcome of monetary reform negotiations. In the early 1940s, a prime concern was finding a medium-term solution to the huge war debts she had accumulated. The problem was never completely solved, for today Britain is still burdened with approximately the same amount of sterling balances held as reserves primarily by former or present members of the Commonwealth.[12] After the 1967 devaluation of the pound sterling, Britain negotiated bilateral agreements with those countries holding sterling in order to halt the process of diversification and to otherwise stabilize the situation. Those agreements expired in September 1973, which means that some new arrangements (possibly involving all members of the EC) must be sought to deal with the problem. This can be viewed as just another reason why Britain looks upon monetary reform as an urgent problem to which the greatest priority should be attached.

The central difference in Britain's role today as contrasted with the Bretton Woods period is that she is now one of nine members of the European Economic Community. As a new member, her role is somewhat delicate; but her long and distinguished history in diplomacy and negotiation are paying off as her leaders appear to have already made a substantial contribution in bringing other members together around common positions on key issues. To the extent that Britain can arbitrate among divergent viewpoints within the EC and can therefore strengthen the actual counterweight role to the United States which Europe has within her grasp, Britain will have once again made a critical and most valuable contribution to monetary reconstruction.

8 Issues and Blocs: III

Reforming the world's monetary system is a matter of great interest and importance for less developed countries (LDCs). At stake is the construction of a monetary system to better serve this group of countries than did the Bretton Woods system. Accordingly, the outcome of the reform negotiations will bear upon the future economic and financial environment within which LDCs both individually and collectively will strive in their quest to achieve economic development objectives.

According to the 1972 Report by the IMF Executive Directors,

The rate of growth in the developing countries is still not sufficient to narrow the gap between them and the industrial countries, and their share of world trade has declined while that of the developed countries has risen. While these unsatisfactory circumstances have been partly attributable to basic economic and other factors in the countries, they have been compounded by difficulties to access to markets and an adequate flow of capital to developing areas.[1]

The problem of gaining easier access to developed country markets is a trade problem and does not fall within the scope of this volume.[2] The second problem is financial in nature and is one stressed at length by the LDCs.

Their position, it will be recalled, was that the hopes initially placed on the World Bank to provide directly or indirectly substantial amounts of both public and private financial assistance never materialized; that the Fund was embued philosophically with a status quo orientation that was contrary to the fundamental LDC desire for change; that the Fund's resources went by and large to help out payments problems confronting the industrial countries, while LDCs themselves were recipients of the Fund's prescription to pursue currency devaluation; that with the advent of special drawing rights, the new international paper reserve asset, allocation was made according to size of members' quotas in the Fund, with the result that LDCs' acute needs for additional foreign exchange continued to go begging.

While the LDCs stand to be affected by—and therefore may be expected to take positions on all matters concerning world monetary reform. three considerations or objectives having to do with shortcomings of the past system are of special importance. One concerns their desire to establish a focus or orientation within any new international monetary system which might be as sensitive to the needs of LDCs as to the needs of industrial countries. The importance of this consideration is based upon the discipline of economic development, a branch of economics which has arisen and flourished since the days of Bretton Woods, and which has resulted in a body of thought and set of policy recommendations distinct from conventional economics long applied to industrial countries.

Another concern of the LDCs is their desire for a commitment on the part of developed countries to a program of increasing the transfer of real resources of LDCs by augmenting the heretofore inadequate flow of economic assistance. They contend this could be accomplished most easily if they were given a larger share of the pie in any future liquidity creation. Specifically, this concerns the proposed SDR-AID link.

A third interest, and perhaps the most important one of all, is that monetary reform embrace a system of stable exchange rates supported in turn by a smooth-functioning adjustment mechanism. The economic environment created therefrom would facilitate economic planning by LDCs and would be conducive to unimpeded international capital flows. These three considerations and other issues of major importance to LDCs will be dealt with in this chapter.

Refocusing the International
Monetary System

In reporting the significant developments occurring at UNCTAD III in 1972, especially the resolution endorsing a link between future allocations of SDRs and international development assistance, Walter Krause commented as to what type of follow-up actions might be expected. The overall intent, he said

is to bring pressure to bear, generally, toward revision in the international monetary machinery more amenable to the interests of developing countries. In specific terms, a twofold thrust is envisaged. First, the leadership structure of the IMF is seen as a target. The hope is to reconstitute that organization so as to shift final decision-making strength, asserted to be now markedly on the side of developed countries, more into balance (or even tipped to developing countries, in keeping with their numerical preponderance).[3]

Indeed, in their long-run objectives to achieve economic development, it is of great importance to LDCs at the current juncture that there be some kind of a reorientation of those institutions that carry out daily operations of the world's monetary system.

This very issue, which has been placed near the forefront of LDCs' concern with monetary reform, underscores a recent turning point in the attitudes with which they view the IMF as an organization and its role in international monetary affairs. For years after disillusionment began setting in over the Bretton Woods system, many developing countries were either indifferent toward or openly critical of the Fund. True, the existing trade and payments system did stimulate very significant growth of trade and world production and contributed to the resurgence of economic activity in such centers as Western Europe and Japan. In particular, a complex network of economic, fiscal, and trade relationships arose among leading industrial countries which had a powerful and occasionally disruptive affect on the monetary system as a whole. Within and among developing countries, basic questions revolving around the distribution of benefits of the system began to be posed in increasingly articulate forms by acknowledged experts. Gradually the idea gained acceptance that a new world economic system was essential. It should be a system designed to further global economic expansion; therefore, it would have to be embodied with clearly defined provisions as to how trade, monetary and financial requirements of LDCs and industrial nations alike might best be served.

All the while, LDC influence in international forums and organizations focused attention on the issue of promoting their own economic and social development, and this resulted in measures and resolutions designed to enhance export earnings and allocate resources in line with internationally agreed objectives. But postwar trade and financial institutions and the monetary system as a whole often did not facilitate implementation of those measures, and in many instances, little or no progress was achieved. General concern about all of this and recognition of the need for reform were made more acute as a consequence of the crisis conditions prevailing after 1968. Two recent developments may be singled out as providing a compelling rationale for LDCs to contribute actively and positively toward reform of the Fund. The first concerned the agreement to issue SDRs, which took place within the Fund and attracted LDC interest from the outset; the second was the 1971 monetary crisis, which was temporarily resolved through negotiations within the Group of Ten outside of the IMF, and without any involvement or participation by LDCs. The disturbing repercussions for LDCs that resulted from that crisis and in the months following its resolution by the Smithsonian Agreement are well known.[4]

International monetary reform is now moving ahead within the Committee of Twenty, a forum established within the Fund. That approach to reform marks an important achievement and an important opportunity for LDCs. Other approaches to reform, centered within the OECD or the Group of Ten, were rejected for various reasons, but one was because those forums were dominated by industrial countries; the implication was that LDCs would have had virtually no representation in the substantive negotiations. An UNCTAD resolution of May 1972 gave strong LDC endorsement of the C-20 proposal, a proposal approved by the IMF Board of Governors on July 28, 1972. To make full and effective use of the opportunities offered by the C-20 (LDCs control nine seats while developed and semideveloped nations control the remaining eleven) will itself be a great challenge to LDCs, for rarely do they find themselves united on any single issue. But it is a challenge they must meet not only to help bring important elements of policy and decision making in world monetary matters back into the Fund where LDCs have a voice, but also to refocus the future orientation of the Fund, or its successor, so that LDCs' needs may be better, more equitably served.

So as to give greater effectiveness to the representation allotted to them in the C-20, the Intergovernmental Group of 24 on international monetary questions was established by UNCTAD in 1972. This group, composed of eight representatives from each of three LDC areas (Latin America, Africa, and Asia), is a forum within which a concerted stand may be thrashed out regarding reform of the monetary system.

In order to achieve a focus or outlook within the reformed IMF (or some agreed upon successor institution) more amenable to their own purposes, the LDCs will have to win the concurrence of other participants in the reform negotiations for at least partial acceptance of their points of view in a number of areas of special interest. Some of those areas will be identified along with the sorts of alterations necessary to put them more in tune with the orientation of the LDCs.[5]

At the top of the list is the LDC representation with the Fund. Both voting power and access to resources of the Fund have been determined by the size of members' quotas in the Fund. LDCs feel that methods by which quotas are determined give them a disproportionately small amount of power vis-à-vis industrial countries, especially in view of the vast populations inhabiting LDCs and the substantial proportion of the world's land masses rightfully claimed by the many sovereign nations in the LDC category. Accordingly, there ought to be a restructuring of quotas, or of decision-making authority, in order to increase the relative influence of LDCs within the Fund. They would thus be given a more equitable role in helping to reach important decisions, and they would have greater recourse than before to the Fund's available resources.

Second, LDCs are especially interested in and concerned about possible resolutions of the liquidity problem. (This matter is discussed at greater length below because of the special significance accorded it by LDCs in the current negotiations on reform.) Some changes in the mechanism for creating international liquidity in the form of SDRs could greatly facilitate the transfer of real resources from developed countries to less developed countries. The focus of attention and interest has been, and continues to be, on proposals that call for a link between the provision of international development assistance and the issuance of SDRs. LDCs believe that a new monetary system more attuned to their concerns should help them to receive increasing amounts of financial assistance and at the same time help them to achieve more and more access to overseas capital markets on easier terms. Resolution of the liquidity problem to include some form of link could contribute both directly and indirectly to those ends.

Another area of import is the IMF General Account, the operation of which might be restructured so as to become a more suitable instrument for combating difficulties prevailing in LDCs' external sectors. Standby credit agreements have normally covered one year; their extension to include longer periods would make them much more useful given the time needed to obtain results in correcting balance of payments disequilibria. The General Account operations might be broadened further to help finance programs of economic development or to alleviate problems stemming from rising external debts. An essential component of such schemes would be to extend the deadlines of repurchase obligations for the loan-receiving countries.

Finally, it has been suggested that the Fund's machinery for compensatory financing and for financing of bugger stocks of basic commodities should be restructured in the light of past experience so as to ensure that the aims for which they were designed are indeed achieved; that is to say, there should be greater flexibility and liberality in granting financing for commodity buffer stocks.[6]

Above all, what is sought is a new monetary system that recognizes and is sympathetic to the specific structural characteristics of various member countries, a system that can respond adequately and flexibly to those characteristics, a system that encourages and facilitates the adoption of domestic policy measures to stabilize payments imbalances with due account taken concerning their possible international ramifications.

Liquidity and the Link with
Development Finance

Two issues here are of interest to LDCs. The first concerns the role of gold and reserve currencies in a new international monetary system; the second has to do with the means by which future liquidity is to be created and how, once created, it is to be distributed to member nations.

As a whole, LDCs do not have a great interest in the role assigned to gold. Few LDCs produce any gold to speak of, and few hold a very large proportion of their reserves in gold. Altogether LDCs hold only 9 percent of the world's monetary gold stock. There does appear to be general support for a reduction in the future use of gold as a means of payment and as a reserve asset. Given the traditional preference for gold on the part of some developed countries, LDCs do not expect (nor appear troubled) that gold may well continue to play some role in any new monetary system and that complete demonetization of gold appears politically improbable.

Greater interest is generated over the question of reserve currencies. LDCs have been interested in and have strongly supported special drawing rights from the outset. Since it is under international control both as to creation and allocation, since it is an international rather than a national asset, it is free from various economic uncertainties and political objections. At the same time there is awareness that replacement of outstanding national currency reserves with

SDRs is something that will in all likelihood take some time to achieve and accordingly that LDCs may be faced with an interim management problem in respect of their existing reserves: that is, having to decide in which currency or currencies to hold reserves and in what instruments they should be placed.

What becomes of reserve currencies will be of prime concern for LDCs for another reason. In many cases, the banking systems arising in developed countries have been mere extensions of banking facilities present in reserve centers. British Commonwealth member countries and several Middle East countries long held financial allegiance to Great Britain and the London financial center; certain African countries formerly members of the French Republic still have large financial holdings in francs in Paris. In all instances, the financial centers, London, Paris, New York, have extended a variety of financial services (helpful in the conduct of international commerce) to depositors. Latin American countries, for example, have held large amounts of their capital in US dollars. This has yielded them not only substantial interest earnings but has also facilitated the process of obtaining commercial credits from US banks. This is precisely the banker role played by a reserve currency country which was discussed in an earlier chapter, and this role will need to be filled in the future by some international institution if not by some financial center or combination of centers such as London, New York, Paris, Tokyo, Singapore, etc. How the role of world banker and financial intermediator is handled by the new international monetary system, therefore, will bear importantly on the evolution of capital markets in LDCs and the future access of those countries to financial markets and financial service in industrial nations.

Within LDCs there is broad support for expanding the SDR mechanism as a part of international monetary reform. What is desired most is a modification of present rules governing SDR creation and distribution so that developing countries might receive a larger proportion of what will be hopefully bigger issues in the future. These aspirations are most often set forth in proposals for a "link" between issuance of special drawing rights and the provision by developed countries of international development assistance.

Two central arguments are advanced for the link proposal.[7] First, since the rationale for SDR allocations has been to meet normally expanding liquidity requirements of the international monetary system, a case can be made for allocating SDRs where the need is greatest, that is, to the LDCs, which have been and still do experience constricting shortages of foreign exchange. If this were done, the LDCs could use SDRs to purchase imports from the developed countries, which would contribute directly to development efforts. Developed countries would still be the beneficiaries of new SDR issues—but on the second round rather than the first—while the LDCs would have also been given a "leg-up" in the form of development assistance.

This leads to the second argument in favor of the link, which is that it would amount to a revitalization of foreign aid. What with the growing disinterest in foreign aid in developed countries (because of pressing domestic problems or balance of payments pressures or both), the SDR-AID link would be a substitute procedure for aid made available traditionally through bilateral channels.[8] Subsidiary merits of the new procedure would be that LDCs as participants in the Fund would have a voice in determining the amount and timing of new SDR issues. Moreover, since SDRs are international reserve assets created on paper by international agreement, they are not subject to limitations stemming from budgetary or financial constraints of any particular developed country or group of developed countries.

A resolution that future SDR allocations be linked closely to international development assistance was brought up and approved at UNCTAD III; a similar resolution received the endorsement of the Fifteenth Session of the UN Economic Commission for Latin America. These actions have been followed up in other forums and in meetings of the Committee of Twenty, with increased pressure exerted by LDCs on developed countries to pass a resolution implementing a link.

The key word is "acceptable." Thus far, some leading developed countries have expressed reservations concerning SDR-AID link proposals for two related reasons. The first is that insofar as the link would "debudgetize foreign aid," it would amount to an unconditional resource transfer and hence a surrender of sovereignty by legislatures in developed countries. This amounts to a question about the political acceptability of the link.

The second reservation is based on economics. A link between SDRs and development finance would amount to a single mechanism serving two important policy objectives: one to increase the amount of liquidity in the world to facilitate trade and payments, the other to provide economic assistance to LDCs. There is no reason why the world's optimum liquidity needs should dovetail with the capacity of LDCs to use effectively (and of developed countries to give) development finance, and therefore, it would be impossible to achieve an optimum solution to both policy objectives simultaneously. Specifically, developed country spokesmen have voiced concern that the link would open the door for unleashing enormous inflationary power internationally by virtue of LDCs' ability to exert pressure collectively through the IMF to obtain more and more development finance via SDR allocations. Sooner or later, the creation of new SDRs would surpass the world's liquidity needs and would feed the fires of world inflation. This concern is probably overstated. LDCs agree that SDRs should be created in accordance with world liquidity needs, not in accord with the financial absorptive capacities of LDCs collectively. LDCs push for the link because it might provide them with financial resources over and above that which they have been receiving from various developed countries and international agencies.

The fact of the matter is that link proposals do not stand up to terse economic scrutiny. In the words of one well-known international economist:

It is unfortunate, in my judgment, that the less developed countries have chosen, and particularly that UNCTAD has chosen, to put so much weight on the link proposal as the way ahead in development assistance, and to support that proposal with obsolete arguments derived from the 1930s.... But I can understand that countries that are thirty years behind the advanced countries technologically find it most comfortable to be thirty years behind them intellectually as well, and to select their approved advisers and spokesmen accordingly—though one might have expected the concept of "leapfrogging" to be as applicable to intellectual as to industrial development.[9]

But the argument for the link does not need to stand on its representing the first best solution to an economic problem; instead, it can be based on the fact that it would offer an important, feasible, and much needed prop on the less-than-ideal international economic stage to help channel more resources to LDCs. The link could offer a way to furnish *additional* financial assistance to LDCs (over and above that now being provided bilaterally and multilaterally) and at the same time a way to inject new liquidity into circulation. In economists' jargon, the argument for the link may be based on its being a "second-best" solution to the liquidity and aid problems rather than a first-best solution.[10] That being the case, and bearing in mind the very high priority LDCs attach to obtaining acceptance of some sort of link proposal in the monetary reform negotiations, how might their appeal best be made and how might objections of developed countries be resolved?

One suggestion made above is that LDCs might press for an increase in their IMF quotas so that future SDR allocations would accord them a proportionately larger share than they have received heretofore. (Side benefits to this approach would include greater LDC access to Fund financing facilities, greater voting power within the Fund and hence a stronger voice in management of the Fund, including operation of the SDR system itself.)

Another suggestion based on pragmatics of current monetary reform negotiations[11] is that since LDCs generally regard as unattractive proposals for more flexible exchange rates among developed countries (see discussion in the following section), they should be granted their wishes on the matter of the link as a sort of consolation prize or as a reward for their acquiescence on resolving the adjustment problem. In some ways, this would be analogous to the inclusion of the "development" aspects of the World Bank in the Bretton Woods Agreement, a decision that was instrumental in getting LDCs to join the Fund more than twenty-five years ago.

Plumtre suggests two other approaches based upon defects in the Bretton Woods system.[12] One stems from the apparent desires of industrial countries to develop balance of payments objectives that are incompatible. They want to achieve current account surpluses that in aggregate substantially exceed their present or probable allotments of financial assistance to LDCs.[13] This implies that there is likely to be a propensity for competitive devaluation and willingness to revalue currencies which would threaten the stability of the international monetary system. This would be alleviated in turn by an increased flow of financial assistance to LDCs either by means of the link or by some other form of transfer.

Plumtre's second approach which might be used to support the link is based upon the chronic deterioration of LDCs' terms of trade and the consequent erosion of their capacity to finance needed imports for their development projects. Such deterioration is not the fault of any country or countries but arises in the main from comparatively slower price increases of goods and raw materials produced and exported by LDCs versus price increases of goods exported by industrial countries. Since LDCs purchase goods and equipment from developed countries, this problem hurts all countries, both developing and developed. Again, it is suggested that the problem could be relieved—combining a sense of justice with expediency—through a decision to allocate more reserve assets to LDCs.

Concerning the question of how developed countries' objections to link proposals might be assuaged, two suggestions may be cited. As for the political problem noted above, liquidity in the form of new SDRs might be channeled, not directly to LDCs with no strings attached, but rather indirectly through multilateral agencies, such as the World Bank Group and regional agencies (Asian Development Bank, Inter-American Development Bank, African Development Bank, and the like). It would then be up to those agencies which have voting representatives from many leading developed countries to ensure that funds allocated were used for appropriate program or project purposes. LDCs do not favor this method of allocating "linked" SDRs. They would greatly prefer to have SDRs given them directly with no strings attached. About the only exception to that point of view had been India, which would be a substantial beneficiary if SDRs were funneled through the International Development Association (the soft loan arm of the World Bank Group).

Another way to ease developed countries concerns would be to limit the annual amount of SDRs allocated directly to LDCs, or indirectly through regional agencies, or both, to 1 percent of the total GNP for all industrial nations, a level of annual foreign assistance giving already accepted in principle. If world liquidity needs thereafter remained unsatiated, more SDRs might be allocated to all countries by some more traditional formula such as size of quotas in the Fund. In any case, these brief suggestions should be taken to indicate that developed countries political and economic reservations concerning the link proposal could be dealt with in an acceptable fashion without seriously debilitating either the developed assistance aspect or the liquidity-creating aspect.

One thing is certain, and that is that LDCs are more united in their stand for some sort of SDR-AID link than they are for any other proposal concerning monetary reform. They view achievement of a resolution implementing the link as being more likely than any other single resolution to make the new international monetary system better suited than the old one to their ongoing needs.

The Adjustment Mechanism

The par value system of fixed exchange rate parities has widespread support among LDCs. Broadly speaking, the reasons behind this view parallel the reasons put forth by developed countries; namely, the well-being and growth of world trade have been well served by fixed rates. On the other hand, floating exchange rates tend to evoke more rather than less government intervention and have on past occasions been accompanied by increased uncertainty at many levels. The essential feature of any adjustment mechanism, and one the LDCs regard as most likely obtainable under a fixed rate system, is stability. The issue in present negotiations is whether greater stability results from fixed exchange rates with large but infrequent adjustments, or from a more flexible mechanism which provides for small and more continuous adjustment.

In past periods when exchange rate instability has prevailed—for example, the years of upheaval between the two world wars and particularly during the 1930s—it was the LDCs with their less diversified economies and unsophisticated financial systems which suffered greatly. World commodity markets, both for agricultural goods and raw materials, took a heavy beating from the start. Moreover, aid programs sponsored by industrial countries and exports of private capital to LDCs were either reduced or dried up altogether, early casualties of worsening overall balance of payments of the more developed nations.

This somewhat superficial stance of LDCs, which tends to associate stability with fixed exchange rate systems and instability with fluctuating exchange mechanisms, was reinforced as a result of the 1971 monetary crisis, the floating exchange rates that ensued, and the eventual realignment of exchange rates embodied in the Smithsonian Agreement. Quite apart from being miffed that substantive negotiations during that time took place within the Group of Ten, and consequently that they were precluded from participating in those negotiations which were of direct, vital interest to them, the LDCs asserted that they stood to be adversely affected in three different ways. First, because some countries had outstanding debts in depreciating currencies that were subject to gold clauses or had nondollar foreign debts and debt service payments outstanding, their liabilities in terms of local currency or in equivalent US dollars increased. Second, since most LDCs reserves were held to a large extent in terms of dollars or sterling or other assets which either declined in value as a result of the crisis or benefited by a small amount, their purchasing power declined. Third, there was concern that LDCs' terms of trade would worsen as a consequence of import prices increasing more than export prices. These adverse effects varied greatly indeed from one country to another depending upon trade patterns, composition of liquidity holdings, and of external debts.

Despite the LDCs' stand, the major issue having to do with the adjustment mechanism is not a choice between a fixed exchange rate system or a flexible system per se; instead, the issue is how to construct an adjustment mechanism flexible enough to avoid financial crises, exchange restraints, and attendant economic dislocations of the past, yet disciplined and smooth enough in its operation so as to maintain a framework of overall stability.

Recalling to mind LDCs' criticisms of the asymmetrical manner in which the adjustment mechanism under the Bretton Woods system worked, we may gain a clearer impression of a general LDC position on the present-day issue of how to improve the adjustment process itself. The criticism voiced earlier was that certain industrial countries with large or perhaps chronic payments surpluses, and others with chronic deficits, managed to avoid international discipline of exchange rate adjustment by virtue of being reserve currency countries or by having easy access to balance of payments credits (both within and outside the purview of the Fund); on the other hand, countries of lesser import economically or in the functioning of the international financial system were subjected to substantially greater international discipline. One of the long-held LDC desires has been, therefore, that the adjustment process be improved so as to operate more fairly and more symmetrically on all members of the system. This in truth implies either the need for greater flexibility of exchange parities themselves (possibly relying on some sort of objective indicators) or that more credits be made readily available to any and all countries encountering payments difficulties in order that they may be given both the means and the time necessary to implement and to realize the fruits of corrective economic measures. If the latter prevails, then LDCs might opt for increased discretionary decisionmaking power for the Fund, together with a stronger LDC role in the Fund.

First, consider some of the LDC attitudes toward greater flexibility, which could be introduced through widening the bands of official support, through some form of crawling peg, or through more frequent parity adjustment. The proposals having to do with widening the margins around par values are looked upon as not being useful for LDCs and as posing possible important dangers to their international trade and investment.[14] Wider margins of developed countries' currencies would likely force LDCs to choose one of the major currencies against which its own currency would be pegged; the choice would not be based on optimum-currency-area considerations if margins were widened by only a small amount. But this might present political problems and could be economically costly besides because of increased foreign exchange risks and higher transaction costs. Wider margins, it is argued, could lead to monetary blocs (that is, a number of countries pledging allegiance, so to speak, to a key currency country; agreeing to peg their currencies to the key currency, and to maintain substantial reserves in the key currency) which could in turn become inward-looking both financially and from a trade point of view. That is, monetary blocs could lead to trade diversion, not trade creation.

Assume that developed countries, through wider margins, were to place greater reliance on monetary policy (induced variations in interest rates) to control domestically generated business cycles, as opposed to imported inflation or deflation, whose effects would be dampened somewhat by exchange rate movements within the widened bands. This could easily cause major debt management problems for LDCs whose currencies were pegged to their currencies. This in turn would add uncertainty and possible disruption to economic planning and investment.

Finally, LDCs generally seem unprepared to take on uncertainties posed by wider margins around their own exchange parities, unprepared to come up with new structures, such as forward markets with experts to operate them, and to handle new problems in reserve currency management. Operational evidence of LDC aversion to wider margins comes from the recent period, the end of 1971, when one-third of the countries posting new central rates (all of them LDCs) rejected the wider margins called for in the Smithsonian Agreement.

The actual merit in these LDC arguments against wider bands is open to question, partly because the empirical evidence is thin and gives little basis for balanced judgment, and partly because some significant theoretical counterarguments have been offered which tend to undercut the LDC position, at least on paper. An important point, however, is that the LDC position is strongly held; and until the true effects of wider banks are proven unambiguously to be substantially less detrimental than feared, LDCs will continue to hold to their position.

With respect to proposals of the crawling peg variety, or proposals for more frequent but smaller changes in parities, the LDC position is neither so adamant nor so consistent. It may be said, however, that either of these means of achieving greater flexibility would be generally acceptable to LDCs so long as stability seemed assured and so long as discipline of the more flexible adjustment mechanism was meted out to all countries alike, deficit and surplus, LDC and DC.

Several Latin American countries have experimented successfully with crawling peg techniques in recent years. Brazil, perhaps the most well known case, has been guided by changes over time in domestic wholesale prices versus world wholesale or import prices in order to determine the degree of periodic minidevaluations; the state of Brazilian reserves has determined the timing of the devaluations. Brazil was led to adopt this means of achieving greater flexibility because of the vulnerability of the country to inflation, of its currency to being overvalued chronically, and because the policy limitations imposed by foreign exchange shortages could be overcome most easily through more flexible exchange rates which required much smaller reserves.

Another argument put forth in favor of this sort of greater flexibility is based on the fact that characteristically within LDCs, skilled management is a scarce commodity.[15] Exchange rate flexibility accomplishes with more automaticity and greater effectiveness what is difficult and time-consuming to do administratively.

The central considerations underlying the case for greater exchange rate flexibility appear to be the extent of inflation domestically and the state of openness of its economy or its stage of development. The higher the rate of inflation sustained and conceded as a cost in achieving more rapid economic advancement, the more there is to be said in favor of frequent exchange rate adjustment so as to avoid any long periods of currency overvaluation which, in the absence of adequate reserves, would mean having to curtail the use of external resources perhaps vital to ongoing development programs.

The second consideration is especially important. Greater flexibility exercised by an LDC with inflationary problems, either in the form of a crawling peg or other small but frequent exchange rate adjustment, imposes a cost-push inflationary effect via rising import prices. For small countries in the early stages of development, where the import content of total product is relatively great and where there has occurred little diversification from an agriculturally based economy, the inflationary effect will be large. In such cases, the adverse terms of trade effect (rising import prices with elastic demand compared to falling prices of exports with inelastic demand) outweigh minor improvements in output or employment. For larger countries (e.g., Argentina, Brazil, Chile, and Mexico) whose economies are more diversified and whose imports account for a smaller share of total product, the cost-push inflationary effect is less significant and the case for greater exchange rate flexibility is reinforced.

These considerations have led some economists to suggest that one resolution of the adjustment problem might be to have two sets of rules, one for major developed countries which might employ a wider band combined with a crawling peg suitable to their general economic performance, and another for LDCs which would be tailored to their economic performances which include relatively higher rates of domestic inflation.[16] If that were the case, that is, developed countries adhering to greater exchange rate flexibility, LDCs' exchange rates would fluctuate more against major currencies. Thus, while the two sets of rules might in one sense help resolve the adjustment problem, LDCs' concerns about stability, in the sense of smoothing their foreign exchange earnings from exports over time, might not be well served.

To summarize, the issue of how best to reform the adjustment mechanism is not one around which LDCs can all rally together with equal enthusiasm. There is indeed a general feeling among LDCs that greater flexibility of any sort is not something that will serve LDC interests. (As elaborated earlier, exceptions to this feeling are held by the larger, more evolved countries such as Brazil, Argentina, and perhaps a few others.) The feeling is based essentially on the terms of trade argument, or some variation of it, which asserts that currency realignment for

LDCs (overwhelmingly of the devaluation variety because of their high rates of domestic inflation) is detrimental because of often experienced adverse effects on terms of trade with other industrial countries. The typical situation arises where exports of LDCs to developed countries outside its currency bloc largely represent primary products for which demand is price inelastic, whereas exports of the developed countries to the LDCs are more price elastic.

Rather than capitulating to the orthodox prescription of devaluation, many LDCs at one point or another have deemed it very much in their interests to battle against the emergence of an overvalued exchange rate with exchange rationing and other techniques, which entail de facto devaluation consequences for domestic economic sectors of lesser importance but not those of primary importance, given the particular objectives of economic development. This policy prescription has emerged from the relatively new field of economic development; it is a prescription that appears to have achieved positive results in a number of countries; it is one in a growing set of policy recommendations, distinct from orthodox economic policy recommendations with which the philosophical orientation of the Bretton Woods system was consistent.

Since this dichotomy exists and has been growing over the past several years, it is not surprising that now, as orthodox thinking moves toward reform proposals offering greater flexibility in one manner or another, that the more revolutionary economic thinking embraced by many LDCs should be leaning in the opposite direction—namely, back towards more fixed exchange rates as a means to achieving maximum advantages from trade, access to developed countries' capital markets, and long-term international capital movements between all nations. The tenacity with which LDCs will adhere to their advocacy of the fixed exchange parity system and narrow margins will depend upon other factors, including what the outlook is for achieving their objectives on other monetary reform issues, and with respect to an emerging consensus among developed countries as to how the adjustment problem might be resolved, how much or how little LDCs interests might be served or impaired.

LDC Blocs

Over the course of the past several years, much has been written about economic blocs. Indeed, some steps have been taken by certain countries to form them. Most often, the result has been loose federations or free trade areas among groups of countries because of old colonial ties or because of geographical proximity. Naturally enough, economic interests of those federations were regarded as being more closely tied with one large industrial country as opposed to another. Thus, Latin-American countries' interests were rather closely associated with the US economy, and those of Africa, the Middle East, South Asia, and Indo-China with one or other of the European powers or Britain.

How the new international monetary system is reconstructed will bear importantly on the question of what lies ahead regarding relationships between the oligopolistic-like industrial countries on the one hand, and the large number of less powerful, poor countries of the world. If the new system embraces more closely the ideals originally envisaged at Bretton Woods (a par value system with elements of greater flexibility, monetary reserves held increasingly in SDRs rather than national currencies or gold, and currency convertibility limiting the ability of all nations to run deficits) then the past privileges accruing to reserve currency countries and the countries with special access to balance of payments finance would be diminished and they would be obliged to make a greater, more timely contribution to the adjustment process. (This is what Alexandre Kafka refers to as the "international option.")[17] While economic blocs of nations experiencing varying degrees of integration might continue and perhaps even grow, there would be little or no likelihood of financial blocs doing likewise. On the contrary, they would be undone over time to the extent that the new monetary system operated successfully. While the monetary system would continue to be characterized by economic bodies of greatly varying strength and importance, the oligopolistic framework toward which the system appeared headed in the 1960s would become less apropos.

On the other hand, the new system may not evolve that way at all. It may instead develop along lines that exacerbate the trend toward larger regional economic units, each unit being composed of one or a few large developed countries and several smaller LDCs. This raises several possibilities. There might be a few large units living and working in harmony, choosing to maintain either stable exchange rates or flexible exchange rates between each other. In the first instance, some sort of international institution would be desired for surveillance over such rates; possibly subsidiary regional institutions would be responsible for supplementing liquidity needs of regional units, or within regional units as well if multiple currencies were maintained within. In the second instance, it might be possible for regional units to allow their currencies to float freely vis-à-vis one another since the relative dependence of any unit on other units would be less than for most individual countries today. In that circumstance, no international body would be necessary. Still, smaller countries especially might feel more at ease if surveillance were exercised by an international institution and not just by regional institutions.

As far as the LDCs' interests are concerned, rejection of the international option and movement toward regional blocs, financial as well as economic, could be a costly matter. At the worst, blocs might arise as a defensive measure in view of the absence of adequate machinery for maintaining orderly trade and payments relationships. If that were to happen, the long-term trend since World War II toward increasing integration in the world economy, a trend that has proved so beneficial for all countries, would be halted or even reversed. But even if blocs were formed under more amicable circumstances, LDCs might have to join one or another bloc whose center was determined by the major developed country or countries belonging to it. This process, if allowed to proceed far enough, could curtail LDCs' access to world markets; i.e., it would limit markets in which they could sell their commodities and thus earn foreign exchange, and would limit access to capital markets from which they could borrow funds to help finance development projects. If so, there would be some fragmentation of political pressures mounted by LDCs in such forms as UNCTAD, UNECLA, CIAP, ECAFE, etc., for world monetary reforms designed to better suit their needs. On the other hand, if the process of monetary bloc formation only went ahead a little further, for example, through creation of an EC monetary bloc, then LDCs very likely would not feel pressured into joining any monetary bloc. The size of an EC currency unit would be similar to the dollar bloc already in existence, and LDCs have proved themselves able to retain their own national currencies and a considerable degree of independence in currency-related decisions in such an environment. Nevertheless, it would appear that LDCs' interests lie very much on the side of monetary reform that embraces rather than rejects the international option and rejects rather than embraces multiple financial blocs.

Special Problems Posed by Oil-Producing Nations

What sets the oil-producing countries apart from other developing countries is their rapidly increasing financial wealth. They are the "haves" as opposed to the "have-nots" because they lay claim to some 60 percent of the world's known oil resources and have been exporting ever increasing amounts of that oil at great profit to industrial Europe, Japan, and now to the United States. A typical barrel of crude oil pumped out of the Persian Gulf costs about 10 US cents to produce but sells for about $2.50 on the Gulf. The other $2.40 is composed of government taxes and royalties of $1.60 and the seller's profit of $.80.[18] Known oil reserves are heavily concentrated in the countries of the Persian Gulf, that is, the United Arab Emirates, Kuwait, Iraq and Saudi Arabia, plus Iran; and remaining or yet undiscovered reserves are believed to be more concentrated still.

America, just like European nations and Japan, is looking toward the Persian Gulf to supply increasing proportions of its fast-swelling demand for oil in the years to come. Many projections have been made as to what the incomes of those few oil-producing countries will be. One recognized expert suggests that their cumulative income from 1973 through 1980 will be over $210 billion and that their cumulative expenditures for the same period will be under $100 billion.[19] Therefore, capital accumulations, initially in the form of foreign exchange earnings, will be over $100 billion by 1980. These potentially massive liquid holdings represent the heart of the problem to which architects of monetary reform must address themselves.

At least two major problems are posed. The first problem is how to persuade the Arab oil-producing countries to go on pumping oil out of the ground when perhaps a few of them (and most certainly Saudi Arabia) can no longer absorb the funds generated from the sales. (If those countries cannot be so persuaded then it appears that a serious world oil shortage will loom in the not too distant future because of inadequate substitute sources of supply.)

The second problem flows from resolution of the first and deals directly with the future international monetary order. The problem is approached first of all by placing petroleum-exporting countries apart from other developing or developed countries in terms of how they would be expected to abide by a balance of payments adjustment mechanism. If they were to behave as other nations under a tight adjustment mechanism, then they would wind up selling oil at an extremely low price, in view of rising world demand and their own more slowly rising domestic expenditures and import requirements. (The usual prescription that their currency be revalued in the face of chronic balance of payments surpluses would only exacerbate those surpluses, because world demand for oil is extremely inelastic.) Such a policy is of dubious merit on equity grounds (since they are exchanging one type of asset, namely oil, for another type of interest-earning asset), and one the Arab countries would never accept, in view of their monopoly-like hold on the world's oil reserves. Therefore, those select few oil-exporting countries with oil reserves in excess of their own development financing needs will be earning large amounts of foreign exchange reserves in the future.

As matters now stand, these countries indicate they want three things as part of any future monetary accord: a value guarantee for their foreign exchange earnings (i.e., a guarantee against unfavorable exchange rate changes), unrestricted use of those reserves in respect of where and in what instruments they are placed, and a high interest rate in return for investing them. But if their foreign exchange earnings rise as expected, then stability of the world monetary system would be seriously threatened by possible shifting of billions of foreign exchange reserves from one financial center to another for whatever reason or set of reasons (political, economic, or financial) these countries deemed sufficient. In order to prevent such a circumstance from manifesting itself, monetary architects are challenged to devise some sort of international investment facility, attractive enough to oil-producing countries to make them want to forego alternative uses of their reserves. One suggestion put forth is that the Fund would provide such an investment facility and that industrial countries would be assessed the interest charges. Then funds placed in the special facility by the oil-exporting countries would be used to further economic development in less developed countries.

Another less grandiose proposal, which might help reduce the problem for the next few years, would be to reach an agreement to the effect that all central banks, including those of the oil nations and other less developed countries, would refrain from investing in or borrowing from the Eurocurrency market. In recent periods, there has been considerable shifting of funds by some central banks in that market, an activity cited as one of the prime factors underlying disequilibrating short-term capital movements.

None of these or other proposals put forth have met with much favor on the part of the oil-exporting countries. They are not anxious to have their financial alternatives constrained in the future. Nevertheless, in the absence of some agreement, their freedom and the exercise of it could threaten the viability of any future monetary system.

Part IV:
Implications

9

The Economic Environment

The outcome of the international reform negotiations, that is, the shape and character of a new international monetary system to be implemented, will have a very considerable impact on the world economic environment. This chapter considers how alternative resolutions of the leading issues posed would affect global economic conditions.

Effects of Monetary Reform on World
Trade and Investment

One of the grave concerns expressed during the 1971 monetary crisis was that the well-being of international trade and investment was in jeopardy since the rules of the game under which the Bretton Woods system had prevailed were in a state of indefinite suspension, if not permanently layed to rest. It was believed that unless early agreement on exchange rate realignment could be secured and the leading countries returned to a Bretton Woods type of monetary system, a worldwide recession along the lines of that which occurred during the early and mid-1930s could follow, simply because without a sound monetary system and payments mechanism, world trade and investment would contract severely.

Those fears were not realized, and indeed world trade continued to expand and to flourish throughout 1972 and 1973 despite waves of speculation, which stemmed in part at least from the absence of an accord on a new international monetary system and which caused substantial and often rapid changes in the existing exchange rate structure. Several factors were responsible for this continuing world prosperity. First, an economic boom had commenced in the United States and was beginning, or about, to take hold in Europe and Japan. This entailed strong demand for imported raw materials and semiprocessed and finished goods to help satisfy domestic needs. Second, there was the factor of growing East-West trade made possible by the continuing thaw in East-West political relations. That development was accelerated by poor agricultural harvests in Russia, in a number of Asian countries, and in Australia as well as elsewhere; accordingly, there were sharp increases in world demand for foodstuffs from those countries that had available supplies, irrespective of the uncertain international monetary situation. Third, there was the unanticipated factor of high adaptability displayed in country after country by commercial traders, managers of multinational corporations, and entrepreneurs. Standard practices of negotiating and writing up trade contracts, of hedging against exchange rate changes that could lead to financial losses, and of acquiring funds for investment purposes were modified as necessary in order to permit trade and investment to continue unimpeded as much as possible.

Despite the fact that international economic prosperity has weathered the 1971 currency crisis and the much longer ensuing period of uncertainty with no monetary system to provide an orderly environment, there is universal agreement that reconstruction of the international monetary system is a prerequisite of future prosperity and to realizing the benefits of growing world economic interdependence while meeting the requirements of national authorities that they retain adequate control over their respective economies.

Resolution of the issue concerning the most appropriate, politically feasible balance of payments adjustment mechanism will indeed affect future world trade and quite possibly investment as well. According to a Ministerial Meeting of the Committee of Twenty, the future exchange rate regime should be based on "stable but adjustable par values," and "floating rates could provide a useful technique in particular situations."[1] The critical points at issue bearing on the future course of trade and investment are "how stable?" "how adjustable;" and "under what particular situations?"

An exchange rate regime with stable but adjustable par values presupposes general availability of financing for temporary periods and in limited amounts for countries in balance of payments deficits. Such financing is essential in avoiding excessive adjustment costs; moreover, it is widely believed that international trade tends to flourish more under expectations of stable exchange rates than under unstable rates. This view is still held despite mitigating factors during the most recent period cited above. If financing of balance of payments disequilibria is too readily available, however, then policy measures directed at either the internal or external sector will be delayed or pursued halfheartedly so that the inevitable adjustment, when it comes, will be larger and therefore more painful because of the magnitude of disequilibria that has been allowed to accumulate. Large but infrequent exchange rate adjustment was the method provided by the evolved Bretton Woods system. There is ample evidence to show that such an exchange rate regime can cause significant sacrifice of domestic full employment objectives, can distort opportunity costs, and can lead to a misallocation of resources—all of which are detrimental to the continuous well-being of international trade and to international investment as well.

If financing for balance of payments disequilibria is less readily available, then adjustment must be more reliant on domestically oriented policies, or externally oriented policies, or both. But adjustment via domestic deflation or inflation can be exceedingly costly in terms of domestic economic objectives, particularly if prevailing domestic circumstances dictate opposing policies. Adjustment via domestic policy changes to effect wage and price patterns is more costly for those economies whose external sectors are small in proportion to their domestic sectors and may therefore be unacceptable for internal political reasons. If adjustment needs result in heavy emphasis being given to commercial policies, such as quotas, tariffs, border taxes, exchange controls, and the like, then again substantial economic and political costs must be born with what can only be adverse consequences for trade and investment. Moreover, resort to controls for balance of payments reasons usually serve to only suppress an imbalance and to delay the need for more fundamental measures. For all of these reasons, an adjustment process that puts greater emphasis than before on exchange rate change may be regarded as more effective in an economic sense.

The successful operation of a more flexible exchange rate regime would be greatly enhanced if the act of parity adjustment were made less political and more symmetrical. Smaller, more frequent exchange rate adjustments, for surplus and deficit countries alike, based upon multilateral consultations and pressures rather than bilateral pressures, and employing objective economic analysis would help in these respects.

While many experts believe that smaller, more frequent parity changes to effect required balance of payments adjustment would be beneficial to the world economic environment as far as the optimum development of trade and investment are concerned, there is the potential danger that if such parity changes are made too frequently, objective indicators may give incorrect signals; these would then create the presumption in favor of policy measures that would in effect be destabilizing and therefore harmful to the trade and investment climate. The problem here is that the terms of trade effects on export and import prices of a country whose exchange rate has just been altered take hold and become visible sooner than do the effects of the value of trade. The lag between these two effects is greater in markets that are relatively less competitive; therefore, the time duration of the perverse signals coming from the balance of payments statistics or the level of foreign exchange reserves is longer for countries whose exports or imports are heavily composed of industrial goods as opposed to raw materials.

The price effects cause a perverse influence on the country's basic balance of payments and also on its official foreign exchange reserves. (That is to say, the basic balance of payments of a depreciating country will actually worsen for a time before the volume effects outweigh the price effects, and vice versa for a country whose currency has been appreciated.) Accordingly, until the full effects of an initial exchange rate adjustment have worked through the trade and payments system, objective indicators will tend to understate the actual impact of parity adjustment. Too frequent resort to parity change as a means of producing balance of payments adjustment runs the risk of overcorrecting a disequilibrium exchange rate, thus causing the reverse price and wage distortions, which can only be disruptive to international trade and investment.

The difficult task in resolving the adjustment problem is to come up with a scheme in which there is greater, but no too great, reliance on exchange rate adjustment so that domestic economic objectives need not be severely compromised and so that restrictive commercial policies or capital controls need not be invoked as a matter of routine. Such a scheme presupposes effective international surveillance of the balance of payments adjustment of each country. While such surveillance and more frequent resort to adjustment via exchange rate alteration represents a certain sacrifice of national sovereignty, it also means greater freedom for national authorities, who would then have one more policy instrument with which they could pursue their economic objectives. To the extent they are able to do so more effectively, and that resort to trade and investment impediments is shunned, prospects for world trade and investment will be greatly enhanced.

Another aspect of monetary reconstruction that could enhance the climate for trade and investment would be to associate the issue of special drawing rights by the Fund with the provision of financial aid to developing countries. There are alternative methods of operating the SDR-AID link. On the one hand, industrial countries might commit themselves to provide untied aid to LDCs, equal to some proportion of SDRs they received at each issue. Alternatively, larger allotments of SDR issues than heretofore might be made directly to LDCs—that is, the proportion of any issue received by LDCs as a group would be greater and the proportion received by developed countries would be less than has been the case in the past. Another proposal is that a definite proportion of newly issued SDRs be placed at the disposal of the International Development Association and/or regional development banks which are specially designed to finance LDCs. In each instance, industrial countries taken as a whole and subject to a time lag would receive their full allocations of SDRs.

The particular method in which the link were operated would not matter so much as would the rate or level at which it were carried out. LDCs receiving additional SDRs would use them to place orders for industrial countries' products. That in itself would enhance the flow of trade between industrial and developing countries and would accordingly make investment opportunities in LDCs relatively more attractive. But a number of other considerations underscore the potential contribution of the link to an improved world economic environment.

As Richard Kahn has suggested, the link, if operating at a substantial rate, could improve the adjustment process and could also help to establish a more rational distribution of the world's monetary reserves.[2] Those countries in which total demand presses most heavily on available productive resources also tend to be countries that experience a surplus balance of payments position. (Japan and Germany are recent cases in point.) To some extent, the authorities of those same countries tend to be most worried about inflation. Where this were true, and to the extent that producers of desired goods and materials had large backlogs of orders, there would be a tendency for less aggressive competition for additional orders coming from LDCs. There would be an opportunity, therefore, for LDCs' demands to be met more quickly and possibly more cheaply by other countries whose resources were underutilized and whose producers were eager to find additional business. The operation of the link would, to the extent demand for goods were placed in the latter category of countries, help alleviate the economic stagnation and unemployment and at the same time would strengthen their balance of payments positions. (Stagnation often has been the result of deflationary policies pursued by government officials when faced with a balance of payments deficit and erosion of reserves. Britain's experience during the mid-1960s is a case in point. Thus, the chance to augment exports without having to provide aid to LDCs first would relieve simultaneously both the external and the domestic problems.) Those economically depressed industrial countries able to win a portion of LDCs' new orders would be improving their reserve positions in that they would be earning SDRs in excess of the shares determined by their IMF quotas.

Looked at from another angle, the link could help remove what has been a serious obstacle against improvement of the adjustment process while at the same time facilitating higher levels of world trade and investment. It has been observed earlier that during the 1960s and to a considerable extent even today, industrial countries that have accumulated very large sums of official reserves are reluctant to contemplate balance of payments deficits and depletion of these reserves. In fact, the balance of payments objectives of industrial countries when taken together indicate a substantial basic balance of payments surplus, net, and a substantial rate of growth in their collective monetary reserves. The collective objectives, in short, are inconsistent unless a mechanism is found for transferring real resources to the rest of the world, namely, to the less developed countries. The operation of the link would help resolve this dilemma since a higher level of aggregate exports of industrial countries to developing countries would occur; moreover, this need not take place in a manner that would aggravate world inflation. And even if it did, the link mechanism could be speedily altered—more speedily in fact than governments acting individually to cut back their aid programs because of excessive domestic demand pressures—by adjusting the level of SDRs allocated to LDCs, however that were done.

In summary, the link could contribute directly to a higher level of world economic activity and therefore to more rapid expansion of world trade and investment. This would be accomplished by giving LDCs the financial means to expand more rapidly and to increase their purchases of goods produced in industrial countries. To the extent that such additional exports helped to relieve stagnant economic conditions existing in certain industrial countries and to foster more rapid economic development in LDCs, the incentives for greater international investment would be improved.

Perhaps the single most important monetary reform consideration that will bear on the future climate for international investment concerns the issue of whether capital movements should be controlled, and if so how and to what degree. Generally, controls on international investment imply controls on long-term capital movements, but some investment takes place in the form of short-term capital flows as well;[3] so we are really talking, potentially at least, about controls on capital movements, short and long term. Any agreement by participants of the monetary reform negotiations to restrict either the inflow or outflow of capital will have a direct, deleterious effect on international investment. The rationale for such controls is that investors too often behave in a way injurious to domestic industry's interests or act in ways that contravene efforts of domestic authorities to stabilize domestic economic activity. The way to overcome these problems is to negotiate ground rules or standards of conduct for multinational corporations or whoever it is who is proposing to undertake some international investment. There are too many benefits to be realized by donors, recipients, and the world generally from encouraging orderly international investment (and hence a more optimum allocation of available capital resources) to resort to controls that would block or otherwise impede capital flows.

Another point to bear in mind is that a considerable portion of disequilibriating capital flows of recent years occurred because of declining confidence in the dollar and expectations of substantial parity changes in it and in other leading currencies. It was only natural that international investors, under those conditions, should seek to safeguard their interests by transferring liquid funds to strong currency centers. Under a new international monetary system, the confidence problem will presumably have been laid to rest and such capital flows will be much less likely to occur. Second, if the adjustment mechanism adopted relies on smaller but more frequent parity changes, there will be much less incentive for speculators or for investors with international interests to transfer funds from center to center—simply because the expected rate of return from any parity adjustment will be much less. Accordingly, problems caused in the recent past by international capital movements might well be substantially reduced under a new monetary system, and application of capital controls might be viewed as "preparations for the last war."[4]

Resolution of the issue of the balance of payments adjustment mechanism is likely to have little or no effect on long-term capital movements,[5] although it is quite conceivable that there could be some effect on short-term capital flows. As for long-term investment, it is believed that one way or another adjustment will occur in the long run, and however it takes place matters little. The existence or absence of controls applied to the initial investment or to recoupment of earnings are deemed far more important, as are other factors not pertaining to characteristics of the international monetary system, such as expectations concerning political stability, long-range economic growth forecasts, wage-price considerations, and the like.

Even if stabilizing in the future, short-term capital flows could be substantial and hence pose problems for national monetary authorities if the adjustment mechanism were one which allowed for relatively infrequent parity changes, or were one in which parity changes on average tended to be rather large (say more than 5 percent), or were one in which timing of parity changes could be predicted with a high degree of accuracy by market operators (which means there would be little or no secrecy as to the substance of the latest international consultations or what the latest objective indicators showed). If the adjustment mechanism were characterized by any or all of these features, then certain governments might be compelled to adopt some form of short-term capital or exchange controls in order to preserve the viability of domestic monetary policy.

Effects of Monetary Reform on
Economic Development

Resolution of several key issues of monetary reform will bear very significantly on the future climate of economic development. A smooth-functioning adjustment process that is by and large free of serious crises is most important in insuring a steady flow of capital into LDCs at moderate rates of interest. If the future adjustment process calls for relatively frequent parity changes on the part of all countries including industrial countries, then the cause of economic development could be hampered, since this would add directly to instability of LDCs export earnings and would jeopardize medium- and long-range economic planning. One way to relieve this potential problem would be to improve the scope of buffer stock schemes and international commodity agreements. This would offer increased insurance as to LDCs export earnings despite greater exchange rate flexibility.

Another key issue of reform that will influence the development climate is whether or not there is a commitment by industrial countries to provide for a continuous transfer of real resources to LDCs. A *link* between SDRs and development finance is the mechanism most talked about thus far for accomplishing this end. But adoption of the link is only one way in which a reformed international monetary system could make better provision than the Bretton Woods system for the needs of the developing countries. What matters most is that there be a substantially stepped-up resource transfer, a transfer additional to what has been provided in the past through bilateral and multilateral channels. This could be handled by developed countries agreeing to increase by some proportionate amount their past contributions of official development assistance to LDCs. Such assistance includes bilateral grants and loans offered on concessional terms and contributions to multilateral institutions. The link itself has been proposed in its various forms because it offers one relatively painless way to accomplish an additional resource transfer amounting to perhaps a few billion dollars annually, and because the basic mechanism of injecting additional reserve assets (SDRs) into the international monetary system has already been established. All that would be required is an agreement to redress the formula for allocating future issues of SDRs. Only if the link were adopted and introduced in addition to—not in substitution for—past and present economic assistance would it assist the cause of economic development. (And even then, the link would have to amount to at least a few billion dollars per year to have any significant impact on development.)

A third aspect of international monetary reform that could have a bearing on the outlook for economic development concerns capital movements. If there were an agreement that all countries must adopt measures to restrict short-term capital outflows, then LDCs would be hampered from attracting funds from abroad. How much of a hardship this might cause development efforts is open to question. However, LDCs have been interested for some time in improving their access to developed countries capital markets but have met with only limited success until fairly recently, when the Eurodollar market has been found to be a welcome source of funds and an outlet for short-term investment. Imposition of short-term capital controls could, therefore, restrict future use of this new-found foreign capital facility.

A related matter concerns the future of financial relationships which have sprung up between LDCs' central banks and leading banks in financial centers such as New York and London which service LDCs' official foreign exchange reserves. If resolution of the consolidation issue required all countries to convert substantial portions of their foreign exchange holdings into some primary international reserve asset such as SDRs, then those financial relationships would be in jeopardy and along with them the important lines of credit which those commercial banks have made available over time to LDCs' central banks. Here again, LDCs' interests could be safeguarded and compensated for, such as by an expansion of a lending facility in the Fund; but the point is that a rigid consolidation arrangement followed by a resumption of convertibility and a tight asset settlement scheme for resolving balance of payments imbalances would force some difficult and sharp changes from past financial practices for LDCs.

Effects of Monetary Reform on Price Levels

Resolution of several key issues of monetary reform stand to have a substantial impact on the behavior of world price levels in the years to come; this includes resolution of such issues as the adjustment mechanism, the issuance of new international liquidity, and disequilibrating capital flows.

It has long been supposed that an exchange rate regime of fixed parities with the ever present concern of balance of payments deficits would result in a major source of discipline for the control of inflation in individual countries. In fact, it may be recalled from previous discussion that Keynes's early concern about the US proposals for monetary reform in the early 1940s was the apparent deflationary bias. Until the middle 1960s, the prevailing view of informed observers was that the Bretton Woods system did indeed possess a deflationary bias caused on the one hand by a one-sided adjustment process (with surplus countries under little or no pressure to adjust their exchange rates in contrast to deficit countries) and on the other hand by an inadequate system of liquidity creation. It was Robert Triffin who cogently argued in the late 1950s that newly mined gold was inadequate to fulfill world liquidity needs and that increasing reliance on the creation of dollar liabilities would prove insufficient and over time would lead to a shortage of international liquidity.

Today, following the breakdown of the Bretton Woods system, more and more experts are concluding that rather than there having been a built-in deflationary bias, the international monetary system instead yielded to inflationary forces that had their origins in domestic economies of important countries, and at the same time, because of the nature of its own institutions, generated inflation on its own.[6]

If the adjustment mechanism adopted under a new monetary system is able to bring approximately equal pressure on surplus and deficit countries to adopt measures to reestablish balance of payments equilibrium and is able to do so without serious imbalances being allowed to accumulate for long periods of time, then the impact of the monetary system on world price levels will tend to be rather neutral. If deficit countries continue to exhibit a strong reluctance to adjust by imposing domestic deflationary measures, they will be forced to endure repeated devaluations of their currencies and thereby swallow the higher than average rates of inflation that they are generating in their domestic economy. Similarly, surplus countries enjoying a better than average price performance and unwilling to pursue inflationary domestic policies sufficient to remove balance of payments surpluses will be forced to revalue their curencies and will not be able to go on exporting deflation and unemployment. The key point is to what extent adjustment pressures are exerted symmetrically on members of the system. Excessive pressure on surplus countries could cause an inflationary bias, while excessive pressure on deficit countries could lead to a deflationary bias.

A second and closely related consideration has to do with resolution of the liquidity problem. If substantial consolidation of excess foreign exchange reserves can be effected, if there can be an agreement to make currencies convertible into primary international assets with payments imbalances to be settled only with those assets, and if future creation of those primary assets can be kept in check so as to just meet the legitimate needs of members who are endeavoring to tide themselves over seasonal or transitory periods of payments imbalances, then the monetary system will be contributing directly to price stability. In that event, no country in deficit will have sufficient reserves to continue living beyond its means for very long and to go on injecting excessive liquidity into the system. It will not be possible for those countries to transmit excess purchasing power abroad.

Concerning the possible adoption of a link between the issuance of SDRs and the provision of international development assistance, the decision to issue SDRs should be based first and foremost on world liquidity requirements. If it were found that absorptive capacities of LDCs exceeded the amount of new liquidity to be created, then, to prevent inflationary tendencies from arising, developed countries bilaterally or multilaterally through regional organizations would have to decide whether to provide additional assistance and if so in what amount. There is no reason to expect that at any moment in time the requirements for additional liquidity should equal requirements of LDCs for assistance. One might be greater than or less than the other. But careful, controlled expansion of international liquidity is a prerequisite for world price stability.

Taking the possible resolutions of the adjustment mechanism and international liquidity creation together, to the extent the latter is carefully controlled and a system of convertibility is enforced, countries will be obliged to pursue promptly a combination of policies of their own choosing which will reestablish balance of payments equilibrium. Accordingly, there will be relatively less opportunity for world prices to take erratic or sustained jumps upward or downward. To the extent that future creation of international liquidity does not accommodate the needs of the system—that is, if either too little or too much is created—then the working of the adjustment mechanism, however technically sound it might be, will be undermined and world price stability will be jeopardized.

During the final decade of the Bretton Woods system, short-term capital movements grew to very large proportions, magnified the pressure of imported inflation in countries that had demonstrated relative price stability, and thereby undercut anti-inflationary policies. The prospect of such capital movements being repeated in the future would cast a shadow over hopes to establish stable world prices. It has been suggested earlier, however, that a reformed monetary system not directly dependent upon the health of a single key currency to ensure its viability may not be subject to anything like the magnitude of disequilibriating capital flows observed in the recent past. The extent to which this suggestion has validity depends to a considerable extent upon smaller, more frequent, and more orderly exchange rate changes. It also depends upon closer approximation to worldwide payments equilibrium and upon restoration of confidence in leading currencies. But even if capital flows proved an encumbrance to efforts by authorities to pursue domestic price stability, various ways up to and including some form of controls or temporary floating of exchange rates might be employed to reduce their impact. While authorities in most countries have met with only limited success in past attempts to control large capital movements, the nature of the problem in the future, if indeed there is a problem, should be greatly diminished.

Reconciliation of Domestic vs.
External Equilibrium

The objective of internal balance or domestic equilibrium in its broadest sense is to maintain a level of aggregate demand sufficiently high for all products in order to sustain full employment (somehow defined), but not so high as to lead to continuing inflation of prices, wages, and other costs. Similarly, the objective of external balance or external equilibrium is to maintain a level of aggregate demand that prevents a deficit or surplus in the balance of payments from arising. Balance of payments equilibrium implies a situation in which there are no restrictions or controls on trade, transfers, or capital movements, but yet "autonomous" payments and receipts just balance each other.[7] Countries endeavor to achieve external and internal balance by manipulating monetary and fiscal policies.[8] Often, the same sorts of policies are required for achieving and preserving both kinds of balance; on the other hand, there may be occasions when there is a conflict in policy requirements.

Within the context of international monetary reform, there are essentially two avenues which may be pursued in order to help reconcile efforts to bring about external and internal balance. The first concerns improved coordination of domestic economic policies among leading countries. While nations pursue broadly similar economic objectives with respect to growth, full employment, and price stability, there has been growing attention in the IMF and elsewhere in the Organization for Economic Cooperation and Development as to the implications for the international monetary system of aberrant financial policies in leading countries. Although expectations to improve policy coordination must be modest because of the worldwide desire to maintain as much national sovereignty as possible, international consultations might serve to further educate authorities about disequilibria present in different parts of the world and changes in national policies that could ease stress or strains. Especially with reference to instability within international capital markets, which has been aggravated by divergent actions taken by government authorities, more consultations with a view to better coordination of policies could well serve the international monetary order.

The trend toward international economic interdependence of the past two decades, epitomized by the unprecedented growth of international trade and investment, must be weighed against another fact of life, which is that national governments are unwilling to sacrifice domestic economic objectives to any great extent in order to achieve external balance. Both can be upheld by what Paul McCracken calls "even small gains [which] can make a consequential contribution to balance between systemic capability for adjustment and the strains imposed upon it."[9] This leads to the second aspect of monetary reform which can help reconcile external and internal balance.

Resolution of the balance of payments adjustment process in such a manner as would, on the one hand, allow for greater use of exchange rate changes than before and, on the other hand, permit equal access for all countries to this policy measure would go far in resolving dilemma situations between external and internal balance. An exchange rate regime that allowed for more frequent changes in currency exchange rates would provide an additional tool of financial policy that could be used to achieve multiple objectives involved in internal and external balance. In this respect, it would make little difference whether the exchange rate regime made use of wider bands, a crawling peg, occasional floating, or simply provided for more frequent parity changes on the basis of objective indicators or international consultations. The important thing would be that the pattern of exchange rates would be more fluid than was the actual case under the Bretton Woods system, and that variations in the prices of national currencies could be used more widely to help restore external balance.

Some experts believe that resolution of the issue of payments adjustment in symmetrical fashion, so as to ensure that all surplus and all deficit countries would be under equal pressure to adjust their payments imbalances, would also help reconcile conflicts between domestic and external equilibrium. The object here would be to make exchange rate policy available to all countries and to make the use of it, or some sufficient substitute, encumbent on all that were experiencing payments imbalances. Under the old Bretton Woods system, surplus countries were reluctant to lose their surpluses by adopting sufficient measures to inflate their domestic price and wage levels or to revalue their currencies. The United States as the key currency country was unable to adjust its exchange rate because to do so would have eroded world confidence in the reserve currency role of the dollar; moreover, many American experts felt that dollar devaluation would have been offset in large part because other countries would in turn devalue their currencies against gold. Thus, there was no way (except by imposing harsh deflationary policies on the domestic economy) that the United States could reconcile external and internal balance; and other countries that could have resolved the dilemma by adjusting their exchange rates were unwilling to do so.

The success of current monetary reconstruction efforts to build into any agreement provisions that will facilitate, if not enforce, better reconciliation of internal versus external balance would in turn make a positive contribution to the world economic environment in its broadest sense. It would mean that nations would be able to pursue jointly and with less conflict than before such domestic objectives as rapid growth and high employment levels at relatively stable prices. And because that scenario could occur, the climate for world trade and investment would be enhanced and threats of world price inflation would be moderated.

Effects of Monetary Reform on Key Currencies

In turning one's attention to the possible impacts of reform on key currencies, it may be helpful to pause briefly and to recall John Williams's key currency approach to monetary reform at the time of Bretton Woods. Currencies of major economic powers needed to be stabilized and to be in the right relationship to one another in order for the international monetary system to function smoothly. If that could be achieved, other lesser currencies would adopt stable relationships with the key currencies; if it could not, then no international agency could reestablish economic order.

With the complex issues and problems that have arisen in the international economic community in the more than quarter century since the Bretton Woods Agreement, Professor Williams's proposals may appear too simplistic to have relevance any longer. However, this is not true at all. The present efforts to reconstruct the international monetary system may very easily and quite appropriately be regarded as efforts to reestablish stable relationships between the key currencies—including the dollar, two or three leading European currencies, and the Japanese yen. To the extent that this succeeds, monetary reform will be a success and other aspects of reform may be looked upon as frosting on the cake. It is precisely the great perception of Professor Williams in revealing to us the critical importance of key currencies, and the nature of their relationship to each other, that we need to be mindful of at the current juncture.

The way the Bretton Woods system evolved, the competitive positions of key currency countries were adversely affected because of defects in the adjustment process and the absence of any means to systematically create new liquidity; accordingly, it became impossible for key currencies to establish stable, tenable relationships with each other, and hence for other currencies to maintain proper relationships with the key currencies. C. Fred Bergsten thought the United States in particular suffered, first because payments pressures prompted or forced currency devaluations, but seldom promoted or forced revaluations; second, because revaluations tended to be smaller and devaluations larger than necessary; and third, because any single devaluation brought pressure to bear on other countries to devalue, because of concern over loss of competitive position, and because devaluation was more feasible politically if carried out in response to similar action by another country.[10]

The bias toward devaluation of other currencies against key currencies, and the willingness of other countries to put up with chronic deficits sustained by key currency countries, was aided and abetted by the absence of any mechanism to create additions to world liquidity in the face of steadily growing need. Hence, deficits of the key currency countries (but especially the dollar), financed by increasing short-term liabilities to foreigners, served the purpose. The pillar of the Bretton Woods system, convertibility of currencies into gold, was allowed to atrophy—at first because key currencies (again, primarily the dollar) were deemed more desirable than gold in a number of respects, and later on because convertibility of key currency liabilities into gold became a virtual impossibility at existing exchange rates and the official gold price.

International monetary reconstruction offers an excellent opportunity to lighten excessive burdens placed upon key currency countries in the past and to provide a more hospitable economic environment in which it will be possible for stable relationships between currencies to be maintained over time. First consider the issue of liquidity creation. Already in the twilight of the Bretton Woods system a mechanism for creating a new form of international liquidity was established: a paper asset called special drawing rights. If that mechanism is made a part of a new world monetary system and if there is agreement that SDRs will serve as the primary reserve asset of all countries, then the burden on key currency countries to sustain payments deficits so that more of their national currency liabilities can function as international liquidity will be relieved. If creation of SDRs is intended to meet 100 percent of all future growth in liquidity requirements, then key currency countries would at once find themselves in a position similar to other countries in that their payments deficits would have to be financed by SDRs or some other acceptable international asset and not in part or wholly by printing national currencies and running up liabilities to foreigners.

A more symmetrical balance of payments adjustment process, and one that at the same time is more responsive to emerging imbalances than the process evolved under the Bretton Woods system, would go far in helping to relieve key currency countries from their previous deficit bias and other surplus countries from their bias toward surpluses. In short, a reformed adjustment process could serve directly the interests of those who seek to preserve orderly exchange rates and balance of payments equilibrium.

With key currencies freed from the previous burden of having to run payments deficits in order to provide the world with additional liquidity, there would be no rationale for not seeking and enforcing an adjustment process that required all members of the system to meet certain standards in the conduct of their balance of payments and to accept exchange rate adjustment if other policy measures proved insufficient to keep trade and payments within those limits. However enforcement were meted out—either by reliance on some set of objective indicators or by emphasing moral suasion based upon regular international consultations—would not matter so much as the willingness of members to be bound by an adjustment process that did not discriminate between a country's overall weight in the international economic community or its status as a surplus or deficit country. With the great bulk of international reserves held in the form of SDRs or some other international asset rather than national currencies, there should be no resistance, as witnessed in the past, by countries holding substantial sums of key currencies to accept adequate corrective measures to eliminate a payments imbalance. In this respect, depoliticizing the adjustment process as much as possible would be especially helpful. But it is an increasingly recognized fact that waste and misallocation of resources occur just as much for a surplus country as for a deficit country; hence, acquiescence to a symmetrical adjustment process should not prove to be so difficult an achievement of reform. Such a process, however, would liberalize key currency countries and would permit them to compete on the same footing with other countries and not as contestants handicapped by chronically overvalued currencies, as has been the case in the past.

Resolution of the issue "How flexible are exchange rates generally to be under a reformed monetary system?" will have an impact on key currency countries in at least two ways. First of all, the greater the reliance on exchange rate change (hence flexibility) as opposed to alternative policy tools to achieve payments adjustment, the smaller will be the official reserve requirements of any given country. On the presumption that key currency countries (especially the United States) hold relatively small amounts of reserves compared to other countries, the transitional problems of their acquiring sufficient international reserve assets, and then reaching a point where conformity to the requirements of a new monetary order would be practicable, would be substantially less if there were greater reliance on adjustable exchange rates. Greater fixity of exchange rates would necessitate larger average reserve holdings in order to tide countries over during periods of seasonal or other short-term payments imbalances, or during transition periods while other corrective policies were being implemented. In that case, the problem would be one of how to provide key currencies with such reserve levels so that they could abide by the new rules of the game.

The second way in which the issue of exchange rate flexibility touches key currency countries has to do with their particular economic structure. A country like the United States with a very small external sector relative to its domestic sector would prefer greater reliance on exchange rate adjustment to achieve balance of payments equilibrium, since that route would require the least painful compromise of other economic policies presumably designed to best achieve domestic economic objectives.

Other key currency countries, such as Britain or Germany, where the external sectors are of substantially greater relative importance, would prefer greater fixity of exchange rates. For them, frequent resort to exchange rate changes could have a more significant, disturbing, uneven impact on the domestic economy, especially if certain industries were heavily export-oriented and others were not, as is often the case. Accordingly, they should prefer to use a combination of monetary and fiscal policies to effect the necessary adjustment of real and nominal aggregate demand and thereby eliminate the existing payments inbalance, since that approach would generally be less painful and more equitable.

Resolution of the interrelated issues of consolidation and convertibility will be important not only for the key currency countries but for holders of reserve currencies as well. Consolidation of existing balances must precede any prohibition or additional holdings of national currencies as reserves, and hence must precede any switchcover to primary reliance on an international reserve currency such as SDRs. In effect, consolidation is a key precondition for a new monetary system to be introduced and for all members to begin operations on an equal, symmetrical basis. Without consolidation, key currency countries would not be able to establish parity exchange rates, for fear that reserves consisting of their national currencies already in the system might be presented for conversion into primary international assets that they do not possess in sufficient quantity; alternatively, setting initial exchange rates for key currency countries which are clearly undervalued and allowing their resulting payments surpluses to be financed by decumulating key currency liabilities to foreigners (i.e., by depleting official foreign holdings of their national exchange) would be a whimsical replay in reverse of recent history.

Proposals for consolidating the dollar overhang (as it is called) range from compulsory conversion of all dollar balances into a special issue of SDRs, to partial or voluntary fundings into medium-term debt which would eventually be amortized by the United States.[11] How consolidation takes place will decide first of all whether the United States is responsible for amortization and, if so, on what terms and conditions. (This will affect the future US balance of payments and future US reserves and the course of the dollar exchange rate.) Second, resolution of consolidation could affect the level of international reserves. To the extent that the present level is regarded as excessive (a very difficult assessment to make), its reduction could alleviate an inflationary bias in the world economy.[12] On the other hand, too much reduction of international reserves through consolidation could impose a deflationary bias on the world economy. Third, the means by which consolidation takes place will decide how rapidly and how completely the dollar overhang will be dealt with. Herein lies part of the answer to the questions of how soon and with what degree of confidence the United States can return to convertibility.

The other part of the answer will be determined by the speed with which the United States is able to rebuild its reserves to a level where convertibility is regarded as a safe risk. This process of rebuilding could take place by a private demand for dollars following some compulsory consolidation of official dollar reserves; it could result in more traditional fashion from US payments surpluses; or there could be a special once-and-for-all increase in US reserves as part of a larger resolution of the consolidation and convertibility issues. To the extent that US reserves can be reconstituted sooner rather than later, and dollar convertibility restored, the prognosis of longevity for a new monetary system would be greatly enhanced. Putting the US balance of payments in order and restoring convertibility are part and parcel of viable monetary reform for the world. As Peter Kenen warns us, if the US reserves are not reconstituted, then the United States could be tempted to tamper with the rules for changing exchange rates in order to protect itself and gradually rebuild its inadequate reserves.[13] If the United States were able to do this, the new system would not be symmetrical, and the ground work would have been laid for future recrimination and possible retaliation by other nations. If the United States proved unsuccessful in its venture, then it would have to break the rules of the game as occurred once before in August 1971, or it would have to resort to controls and domestic policies offensive to US trading partners.

The future role of key currency countries in a reformed monetary system is likely to differ substantially from the critical role assumed by them in preceding years. If some or all of the high goals of reform are realized, key currency countries would have rights and obligations more similar to those of other members. Their currencies might still be used frequently for transactions purposes and perhaps also for purposes of official intervention; but because their currencies might no longer be held in large amounts as official reserves, they would not be obliged to play passive roles as far as balance of payments adjustment was concerned. Finally, key currency countries, because of their relatively large economic strength, will continue to have a significant impact on the world economic environment; accordingly, their pursuit of responsible economic policies will positively affect the climate of operation for all other nations.

Effects on the Eurocurrency Market

The Eurocurrency market is a highly competitive deposit and loan market for dollars and other reserve currencies held in countries other than the one that the currency (in which deposits are denominated) originated in. The Eurocurrency market, roughly three-quarters of which is composed of US dollars, has grown rapidly in recent years, and a wealth of literature has been published in the form of explanation and analysis of its business and its impact on economic policy.[14]

Of interest and relevance for present purposes is the fact that the Eurocurrency market, which possesses some of the essential characteristics of an international money market, has been the vehicle for short-term capital movements that on a number of past occasions have undermined national monetary policy.[15] In fact, the pursuit of independent monetary policy for the purpose of stabilizing domestic economic activity has been next to impossible for some of the leading European countries, and in recent years has even caused sizable headaches for the US Federal Reserve. Italy and Germany have been in the forefront of those countries attempting to devise measures to deal with such problems.[16] Their efforts have met with some success in moderating capital flows that might have otherwise occurred; but given the ingenuity of today's speculators and the massive amounts of liquidity which have been mobilized on very short notice, government efforts have fallen short of their mark, which goes a long way in accounting for the present state of floating currencies since the spring of 1973.

In light of recent experience and the shortcomings of efforts by authorities to keep short-term capital movements in the Eurocurrency market from totally frustrating domestic monetary policy and successfully challenging the mechanism of fixed exchange rate parities of the Bretton Woods system, how might international monetary reform affect the Eurocurrency market? First of all, to the extent that a new adjustment mechanism includes provision of wider bands, smaller but more frequent changes in parities, and greater symmetry of adjustment itself, the integration of national money markets through the Eurocurrency market will be rendered somewhat less perfect than before. Accordingly, forward exchange rate discounts and premia will be greater, and this in turn will leave more scope for divergence of domestic interest rates from those in foreign centers. In effect, therefore, resolution of the issue of balance of payments adjustment along the lines just suggested should give a degree of added independence to domestic monetary policy. Greater fixity of exchange rates and reliance on other means of payments adjustment would lead in the opposite direction.

More fundamentally, the potential for conflict will exist as long as the international money market and international banking continue to grow in the absence of international institutions and mechanisms to regulate and control them. Any possible contribution in these areas emanating from monetary reform negotiations is very difficult to anticipate or foresee at present. As Otmar Emminger stated in a paper referred to earlier, "We know now all the questions involved [in the field of disequilibrating capital flows] ... [but] no panacea has as yet been found dealing with the crucial problem in a future monetary system."[17] For now, the philosophical, institutional, and administrative differences between even the leading countries are too great. The best hope for the medium term is that monetary reform itself will establish confidence in the world economic environment and that massive capital movements of the past will not arise.

Aside from systematic internationalization of banking regulations, there is one area of monetary reform that could help reduce volatility of the Eurocurrency market and its contribution to disequilibrating capital movements. The Eurocurrency market is comprised not only of private individuals and commercial banks that deposit the monetary base for the development of credit, but it is also comprised of many central banks that do the same. In fact, recent actions of some central banks to diversify some of their reserves held in dollars and placed in the Eurodollar market into other national currencies have contributed in a major way to volatility of the market. Any resolution of this problem to establish a code of conduct for central bank participation in the Eurocurrency market would add directly to greater stability.

If no direct resolution were possible, the potential problem might still be alleviated by mandatory consolidation of dollar reserves or all national currency reserves, or by some voluntary scheme of consolidation that would prove sufficiently enticing to countries otherwise wishing to retain the right to decide how to order their portfolio of official reserves. For the longer term, and recalling the outlook for large payments surpluses and reserve accumulation by a few of the large oil-producing countries, there will have to be provision for an international investment facility or reserve asset capable of attracting and making orderly, effective use of those financial resources. The alternative of even more massive funds being shifted from one financial center to another depending upon changing interest rates or political considerations is ominous.

10 Relative Status of the Participants

This final chapter examines in broad fashion what countries or power blocs stand to gain or lose from the possible monetary reform arrangements. Of course, what appears to be an advantage to the national interest of a particular country may not be an advantage to other countries or to the monetary order as a whole. We shall consider in turn the oil-producing countries, other developing countries, industrial countries including the European Community, and finally, the United States.

The Oil-Producing Countries

By all forecasts, world demand for crude oil is going to expand at an ever more rapid pace in the years to come. Some of the largest oil deposits lie in the Middle East—particularly Saudi Arabia, Iran, and Iraq. Those countries, all in the rank of less developed countries, stand to earn vast amounts of foreign exchange by simply selling their crude oil to international oil companies, which in turn refine it and market the finished products in various industrial and semi-industrial nations all over the world. Some oil-producing countries will be in the position of earning more foreign exchange than they could possibly need to sustain their economic development; a few will encounter excessive foreign exchange earnings and over time may accumulate extremely large foreign exchange reserves, by any standards, as a result of continued payments surpluses.

The problem to be resolved is: How should those stores of foreign exchange be dealt with so that they will not become a serious destabilizing force in the future? Oil-producing countries have steadfastly maintained that they intend to keep open their options as to where and how their foreign exchange reserves may be invested. This could mean that changes in interest rate differentials, changes in other economic factors or political factors could cause huge sums of those countries' exchange reserves to be moved from one center to another, an event that could be very disruptive to an existing exchange rate structure and indeed to the viability of the international monetary system itself.

Other nations, chiefly the developed countries whose financial centers would be the recipients of oil-producing countries' investment funds, have been increasingly concerned with this potential problem; yet it appears that the oil-producing countries are in the driver's seat, for they are the ones with the vast crude oil resources which industrial countries need so badly. Furthermore, they are not going to give up the oil unless they can get what they believe to be a fair price and then are able to use the proceeds in ways that best serve their national interests. An amicable resolution of the problem which now rests on the doorstep of the developed countries must mean that the payoff for the oil-producing countries must be greater than no resolution and continuation of past practices according to which the foreign exchange proceeds were invested in London, New York, or elsewhere.

Alternative schemes mentioned earlier in this volume included establishment of an investment fund in the IMF in which oil-producing countries would place their excess reserves; another concerned an agreement among central banks whereby all countries—developed and underdeveloped—would agree to abstain from investing in or borrowing from the Eurocurrency market. Aside from the practical matter that the ground work for either of these alternatives does not appear to have been laid, neither of the proposals (and especially the latter) appears to be conceived of or framed in a way to make them irresistible to the oil-producing countries.

Because of rich natural resource endowment, this group of nations is in a position of not being able to lose in the process of monetary reform, and possibly of making a sizable financial gain—if not as part of an original reform agreement, then quite probably as an addendum to it at some early time in the future when their official foreign exchange reserves will begin to climb sharply (if forecasts are at all accurate). This should not be viewed as a small group of countries of little economic or political consequence "holding up" the rich countries of the world for ransom; instead, it is a matter of the former group holding out for the freedom to invest their justly earned foreign exchange in ways they see fit—just as governments of other countries have been allowed to do over the years. And if they are to relinquish part or all of that freedom, then quite understandably they want to be compensated for doing so.

Other Less Developed Countries

Contrary to what has occurred previously (in the negotiations leading up to the Bretton Woods Conference, then in the conference itself, and in the resolution of the 1971 monetary crisis which took place within the Group of Ten), LDCs are adequately represented in the Committee of Twenty, which will decide the shape of a reformed monetary system.

LDCs stand to gain what they thought they had gained—but had not—at Bretton Woods by becoming members of the World Bank; that is to say, if there is adoption of some form of SDR-AID link as a part of a monetary reform agreement, and if that link is superimposed on current levels of bilateral and multilateral economic assistance, they will have won an additional transfer of resources from the rich industrial countries from whom they will ultimately purchase goods and services with SDRs in order to advance their economic development schemes. The link would be a most important gain in two respects. First, it would be a psychological gain for LDCs as a group, for it has been from the outset the single most important issue basically supported by all. Second, depending on the magnitude of the link, it could provide significant economic benefits for countries in chronic short supply of foreign exchange reserves. If the gap between developed and developing nations is to begin narrowing and not go on widening—in short, if more and more LDCs enter the takeoff stage of economic development—a number of complex social, cultural, and economic forces must come in to play; but one that can facilitate and speed the process along is for developed countries to make available to LDCs a larger share of their resources than they have contributed in the past. This transfer need not occur through a link mechanism; however, the link is presented as one means of achieving the desired result, and it may be included as part of a monetary reform agreement.

LDCs might also gain from monetary reform if there were provisions calling for reinforcement of buffer stock schemes and if international commodity agreements and IMF financing schemes were shaded in favor of raw materials producers and LDCs generally. The benefits to LDCs in these instances would be greater assurance of a steady stream of foreign exchange earnings from exports; and, in the event of seasonal or other short-run economic adversity, they would have a more ample source of funds on which to draw to support their exchange rate and important ongoing development projects.

Some of these potential gains from monetary reform would be offset if the large industrial countries agreed to an adjustment mechanism calling for greater exchange rate flexibility and if, at the same time, it was agreed that exchange rates would be permitted to fluctuate within a wider margin, or band, as was the case in the Smithsonian Agreement. If there were a widespread concurrence of opinions that the band should be wider than 2¼ percent either side of parity—say, 3, 4, or even 5 percent—then LDCs might feel forced to choose a key currency to which they would peg their own currencies. This could be economically harmful in that it would promote the formation of monetary blocs; those blocs in turn could easily become inward-looking trading blocs causing costly trade diversion as far as LDCs interests were concerned.

Adoption by the large developed countries of greater exchange rate flexibility, wider bands, or both, presents a twofold problem to LDCs. First, it causes uncertainty as to what foreign exchange earnings are to come about from sale of their agricultural produce and other raw materials. This type of uncertainty is distinct from uncertainty of world prices for those same products that, in the absence of stabilization agreements of buffer stock schemes, are determined by supply and demand on a world level. Second, if wider margins or greater exchange rate flexibility are pursued by major countries, then in all likelihood, policy makers would place greater reliance on instruments of domestic monetary policy. That in turn could mean greater fluctuations in interest rates, and therefore, LDCs ability to borrow or to refinance large external debts would be jeopardized. Realization of either or both of these problems, if severe enough, would be the rationale for LDCs deciding to peg their currencies to one or another key currency.

Depending upon the manner in which the issues of consolidation and convertibility are treated in any monetary accord, LDCs could stand to forfeit benefits stemming from their past financial practices. For example, if all parties of the new monetary reform agreement were obliged to consolidate their foreign exchange reserves (except for some minimum level of working balances for official intervention purposes) into new primary international assets such as SDRs, then LDCs would have to withdraw foreign exchange balances deposited in leading financial centers such as New York and London, and in doing so they would lose their credit lines that depend upon those deposits. Similarly, if there were an agreement whereby national central banks would neither lend to nor borrow from the Eurodollar market, certain LDCs that have made use of those facilities in the past would be precluded from doing so in the future. These possible losses could be minimized, however, if some of the possible gains already mentioned were realized.

The matter of there being some kind of structural reform of the International Monetary Fund, so that LDCs interests could be better served, has been discussed in an earlier chapter. What the LDCs call structural change—such as changes in quotas or weight accorded to countries voting on important issues, or appointment of another Deputy Managing Director of the Fund from a developing country—others refer to as operational change. Whether concessions of these sorts are included in a new monetary reform agreement remains to be seen. But the fact that LDCs are now represented in the formal body conducting the reform negotiations is evidence itself of the increasing political importance they are achieving. If this momentum continues, and there is no reason to believe it will not, then it would seem to be only a matter of time before international institutions are modified to give LDCs the kind of representation and the increased benefits they feel are rightfully theirs. For such changes to take place, LDCs will have to demonstrate a commensurate ability to accept responsibilities and to make their contribution to a more stable economic world order.

The European Economic Community

A major gain for European countries resulting from monetary reform would be relief from exchange rate instability and disequilibrating capital flows and hence an opportunity for them to regain control of domestic monetary management. One country after another, and on occasions several at once, have been recipients of very large amounts of short-term capital inflows and other more disguised currency speculation. Attempts to control those inflows have met with only very limited success.[1] These disruptive forces have been harmful to the EC goal of establishing a monetary and economic union by 1980. Thus, a more stable economic environment will result: if monetary reform is able to recreate an atmosphere of confidence generally; if an agreement can be reached which limits central bank borrowing and lending in the Eurodollar market and prevents further diversification of their foreign exchange reserves into Eurocurrencies; if there is an adjustment mechanism that provides for smooth exchange rate changes in the world without generating financial crises of recent proportions; and if the official reserve role of national currencies can be phased out and in its stead an international liquidity mechanism can be established to create only the amount of international reserve assets needed by the world as a whole to maintain stable exchange rates, convertibility of currencies, and a tight asset settlement of payments imbalances.

Achieving a monetary and economic union will be a technically complex, long-drawn-out process, difficult for EC participants to achieve even under ideal international economic conditions. Yet, if Europe is successful in its efforts, there could be gains for the rest of the world in the sense that Europe would become a more cohesive, politically integrated unit and, therefore, a more effective representative at international meetings. What comes to mind here is the frequent situation in the past of EC members being divided on many international issues and the stalemates that have resulted. An EC speaking with a more unified voice could play a constructive and leading role in promoting a better world order. Second, European integration in the form of a union could lead to reduced international economic instability, and here again the rest of the world would share in the benefits.

But a European union could also create some losses for the rest of the world in the form of further trade diversion, greater competitive strength of the EC vis-à-vis other leading industrial countries in third country markets, and increased bargaining power in international monetary affairs at the expense of others. Accordingly, it is impossible to predict at this current juncture whether European union would be an overall net gain for the world economy.

One of the foremost issues put before architects of monetary reform is to devise a system that strikes the right balance between the desire for greater economic integration of the world on the one hand and the desire to maintain national independence on the other. Europe would like to discipline the United States by eliminating the reserve currency role of the dollar, by making all currencies convertible into primary international assets such as SDRs, and by requiring that balance of payments imbalances be settled only with primary reserves—not national currencies. Furthermore, for their having helped to finance past US payments deficits in the name of maintaining monetary order by purchasing surplus dollars on foreign exchanges, Europe would like to extract its "pound of flesh" from the United States by striking an accord to consolidate the dollar overhang in a manner that would require the United States to continue to bear some kind of responsibility until consolidated dollars had been amortized. (This refers to Europe's desire to see the US effect a balance of payments surplus for some period of time—but a surplus that, through more effective use of capital controls, does not entail such a large surplus balance of trade as the United States intends.)

But overzealous efforts to force discipline on others in the name of economic integration, if successful, could lead to a situation in which countries were either unable or unwilling to abide by the rules of the system, in which case the system would break down again as it did in August 1971. Thus, if US official reserves were not adequately reconstituted, either as a result of return capital flows following a monetary accord or as a result of a special issue of SDRs to the United States to achieve the objective of replenishment, the United States could not restore dollar convertibility without a great deal more exchange rate flexibility or resort to more floating than Europe would like to allow. Thus, also, it has been a fact of life for US political leaders that they would not accept external pressure to restrain the domestic economy when unemployment was the key domestic problem, nor would they accept external pressure to expand the domestic economy when inflation is already a problem. In such dilemma situations, the United States and probably a good many other countries as well, including some European nations, would insist on their right to place national independence ahead of international unity by resorting to an exchange rate adjustment, currency float, or to trade or capital controls.

The lesson is that too much integration and not enough independence is likely to foredoom any reformed monetary system; the likely direction of countries in that event might be toward formation of regional units consisting of currency blocs possibly characterized by joint defensive efforts to raise barriers to economic intercourse against a hostile world. On the other hand, too easy capitulation to narrow vested interests in the name of national independence might disrupt the record compiled over the last quarter century of rapid sustained growth in trade and international capital movements and might lead possibly to a decline in the material welfare of the world economy.

Depending on the precise resolution of issues surrounding the balance of payments adjustment process (and settlement of the question of whether or not nations should impose controls on short-term capital flows) some EC countries might stand to lose their chronic trade surpluses of recent years, surpluses that have provided solid stimulation to domestic industries. With a symmetrical adjustment process, in which objective indicators played an important role and resort to exchange rate changes were not submerged too deeply, the danger would be that a sharp deflationary effect causing pockets of unemployment and idle resources might arise in reaction to quick disappearance of those European countries' trade surpluses. If there is to be a transition away from large trade surpluses it should be allowed to take place gradually, say over a period of two years, so as to ease the internal adjustment process both as far as those affected European producers may be concerned and, if it is, the case that European imports showed sharply rising tendencies, as far as foreign producers may be affected.

Such a possibility of swift and rather substantial inflationary or deflationary impacts befalling domestic sectors of countries with relatively large trade or external sectors reveals why it is in their interest to rely more on international consultative machinery rather than objective indicators which, even if programmed for gradual payments adjustment, by their nature categorize each situation as black and white. It would be to the advantage of such countries to have some kind of discretionary authority to play a role in any adjustment process so that excessive strain on a country's domestic sector as dictated by presumptive indicators of change might be avoided or phased in gradually. All of this goes to say that countries with relatively substantial external sectors will be better off if the adjustment process is one that gives them time to pursue appropriate monetary and fiscal policies and therefore does not force them to resort to exchange rate changes at an early stage, since doing so would confront the national authorities with additional problems of differential changes in income distribution and compounded political burdens.

Out of current efforts to reform the world's monetary system, nations comprising the European Community could emerge as a formally recognized economic power, equal to the United States, with neither power benefiting from rights nor burdened by obligations the other does not also possess. This would be a boon not only to Europe's own ego and prestige in the world, but also to other nations participating in the world economy; for if Europe were able to play its new role responsibly and effectively, the world would have moved ahead in its collective ability to resolve emerging problems in the future.

Other Developed Countries

Although developed countries outside of the European Community have considerably less impact on reform negotiations than either the EC or the United States, they will be affected directly by the resolutions on some or all of the key issues. Most developed countries such as Austria, the Scandinavian countries, Switzerland, Japan, and Canada have economic interests closely identified with other large industrial countries. They would all stand to gain from an adjustment mechanism that provided for greater exchange rate stability rather than greater flexibility. Their situation is similar to that of less developed countries; for if leading industrial powers pursue exchange rate stability, then other countries need not peg their currencies to any one key currency in particular, nor need they concentrate their commercial interests on that particular country, possibly foregoing marginal if not substantial market opportunities elsewhere. Instead, with key currencies generally stable, other developed countries would be in a better position to conduct their international trade and commerce to maximum advantage—both for themselves and for others.

Another reason why other developed countries would prefer exchange rate stability is that their trade and payments contracts usually call for payment in some foreign currency such as the US dollar. This trend is likely to continue for some time to come, regardless what new role may be assumed by SDRs or what kind of consolidation agreement may be reached. The dollar and a few other key currencies will continue to dominate settlement of international transactions in the future; therefore, exchange rate stability creates an atmosphere of greater certainty in which international traders and financiers can conduct business. Exchange rate flexibility—especially for leading currencies used frequently in international transactions—would necessitate more frequent covering of exchange risks through forward exchange market transactions. Aside from the added costs involved, forward exchange markets tend to be thin and underdeveloped outside of leading financial centers; indeed, it would take time to train dealers and to create viable forward markets whose operations were routinely understood by businessmen as well as financial experts and which operated at moderate expense. Finally, when supply of forward foreign exchange were not counterbalanced by a corresponding demand, government intervention would be required to restore equilibrium and to relieve the burden of a large foreign exchange risk from traders who might otherwise be forced to suspend their operations.

Australia is an example of a developed country that, by virtue of being endowed with rich natural resources, exports large quantities of various raw materials to other developed countries and therefore favors relatively fixed exchange rates for reasons similar to LDCs. If the large industrial countries with whom she trades embraced greater exchange rate flexibility, Australia would be forced to tie its rate of exchange to one of them. Today it would be tied presumably to the dollar; in five or ten years, however, it might be the Japanese yen, for Australia is conducting an ever increasing share of its trade with that country. Australia's interests would be hurt, however, were she forced to choose between one or the other currency.

Canada's case is somewhat different. With two-thirds of her total trade being conducted with the United States, and given the critical role US financial markets play in the well-being of the Canadian economy, there is no doubt as to where her interests lie. And if the US dollar and other currencies were more flexible vis-à-vis each other, then it is logical that the Canadian dollar would be tied de facto if not de jure to the US dollar. While such a development would cause less of a loss for Canada than it might for a number of other developed and semideveloped nations, there would be a clearly adverse political reaction to such an overt admission of dependence on the United States.

One of the biggest conceivable gains for Canada stemming from a new monetary accord would be for floating exchange rates to be recognized as a legal, dignified policy. This would allow Canada to continue its past practice of keeping its currency very close to a given rate of exchange to the dollar over time by pursuing a monetary policy that would be in close contact with US monetary policy. In years gone by, this practice gave the illusion of independence, which was politically beneficial, while it established a pattern of (for all intents and purposes) a fixed US-Canadian dollar exchange rate, which enhanced trade and was consistent with the high degree of integration between the two economies. Floating currencies in particular situations or for less important currencies could be possible without its becoming commonplace, and this is what Canadians would hope for.

Another practice that Canada would like very much to carry over from the past (at least for its own operations) is free movement of capital across national boundaries. If monetary reform embraced a code restricting such movements, Canada's interests could be impaired, and seriously so if exceptions were not granted in view of her great reliance on the United States as a source of capital.

A final point to note about Canada's interests in the outcome of monetary reform is that of all the industrial countries, Canada would be one of those least hurt should the one-world solution fail to materialize and the monetary order were to give way to regional blocs. In that event, Canada would certainly be expected to join forces with the United States; but since a huge proportion of her external transactions already take place with that country, the welfare loss stemming from trade diversion and cutbacks in other international transactions would be minimized.

Japan's case is substantially different from that of Canada. Japan is truly a country with global interests; roughly 30 percent of her trade is with the United States; another 30 percent takes place with South and East Asian countries; about 15 percent is with Western Europe; and the balance is with South America, Africa, and the Middle East. Anything other than a one-world solution to monetary reconstruction would be costly for Japan. Similarly, Japan's interests in the upcoming trade negotiations, which were opened formally in Tokyo in September 1973, are very great. Japan's economic well-being rests on having access to the world's markets both to gain needed raw materials, in respect of which her own endowment is very meager, and also as an outlet for her increasingly sophisticated product lines to pay for those imports.

The idea, therefore, of regional blocs—one of which would surely be a yen bloc—does not arouse positive enthusiasm in Japan. There is widespread opposition to the yen being used as a reserve currency, since it would jeopardize the authorities' grip on domestic monetary policy and would pose other problems similar to those that have confronted British and American authorities in the past when their currencies were used as reserve currencies. Within private financial circles, however, and increasingly so within the government, there is support for Tokyo's becoming a key financial center not only for the Pacific and Far East countries but even for countries further afield. This development, however, might well take several more years to come to fruition. In all these respects, an international currency, such as SDRs, which would be the numeraire of the system and primary reserve asset for all countries, makes sense for Japan.

A quality Japanese traders and financiers have displayed time and again over the course of the past three years has been "adaptability." They have continued to prosper internationally despite a great amount of monetary uncertainty and a substantial appreciation of their currency vis-à-vis almost every other currency except the German mark. That quality plus other virtues that have helped the Japanese achieve an unprecedented record of growth and economic expansion over the last quarter century should help Japan to minimize any aspects of monetary reform resolutions that might run contrary to her immediate interests, and to maximize those opportunities that might be offered.

On more specific matters, Japan would gain from a payments adjustment mechanism that emphasized exchange rate stability. Although all new contracts for shipbuilding have recently become yen-denominated, most other trade contracts and many other transactions continue to be denominated in foreign currency (mainly US dollars). While these practices persist, Japanese traders and bankers will continue to have a strong preference for fixed exchange rates which will minimize foreign exchange risks. Japan would also prefer greater fixity of exchange rates because her ability to impose exchange and capital controls and to make them relatively effective ranks at the top of all other developed countries. Controlling disequilibrating capital flows by nonmarket methods (that is, by imposing measures to stem inflows or outflows rather than resorting to floating exchange rates) is a game she has played with dexterity in the past and is prepared to play again in the future.

A substantial SDR-AID link would also redound to Japan's benefit. In recent years, Japan has shown increasing interest in a number of developing countries in Africa and Latin America, and her interest has been reciprocated. Providing LDCs with a greater financing capability would therefore create additional trade for Japan with those countries. It is important from Japan's standpoint, however, that an SDR-AID link be constructed carefully and administered responsibly; for if confidence in SDRs were jeopardized by too large a link, then there might be a fallback to an earlier situation where national currencies served as official foreign exchange reserves, or even a resort to currency blocs, either one of which would be contrary to Japan's interests.

The United States

The United States would gain substantially from a reformed international monetary system that in the first place would permit all members, including itself, to alter exchange rates when confronted with a balance of payments disequilibrium. Second, the United States would gain, along with other countries, from a system that would create by an independent mechanism, not reliant upon payments deficits of any key currency country, a truly international form of liquidity as it was needed. In past years, the United States was saddled with an overvalued currency which fostered a deteriorating trade balance and cost jobs domestically for those in affected industries; to the extent that the overvalued dollar caused a deflationary bias not offset by domestic monetary and fiscal policies, there resulted underutilization of labor and other resources. Moreover, the overvalued dollar was a major factor causing erosion of the wide domestic base of support for a liberal trade policy and, in part at least, undermining support for continuing US economic assistance to less developed countries. The dollar remained in its overvalued state because of the special reserve currency status accorded it, because there was no effective alternative for meeting additional world liquidity needs, and because other countries with payments surpluses were unwilling to correct the existing disequilibrium.

It is in the US interest, for reasons based both on domestic and foreign policy grounds, that international monetary reform provide a balance of payments adjustment process that permits (indeed requires) members to undertake effective policy measures to remove balance of payments disequilibrium. Specifically for the United States, this implies active resort to exchange rate adjustment rather than trade controls (which are inefficient and lead to retaliation by others), or capital controls (which US authorities are ill-equipped to enforce and are opposed to on philosophical grounds), or changes in domestic financial policies beyond those required for internal reasons. To be effective, the United States believes such an adjustment process must be based on a set of guidelines indicating which countries should adjust and by how much, and supported by international sanctions against those members who failed to comply.

In order for the United States to be subject to that kind of adjustment process, the reserve role of the dollar would have to terminate; in its stead would be an international currency such as SDRs, appropriately defined so that its value would not hinge on the well-being of any one country's or bloc of countries' balance of payments. Such an international currency would be capable, therefore, of commanding as much if not even greater confidence than any national reserve currency did before.

A monetary system possessing those general characteristics, and at the same time symmetrical in its apportionment of responsibilities and obligations to members, would, according to US experts, permit the United States greater freedom to concentrate various tools of financial policy on attaining domestic economic objectives. Second, such a system would expose to the public view the full economic costs of those domestic policies on the external payments position of the United States. Third, such a system would provide the administration, the

Congress, and the American public with a more accurate picture as to what alternative foreign policy courses would cost; accordingly, there would be a more rational basis for making decisions on domestic spending versus expenditures abroad. Whatever the resolutions of major monetary reform issues may be, there is extremely little likelihood that US ability to carry out foreign policy objectives will be compromised. The gain, however, would be to reveal to US policymakers and to friendly governments abroad what the true price tags were, which should make for improved political and military decisions on the part of the United States and all other countries belonging to the monetary system.

United States commercial and financial interests stand to be well served by a monetary reform agreement that encourages freer trade and open capital markets, that carefully defines the "particular situations" in which trade, exchange, or capital controls may be used, and that provides the necessary international surveillance to ensure that such techniques of market intervention are not abused. One of the long-standing complaints of US traders has been that their access to foreign markets has been hampered by such things as an overvalued dollar, nontariff barriers which restrict imports, and near-concessional financing arrangements offered by their competitors. While a monetary accord cannot span all these vital areas, it can set the tone for a monetary order which—perhaps through other related international institutions—would establish ground rules and would work to achieve a standard code of behavior in order to reduce the chances for any country or bloc of countries gaining an unfair competitive advantage.

As for US financial interests, the importance of New York as a key financial center could be enhanced by a reformed monetary system in which capital controls were the exception rather than the rule and the dollar was maintained at or near equilibrium over time as a result of exchange rate adjustment. According to many financial experts, a good deal of business that has gone to the Eurobond market since 1963 when the interest equalization tax was first imposed could be expected to switch back to New York. Thus, while the role of the United States as an exporter of long-term capital would be strengthened, there would probably be a substantial inflow of short-term capital, net, and a steadily increasing inflow of direct and portfolio investments from abroad. The prospects for such inflows (the latter two having become increasingly evident in the recent period) might be enhanced all the more in consequence of US financial policies being freed to concentrate on achieving domestic economic objectives of steady growth, stable prices and low unemployment. A short-term capital inflow is something that most financial centers would expect under relatively stable monetary conditions, simply as a result of their serving a financial intermediation role for foreigners.

A critical question that must be faced in monetary reform negotiations is, What trade-off should there be between exchange rate changes and official exchange market intervention to maintain stable exchange rates? The question should be posed on a global level for all nations collectively; and should be posed for individual nations. While there is no one right answer, resolution of the matter will have an impact on each and every country. As far as the present US interests are concerned, more exchange rate flexibility is to be preferred. On the other hand, intervention to support exchange rates could achieve substantial redistribution of international reserves as capital flows take place. And if there are large flows of short-term funds back to the United States, as many expect to occur once a monetary reform agreement has been reached, and if it had been agreed that the US government could intervene in the exchange market to support a given exchange rate rather than allow the dollar to appreciate, then US reserves could be easily and perhaps quickly replenished to an amount thought to provide reasonable safety.

The importance of replenishing US reserves so as to allow this country to participate in a system of stable but convertible currencies (that is, convertible into international reserve assets) has been discussed before. Thus, if a way were found to reconstitute US reserves, then any possible loss to the United States from maintaining greater exchange rate stability would be reduced. And at the same time, with greater probability that the United States could adhere to a new international monetary system, the chances of that system not only surviving but enduring for some time to come would be enhanced.

It is important that resolutions be reached deliberately and carefully on these issues: How much exchange rate flexibility versus how much stability? Which countries should intervene in exchange markets? When? And by how much? Decisions on these matters are of great importance to the United States and to all members of the monetary system. Provided the necessary amendments are made concerning exchange rate adjustment, so that the United States (and others) can adjust the value of its currency in line with the needs of its underlying balance of payments position, then an obligation of convertibility need not be regarded as a loss or a burden on the United States. Similarly, if the question of providing a link between SDRs and providing additional development assistance to less developed countries were resolved in a way that safeguarded world confidence in SDRs as the primary reserve asset, then the United States need not be regarded as having lost in any sense, since its main concern would have been laid to rest.

Resolution of the key issues confronting international monetary architects, whether or not they accord closely with US proposals, can be construed as an overall gain for this country as long as the resulting system is one whose rules the United States adheres to faithfully over time. On August 15, 1971, the United States concluded that the evolved Bretton Woods system was too costly to warrant its further participation; therefore, any new system agreeable to the United States must be concluded as one that better serves US interests than the system did which existed prior to August 15, 1971, or than have the loose arrangements that have existed in the months since that date.[2] The same comment cannot necessarily be made for any other country or bloc.

Summary

In international negotiations such as those concerning international monetary reconstruction, economics and politics are inextricably mixed. Compromise solutions pleasing few but acceptable to many are likely to result. The final assessment concerning which countries or blocs gain or lose and by how much is up to the reader to make, once resolutions of major problems and issues identified in this volume have been negotiated and announced publicly. It is to be hoped that each country or bloc gains something of value and that whatever losses must be sustained can be minimized. For only if such a statement can be made about an ultimate monetary accord is it likely to prove durable.

Addendum: The 1973 Annual Fund-Bank Meeting

During September 24-28, 1973, the Annual IMF-IBRD meeting was convened in Nairobi, Kenya. For months it had been the anticipation and hope of many experts that a detailed outline of a reformed international monetary system could be drawn up and agreed upon by the Committee of Twenty, and then presented at the 1973 Annual Meeting. That would have made it feasible for the C-20 to iron out differences in remaining details and to have the necessary legal language drawn up amending the IMF Articles of Agreement. Those formal amendments, it was presumed, could have been put to a vote *ad referendum* at the 1974 Annual Meetings, with ratification by national legislatures and parliaments to take place over the course of the ensuing months. Parts of the reformed monetary system could have gone into effect in late 1974 or early 1975, and the entire system could have been operative when the Annual Meetings took place in September 1975.

But during the few weeks prior to the Nairobi Conference it was becoming clear that the first act of such a scenario was not going to materialize. The persisting differences in views between participants at a meeting of the deputies of the C-20 in Paris in early September, and then again at a meeting of the ministers in Washington soon thereafter, made it plain that a detailed outline of a new system could not be prepared in time.

Instead, it was decided that C. Jeremy Morse, Chairman of the Deputies of the Committee of Twenty, would prepare a "First Outline of Reform." That outline represented Morse's view of the current state of negotiations but did not represent a commitment on the part of the C-20 ministers to the language of the outline. On September 24, the "Outline" was presented formally to the Governors of the Fund and Bank. It was much more of a status report than it was a blueprint or an outline for reform. It recorded both agreement and disagreement on various issues; it recorded suggestions not generally accepted; and it pointed out where there was need for further detailed study.

The introductory section of the "Outline" describes the essential characteristics of a new international monetary system, characteristics endorsed with near unanimity. That portion read:

It is generally agreed that there is need for a reformed world monetary order, based on cooperation and consultation within the framework of a strengthened International Monetary Fund, that will encourage the growth of world trade and employment, promote economic development, and help to avoid both inflation and deflation. The main features of the international monetary reform should include:

(a) an effective and symmetrical adjustment process, including better functioning of the exchange rate mechanism, with the exchange rate regime based on stable but adjustable par values and floating rates recognized as providing a useful technique in particular situations;

(b) cooperation in dealing with disequilibrating capital flows;

(c) the introduction of an appropriate degree and form of convertibility for the settlement of imbalances, with symmetrical obligations on all countries;

(d) better international management of global liquidity, with the SDR becoming the principal reserve asset and the role of gold and of reserve currencies being reduced;

(e) consistency between arrangements for adjustment, convertibility, and global liquidity;

(f) the promotion of the flow of real resources to developing countries.

It is recognized that the attainment of the purposes of the reform depends also upon arrangements for international trade, capital, investment, and development assistance including the access of developing countries to markets in developed countries; and it is agreed that the principles which govern the international monetary reform and arrangements in these related areas must be consistent.[a]

Broad agreement among C-20 participants ceases after generalities have been uttered. In many instances there is discord over the operational provisions of the reformed system. Views of major participants diverge on such issues as the scope for floating exchange rates, the precise valuation of SDRs, the future role of the International Monetary Fund, the SDR-AID link.

Major attention in these diverging views continues to be focused on the adjustment process and on convertibility. The lines remain drawn much as has been described in the foregoing text. The United States continues to endorse a system that relies heavily on presumptive indicators, although it concedes there could be some form of assessment by Fund members which could presumably override the indicators in some cases. Europeans and others continue to argue for major reliance on an IMF assessment procedure to determine when and where adjustment is needed, and they remain skeptical about any majorsuse of presumptive indicators. As for the other major issue, convertibility, the United States favors a system in which countries have the *right* to present as foreign currency balances for conversion into primary reserves, with issuing countries bearing the obligation to convert such balances presented to them. On the other hand, Europeans and others continue to favor a *mandatory*, full asset settlement system for all countries, wherein no financing of deficits would be permitted by increasing liabilities of national currency balances.

The next step in the movement to reform is for technical groups of the deputies of the C-20 to meet in an effort to gain a more thorough understanding of the complex and difficult issues of monetary reform that remain unresolved. It is hoped that their efforts will pave the way for settlement of operational provisions, for agreement of principles, and ultimately for final agreement of the

[a]A copy of the "First Outline of Reform" in its entirety may be obtained from the International Monetary Fund, Washington, D.C.

whole range of issues of reform. Four technical groups will now go to work: one on future arrangements for adjustment and convertibility, including the details of an assessment procedure and the structure of presumptive indicators; another on intervention and asset settlement, including a possible multicurrency intervention system; a third on global liquidity, or primary reserve assets, and consolidation and management of currency reserves; and a fourth on the transfer of real resources, i.e., the proposed SDR-AID link, and other proposed credit facilities that would favor less developed countries.

As for the timing of the movement to reform, ministers of the Committee of Twenty have committed themselves to a date, July 31, 1974, by which time they intend to have resolved all issues. If that timetable holds, a blueprint of monetary reform, if not the actual proposed system with all its legal trappings, could be presented to the 1974 Annual Fund-Bank Meeting in Washington, D.C. Thus, it appears at this juncture that realization of monetary reform has been pushed back by perhaps one year.

Notes

Chapter 1
The Current Juncture

1. For a brief account of what did occur at the Nairobi meetings held during September 24-28, 1973, see the Addendum.

2. IMF, *Annual Report*, 1973 (Washington, D.C.).

Chapter 2
The Spirit of Bretton Woods

1. For further definition and explanation of the gold standard and variations thereof, see Lester V. Chandler, *The Economics of Money and Banking*, 3rd ed., (New York: Harper and Bros., 1959), chapter 19.

2. Leland Yeager, *International Monetary Relations* (New York: Harper and Row, 1966), p. 255.

3. The actual end of British free trade is placed at 1931. (Ibid., p. 274.)

4. William Scammell, *International Monetary Policy* (London: Macmillan, 1957), p. 52n; and Yeager, p. 278.

5. Ibid., p. 279.

6. Ibid., p. 286.

7. Ragnar Nurkse, *International Currency Experience* (League of Nations, 1944), p. 117.

8. William A. Brown, Jr., *The International Gold Standard Re-Interpreted* (New York: NBER, 1940), II, p. 805.

9. Yeager, p. 290.

10. Bank for International Settlements, *Tenth Annual Report*, 1939-40, pp. 18-25.

11. J. Keith Horsefield, *The International Monetary Fund 1945-65*, vol. I: "Chronicle" (Washington, D.C.: International Monetary Fund, 1969), p. 7.

12. Ibid., pp. 8-9.

13. Yeager, p. 332.

14. Yeager, p. 335. Reference to William Ashworth, *A Short History of the International Economy* (London: Longmans, Green, 1952), pp. 227-28; and Bank for International Settlements, *Eighteenth Annual Report*, 1947-48, p. 15.

15. John Maynard Keynes, *The General Theory of Employment, Interest and Money* (London: Harcourt, Brace, 1936). In America, Alvin Hansen was the torchbearer and interpreter for such new thinking even before Keynes's book was published.

16. Horsefield, p. 10.

17. Lawrence B. Krause, *Sequel to Bretton Woods—a Proposal to Reform the World Monetary System.* A Staff Paper (Washington, D.C.: The Brookings Institution, 1971), p. 7.

18. See Harley Notter, *Postwar Foreign Policy Preparation, 1939-45* (Washington, D.C.: Department of State, 1949).

19. Promulgated on August 14, 1941, at a conference between President Roosevelt and Prime Minister Churchill.

20. See Dean Acheson, *Present at the Creation—My Years in the State Department* (New York: Norton and Co., 1969), p. 29.

21. Horsefield, p. 12.

22. Ibid., vol. 1, chs. 1 and 2; and vol. 3.

Chapter 3
The Record: Emerging Criticism

1. According to Walter Krause (*International Economics* [Boston: Houghton Mifflin, 1965], pp. 358-59), two considerations were highly pertinent in this decision. First, the problems then facing resumption of free multilateral trade were so great at the time that minor exchange rate adjustments would have made only scant difference. Fundamental problems lay in the areas of production and transportation. This view was also reflected in the IMF *Annual Report*, 1947 "Statement Concerning Initial Par Values," Appendix (Washington, D.C.: 1947). Second, existing exchange rates were accepted because of concern that exchange depreciation would serve mainly to aggravate postwar inflationary problems with which many countries were faced at that time.

2. Article IV. 5f.

3. Robert Triffin, *National Central Banking and International Economy*, Postwar Economic Studies, No. 7 (Washington, D.C.: Board of Governors of Federal Reserve System, 1947), p. 77.

4. IMF *Annual Report*, 1948, Washington, D.C., pp. 48-49.

5. J.W. Beyen, *Money in Maelstrom* (New York: The Macmillan Co., 1949), pp. 202-3.

6. IMF *Annual Report*, 1948, pp. 22-23.

7. IMF, *Fourth Annual Report on Exchange Restrictions*, 1953, p. 9.

8. Ibid., p. 7.

9. Walter Krause, *International Economics*, ch. 9; and Walter Krause, *Economic Development* (San Francisco: Wadsworth Publishing Co., 1961), pp. 374-81.

10. Krause, *International Economics*, p. 371.

11. Robert Triffin, *Gold and the Dollar Crisis* (New Haven, Conn.: Yale University Press, 1961), revised edition.

12. Krause, *International Economics*, pp. 363-64.

13. See IMF, *Fourteenth Annual Report on Exchange Restrictions*, (Washington, D.C. 1963), p. 1, and IMF, *Annual Report*, 1963 (Washington, D.C. 1963), p. 10.

14. See J. Keith Horsefield, *The International Monetary Fund 1945-65* (Washington, D.C.: International Monetary Fund, 1969), pp. 536-40.

15. Emile Despres, Charles P. Kindleberger, and Walter S. Salant, "The Dollar and World Liquidity—A Minority View," *The Economist* Feb. 5, 1966, pp. 526-29.

16. Hal B. Larry, *Problems of the U.S. As World Trader and Banker* (National Bureau of Economic Research, 1963).

17. E.M. Bernstein, "Contingency Planning for U.S. International Monetary Policy," Statements by Private Economists submitted to Subcommittee on International Exchange and Payments of Joint Economic Committee, 89th Cong., 2nd Sess., 1966, Washington, D.C., pp. 3-5.

Chapter 4
The Record: Crisis

1. Harry G. Johnson, *The World Economy at the Crossroads* (London: Oxford University Press, 1965), p. 24.

2. Ibid., pp. 24-25.

3. Robert Triffin, "International Monetary Collapse and Reconstruction," *Journal of International Economics*, 2: 4 (Sept. 1972), pp. 375 ff.

4. Johnson, p. 30.

5. Robert Triffin, "Neither Gold Nor the Dollar," in Lawrence H. Officer and Thomas D. Willett, eds., *The International Monetary System—Problems and Proposals* (Englewood Cliffs, N.J.: Prentice-Hall, 1969), p. 5.

6. Harry G. Johnson, "Political Economy Aspects of International Monetary Reform," *Journal of International Economics*, 2: 4 (Sept. 1972), p. 413.

7. Robert Triffin, *The World Money Maze—National Currencies in International Payments* (New Haven: Conn.: Yale University Press, 1966), p. 233, quoting an unnamed Treasury official.

8. See "White House Message on Balance of Payments and Gold," February 6, 1961, reprinted in Seymour Harris, ed. *The Dollar in Crisis*, (New York: Harcourt Brace and World, Inc., 1961), pp. 295-307.

9. For example, see Herbert G. Grubel, *World Monetary Reform: Plans and Issues* (Stanford, Calif.: Stanford University Press, 1963). Also of interest and importance was the debate betwen Professor Robert Triffin of Yale and Oscar Altman of the IMF staff. See selections in Seymour Harris.

10. Charles Coombs, "Treasury and Federal Reserve Foreign Exchange Operations," *Federal Reserve Bulletin*, March 1965, pp. 379-82.

11. Harry G. Johnson, "The Sterling Crisis of 1967," the C. Woody Thompson Lecture, Annual Meeting of Midwest Economic Association, April 18, 1968.

12. That program was necessitated by the sterling devaluation, which adversely affected the US balance of payments and indirectly undermined confidence in the entire international monetary system. See Lawrence B. Krause, "Recent International Monetary Crises: Causes and Cures," in Warren L. Smith and Ronald L. Teigen, eds., *Readings in Money, National Income, and Stabilization Policy*, revised edition (Homewood, Ill.: Richard D. Irwin, 1970), pp. 556-70.

13. Ibid.

14. Ibid.

15. Harry G. Johnson, "The Sterling Crisis of 1967," p. 22.

16. Robert Triffin, "International Monetary Collapse and Reconstruction," p. 379.

Chapter 5
Events of 1968-1972

1. For a comprehensive account of what those policies were, see *Economic Report of the President*, January 1972 (Washington, D.C.: Government Printing Office, 1972).

2. This refers to a process by which short-term funds would be transferred from one center to another in order to take advantage of an existing interest rate differential for some period of time and would then be remitted to the home center. The gain from the transaction could be determined and insured in advance if an appropriate transaction in the forward exchange market were made simultaneous with the initial transfer of funds.

3. For further details on the Triffin plan, see *Gold and the Dollar Crisis*, revised ed. (New Haven: Yale University Press, 1961), and "Updating the Triffin Plan," ch. 9 in Triffin, *The World Money Maze–National Currencies in International Payments* (New Haven: Yale University Press, 1966).

4. "Guidelines for International Monetary Reform," Hearings Before the Subcommittee on International Exchange and Payments of the JEC, 89th Cong., 1st Sess., Part 2, 1965, pp. 230-31, 245-46, 257-58, 269-70. Adapted and reprinted in Krause and Matthis, eds., *International Economics and Business: Selected Readings*(Boston: Houghton Mifflin, 1968), pp. 183-88. The Bernstein plan highlighted here comes from Edward M. Bernstein, "The Gold Crisis and the New Gold Standard," *Quarterly Review and Investment Survey* (New York: Model, Roland and Co., Inc., first half, 1968), pp. 1-12.

5. From statement by Emile Despres in *New Approach to United States International Economic Policy*, Hearings before the Subcommittee on International Exchange and Payments of the JEC, 89th Cong., 2nd Sess., 1966 (Washington, D.C.: Government Printing Office, 1966), pp. 39-42.

6. George Halm, "Toward Limited Exchange Rate Flexibility," Princeton University, *Essays in International Finance*, No. 73, March 1969, pp. 4-5.

7. See proposals by James E. Meade, *The Three Bands Review*, Sept. 1964 and June 1966; John H. Williamson, "The Crawling Peg" Essays in International Finance, no. 50, 1965; J. Carter Murphy, *The National Banking Review*, Dec. 1965 and Sept. 1966; E. Ray Canterbery, *Economics on a New Frontier*, 1968; William Fellner in Fellner, Machlup and Triffin, eds. *Maintaining and Restoring Balance in International Payments*, Princeton, 1966; and George N. Halm, "Toward Limited Exchange Rate Flexibility," Essays in International Finance, No. 73 (Princeton: March 1969).

8. Ibid., p. 16-17.

9. *Approaches to Greater Flexibility of Exchange Rates*—The Bürgenstock Papers, George N. Halm, ed., (Princeton, N.J.: Princeton University Press, 1970).

10. Report of the Executive Directors to the Board of Governors of the IMF, *The Role of Exchange Rates in the Adjustment of International Payments* (Washington, D.C., 1970). See also George N. Halm, "The IMF and Flexibility of Exchange Rates," Essays in International Finance, No. 83 (Princeton: March 1971).

11. Press communiqué released from Bürgenstock, Switzerland, June 19, 1969, reprinted in *Approaches to Greater Flexibility of Exchange Rates*—The Bürgenstock Papers, George Halm, ed., p. vii.

12. See Jacques Rueff, "The Rueff Approach" in Randall Hinshaw ed., *Monetary Reform and the Price of Gold* (Baltimore: The Johns Hopkins Press, 1967), pp. 39-46.

13. The classic article is by Milton Friedman, "The Case for Flexible Exchange Rates," *Essays in Positive Economics* (Chicago: University of Chicago Press, 1953). See also Friedman's "Statement by Private Economists," submitted to the Subcommittee on International Exchange and Payments of the JEC, 89th Cong., 2nd Sess., 1966 (Washington, D.C.: Government Printing Office, 1966), pp. 30-36, and James E. Meade, "Exchange Rate Flexibility," in *International Payments Problems* (Washington, D.C.: American Enterprise Institute for Public Policy Research, 1966), pp. 71-80.

14. Lawrence B. Krause, "Sequel to Bretton Woods—A Proposal to Reform the World Monetary System," a staff paper (Washington, D.C.: The Brookings Institution, 1971). Other prominent proposals not discussed here include ones by Franco Modigliani and Hossein Askari, "The Reform of the International Payments System," Essays in International Finance, No. 89 (Princeton: Sept. 1971), and Michael V. Posner, "The World Monetary System: A Minimal Reform Program," Essays in International Finance, No. 96 (Princeton, Oct. 1972).

15. The other two very important issues to surface at UNCTAD III concerned preferential tariffs (according to which manufactured goods produced in LDC's receive favorable tariff treatment in gaining access to developed countries' markets) and problems associated with the growing importance and power of multinational corporations in the world. For a discussion of these issues, see

Walter Krause, "World Trade and Development: The View From UNCTAD III," *Arizona Business* (Aug.-Sept. 1973).

Chapter 6
Issues and Blocs: I

1. See C. Douglas Dillon, "The United States Balance of Payments," statement before the Joint Economic Committee, *Hearings*, Part I, Current Problems and Policies (Washington, D.C.: 1963), p. 28.

2. See Herbert G. Grubel, "The Benefits and Costs of Being the World Banker," *National Banking Review*, 2: 2 (Dec. 1964), pp. 197-205. For a contrasting view, see Henry N. Goldstein, "Does It Necessarily Cost Anything to be the 'World Banker'?" *The National Banking Review*, 2: 3 (March 1965), pp. 411-15.

3. William B. Dale, "The International Monetary Fund and Greater Flexibility of Exchange Rates," in C. Fred Bergsten and William G. Tyler, eds., *Leading Issues in International Economic Policy* (Lexington, Mass.: D.C. Heath and Co., Lexington Books, 1973), pp. 3-4.

4. This plan was propounded by Secretary Shultz at the 1972 Annual Fund-Bank Meeting in Washington, September 26, 1972. See *Summary Proceedings Annual Meeting, 1972* (Washington, D.C.: IMF 1972).

5. The details of the US proposal for using reserves as an indicator of the need for balance of payments adjustment appear in an appendix to chapter 5 of the *1973 Annual Economic Report of the Council of Economic Advisers* (Washington, D.C.: Government Printing Office, 1973).

6. See, for example, Henry C. Simons, "Rule Versus Authorities in Monetary Policies," *Journal of Political Economy*, 44:1 (Feb. 1936), pp. 1-30; and Lyle E. Gramley, "Guidelines for Monetary Policy—The Case Against Simple Rules," a paper delivered at the Financial Conference of the National Industrial Conference Board, New York, Feb. 21, 1969, reprinted in Smith and Teigen, eds., *Readings in Money, National Income and Stabilizing Policy* revised ed. (Irwin, 1970), pp. 488-95.

7. Speech delivered September 26, 1972, at the Annual Fund-Bank Meeting in Washington, D.C.

8. Ibid.

9. Ibid.

10. Alexandre Kafka, "The IMF: The Second Coming," Essays in International Finance, No. 94 (Princeton: July 1972), pp. 36-38.

Chapter 7
Issues and Blocs: II

1. Communiqué of the Committee of the Board of Governors on International Monetary Reform and Related Issues, March 27, 1973. Italics are mine.

2. "Inflation and the International Monetary System," a paper presented by Otmar Emminger, Deputy Governor of the Deutsche Bundesbank, in Basel, Switzerland, June 16, 1973.

3. See Harry G. Johnson, "Problems of European Monetary Union," *Journal of World Trade Law*, 5: 4 (July-August 1971), pp. 377-87. Johnson suggests there are two main motives for Europe's stated intentions: first, to "persuade, cajole or blackmail the members of the Community into the adoption of central coordination of monetary and financial policies," and hence fulfill the economic prerequisite to political unification; second, to escape from US dollar domination by creating a rival international currency. Johnson is dubious about the sincerity of Europe's intentions to establish monetary union. See also the excellent article by Ronald I. McKinnon, "On Serving a Common Monetary Policy in Europe," *Banca Nazionale del Lavoro Quarterly Review*, No. 104 (March 1973), pp. 3-20.

4. The Werner Report of October 1970 to the EC countries laid down the program for achieving the union in a series of stages through progressive and mutually supportive policies of harmonization, standardization, and unification.

5. This postulate is advanced by advocates of the policy of "benign neglect," G. Haberler and T. Willett, "A Strategy for U.S. Balance of Payments" (American Enterprise Institutes, Washington, D.C., 1971), and Lawrence B. Krause, "A Passive Balance of Payments Strategy for the U.S." Brookings Papers on Economic Activity, No. 3, 1970; and also by those who reject that policy—for example, Arthur F. Burns, "Some Essentials of International Monetary Reform," Federal Reserve Bank of N.Y. *Monthly Review*, June 1972 (address to the 1972 International Banking Conference, Montreal, Canada, May 12, 1972). Burns stated that the "international monetary system will have to respect the need for substantial autonomy of domestic policies. . . . No country . . . should have to accept sizable increases in unemployment to reduce its deficit. Nor should a surplus country have . . . [to accept] high rates of inflation [to reduce its surplus] ."

6. By way of further elaboration, Gottfried Haberler in a recent paper, "International Aspects of U.S. Inflation" in *A New Look at Inflation* (American Enterprise Institute, 1973), has identified an "inflation transmission multiplier" to explain the empirically observed phenomenon that inflation in the United States is transmitted in a significantly amplified manner to certain other countries, namely industrial countries with average annual growth in productivity (output per man hour) substantially greater than in the United States. According to Haberler's evidence, rapidly growing economies of Germany, Italy, and Japan displayed greater divergences in rates of increase in domestic consumer prices vs. domestic wholesale and export prices than have the slower growing economies of the United States and Canada. The reason is that all consumer price indices are heavily weighted with services which are on the whole labor intensive and have slower productivity growth than manufacturing industries, and because rapid domestic expansion and export growth of those economies have resulted in large part from great success of manufacturing

industries. The economic consequences of the divergence between consumer prices and wholesale or export prices are that consumer prices in rapidly growing economies must rise substantially faster than those in the United States if balance of payments equilibrium is to be maintained at fixed exchange rates. This is because prices and price levels of internationally traded goods are linked closely and tend to move together.

7. See William D. Nordhaus, "The Worldwide Wage Explosion," Brookings Papers on Economic Activity, No. 2, 1972, for a discussion of sources and theories of explanation underlying interrelationships of wage rate changes during recent years.

8. Ibid. Nordhaus analyzing econometric evidence on lags concludes that the rise in world prices was the most significant causal factor of wage explosion occurring in non-US countries. Nordhaus poses the question: "How does the United States exert such a powerful influence on prices abroad?" He replies, "Paradoxically, the answer is because the United States is the only country that does not (or cannot afford to) care seriously about the effect of its price level on its external position."

9. US reserves consisting mostly of gold but also some SDRs, foreign exchange and a net position with the Fund, amount to $14.35 billion. Source: IMF International Statistics (July 1973).

10. Statement by the Governor of the Fund for the United Kingdom, Anthony Barber, 1971 IMF Annual Meeting, Sept. 27, 1971. See Summary Proceedings—Annual Meeting 1971 (Washington, D.C.: IMF).

11. Ibid.

12. In 1949, $6.9 billion worth of sterling was held in the form of world monetary reserves. In 1971, the figure was $7.2 billion. Source: IMF, International Financial Statistics.

Chapter 8
Issues and Blocs: III

1. Report by the Executive Directors to the Board of Governors, Reform of the International Monetary System (Washington, D.C.: IMF, Sept. 1972), p. 66.

2. For a summary of what has been done to meet this problem and where matters stand as of 1972, see Walter Krause, "UNCTAD III, World Trade and Development," Arizona Business, Aug.-Sept., 1972.

3. Ibid., pp. 7-8. By permission of Bureau of Business and Economic Research, College of Business Administration, Arizona State University. The second purpose he referred to was to attain implementation within the IMF of the resolution binding SDRs to development assistance. See the section following in this chapter.

4. See Alexandre Kafka, "The IMF: The Second Coming," Essays in

International Finance, No. 94 (Princeton: July 1972), esp. pp. 4-6; and Walter Krause.

5. These and other special areas of interest to LDCs emerged at the Fifteenth Session of the UN Economic Commission for Latin America held in Quito, Ecuador, March 23-30, 1973.

6. See "Aspects of the Reform of the International Monetary System Information." Note by ECLA Secretariat prepared with cooperation of Carlos Masad, Fifteenth Session of United Nations Economic Commission for Latin America, 1973.

7. Walter Krause, "UNCTAD III: World Trade and Development," *Arizona Business*, Aug.-Sept., 1972.

8. See M.E. Bond and F. John Mathis, "The Disinterest in Foreign Aid: An Appraisal," *Kyklos*, 1970, pp. 446-70.

9. Harry G. Johnson, "The Link that Chains," *Foreign Policy*, No. 8 (Fall 1972), pp. 116-17.

10. Jagdish, Bhagwati, "The International Monetary System: Issues in the Symposium," *Journal of International Economics*, 2: 4 (Sept. 1972), p. 322.

11. Offered by A.F.W. Plumptre, "Reform of the International Monetary System: Some Points of Special Interest to Developing Countries of the Commonwealth," a paper prepared for the Commonwealth Secretariat (FMM(72)8), Sept. 1972.

12. Ibid.

13. See "Reform of the International Monetary System," Report of the Executive Directors of the IMF, Sept. 1972, p. 8.

14. See Alexandre Kafka, "The IMF: The Second Coming," Essays in International Finance, No. 94 (Princeton: July 1972), p. 13. An IMF study SM/70/90, dated May 12, 1970, "Effects of a Slight Widening of Exchange Rate Martins Around Par on Primary Producing Countries with Special Reference to Developing Countries," also reached a negative conclusion. Resolutions of UNCTAD and other groupings of developing countries have also resisted such proposals.

15. Individual Observations by Robert Campos in *Latin America and the Reform of the International Monetary System*, Inter-American Committee on the Alliance for Progress, General Secretariat (OAS: Washington, D.C., p. 83, Results and Proceedings of a meeting convoked by Chmn. of CIAP and the Exec. Secretariat, Jan. 1972.

16. Stephen Marris, "The Bürgenstock Communique: A Limited Examination of the Case for Limited Flexibility of Exchange Rates," Essays in International Finance No. 80 (Princeton: May 1970), p. 51 and CIAP, p. 26, *Latin America and the Reform of the International Monetary System.*

17. Alexandre Kafka, "The IMF—The Second Coming," Essays in International Finance, No. 94 (Princeton: July 1972), p. 36-38.

18. *The Economist*, July 7-13, "Survey: The Phony Oil Crisis."

19. James E. Akins, "The Oil Crisis: This Time the Wolf is Here," *Foreign Affairs* (April 1973), pp. 462-90. Another informed observer who agrees that OPEC (Organization of the Petroleum Exporting Countries) countries will experience soaring revenues, is M.A. Adelman. See his book, *The World Petroleum Market* (Johns Hopkins University Press: 1973).

Chapter 9
The Economic Environment

1. Communiqué of the Committee of the Board of Governors on International Monetary Reform and Related Issues, IMF Press Release, No. 964, March 27, 1973.

2. Richard Kahn, "The International Monetary System," Special Invited Lecture, 85th Annual Meeting of the American Economic Association, Toronto, Ontario, Dec. 28-30, 1972, in AEA *Papers and Proceedings*, 63:2 (May 1973), pp. 181-88.

3. Japan is the prime example of a country that by design set out to restrict severely all types of capital inflows during the last quarter century and which was successful in doing so. See my book, *Japan: Financial Markets and the World Economy* (New York: Praeger, 1973), chapter 10.

4. Capital flows have come under considerable criticism for being destabilizing rather than stabilizing. The other view is that speculators' judgment about the present strength or weakness of a currency more often than not tends to be right and that of government authorities more often than not tend to be wrong. See Gottfried Haberler, "The Case Against Capital Controls for Balance of Payments Reasons," prepared for the Geneva Conference on Capital Movements and their Control, June 15-16, 1973 (to be published).

5. If countries were somehow permitted to retain overvalued or undervalued currencies for long periods of time, there could be some distortion in the pattern of long-term investment. However, the possibility that the future adjustment mechanism will work this way appears to be remote as of this writing.

6. See the important paper by Otmar Emminger, "Inflation and the International Monetary System," May 31, 1973. He contends that there was a combination of trends and forces in the international monetary system which made for a very strong inflationary bias. He includes in his list a one-sided balance of payments adjustment process in which discipline was nonexistent, a rigid parity system based upon a structurally weakening dollar, destabilizing capital flows, and uncontrolled expansion of international liquidity. See also, Harry G. Johnson, "Inflation and World Trade: A 'Monetary' View," *Journal of World Trade Law* (Jan.-Feb. 1972), pp. 9-19.

7. See James E. Meade, *The Balance of Payments* (London: Oxford University Press, 1962), chapter 1.

8. For a survey of the literature on the problem of external-internal balance, see Marina von Neumann Whitman, "Policies for Internal and External Balance," *Special Papers in International Economics*, No. 9 (December 1970) International Finance Section, Princeton University.

9. Paul W. McCracken, "Domestic Economic Policy and Convertibility," *Papers and Proceedings* of the Eighty-Fifth Annual Meeting of the American Economic Association, Toronto, Dec. 28-30, 1972, p. 204.

10. C. Fred Bergsten, "The United States and Greater Flexibility of Exchange Rates," in George N. Halm, ed., *Approaches to Greater Flexibility of Exchange Rates–The Bürgenstock Papers* (Princeton, 1970), p. 68. The same might also be said for the other key currency in the postwar world, the pound sterling.

11. For reference to further discussion of consolidation proposals, see Peter B. Kenen, "Convertibility and Consolidation: A Survey of Options for Reform," *Papers and Proceedings*, Eighty-fifth Annual Meeting of the American Economic Association, Toronto, Dec. 28-30, 1972, pp. 189-98.

12. See Robert V. Roosa, "Approaching the International Reform," in *The Smithsonian Agreement and its Aftermath* (New York: Council on Foreign Relations, 1972). Roosa minimizes the essentiality of consolidation because he believes that once confidence is restored most of the recent growth in official dollar holdings will flow back into private hands.

13. Peter Kenen, op. cit.

14. For a brief, clear description of some of the market's basic features, see Alexandre Lamfalussy, "The Eurodollar Market," *Journal of World Trade Law*, 5: 4 (July-August 1971), pp. 338-96.

15. The size and extent of the Eurocurrency market exerts a strong integrative influence on national money markets. There are great similarities of Eurocurrency loans and deposits from country to country in respect of legal characteristics, types of maturities, repayment features and the like. Interest rates charged to similar borrowers and rates offered by similar intermediaries in different countries closely coincide. Eurocurrency loans and deposits are largely denominated in U.S. dollars. See Alexander K. Swoboda, "Multinational Banking, Euro-dollar Market and Economic Policy," *Journal of World Trade Law*, 5: 2 (March-April 1971), pp. 121-30; and A.K. Swoboda, *The Euro-dollar Market: An Interpretation*, Princeton Essays in International Finance, No. 68, Feb. 1968.

16. Measures have consisted of providing commercial banks with special incentives for placing in the Eurocurrency markets liabilities incurred to residents and nonresidents, forward exchange market operations designed to stimulate covered outward arbitrage, imposition of high reserve requirements against liabilities of commercial banks to nonresidents not offset by claims on nonresidents, and 100 percent reserve requirements on additions to net liabilities to nonresidents. The Federal Reserve itself has experimented with various measures, including those provided under the Voluntary Foreign Credit Restraint Program and attempts to have the US Eximbank reabsorb dollars which had flowed abroad by issuing its own short-term notes in Europe.

17. "Inflation and the International Monetary System," May 31, 1973.

Chapter 10
Relative Status of the Participants

1. See Alexander K. Swoboda, "Multinational Banking, The Euro-dollar Market and Economic Policy, *Journal of World Trade Law*, 5: 2 (March-April 1971), pp. 125-28 and Guido Carli, "Euro-dollars: A Paper Pyramid?" *Banca Nazionale del Lavoro Quarterly Review* (June 1971), pp. 95-109.

2. Maintenance of the status quo of floating exchange rates with no agreement on ground rules for official intervention is one possible alternative to constructive, systematic monetary reform.

Index of Names

187

Index of Subjects

About the Author

Wilbur F. Monroe is an international economist with the U.S. Department of the Treasury. He has served as assistant financial attache in the American Embassy in Tokyo and has been a guest scholar at the Brookings Institution. He received the Ph.D. in economics from the University of Iowa in 1969, having done some study at the London School of Economics and Political Science. Dr. Monroe is the author of *Japan: Financial Markets and the World Economy* and a number of articles on international economic and financial topics which have appeared in professional journals.